New Women *of the* Old Faith

To Catherine,
with gratitude for all
you do to support
our "sisters" in the Church,

Warmly,

Kathleen D. Cummings
Michigan City, Ind.
July 2011

KATHLEEN SPROWS CUMMINGS

NEW WOMEN

of the OLD FAITH

GENDER *and* AMERICAN CATHOLICISM

in the PROGRESSIVE ERA

The University *of* North Carolina Press CHAPEL HILL

© 2009
THE
UNIVERSITY
OF NORTH
CAROLINA
PRESS

All rights reserved

Manufactured
in the United States
of America

This book has been
made possible in
part by support
from the Institute
for Scholarship in
the Liberal Arts,
College of Arts and
Letters, University
of Notre Dame.

Designed by Courtney Leigh Baker and set in Whitman
with Sackers Gothic Display by Keystone Typesetting, Inc.

Title page and chapter opening illustration
© iStockphoto.com/Grigory Bibikov

The paper in this book meets the guidelines for permanence
and durability of the Committee on Production Guidelines
for Book Longevity of the Council on Library Resources.

The University of North Carolina Press has been a member
of the Green Press Initiative since 2003.

Library of Congress Cataloging-in-Publication Data
Cummings, Kathleen Sprows.
New women of the old faith : gender and American
Catholicism in the progressive era /
Kathleen Sprows Cummings.
    p. cm.
Includes bibliographical references and index.
ISBN 978-0-8078-3249-3 (cloth : alk. paper)
1. Women in the Catholic Church—United States—History.
2. Sex role—Religious aspects—Catholic Church—History.
3. Sex role. 4. Catholic Church—United States—History.
5. Progressivism (United States politics) I. Title.
    BX1407.W65C86 2009
    282'.7308209034—dc22
    2008031980

Parts of this work have been reprinted in revised form from "The 'New
Woman' at the 'University': Gender and American Catholic Identity
in the Progressive Era," in *The Religious History of American Women:
Reimagining the Past*, edited by Catherine A. Brekus, © 2007 by
The University of North Carolina Press, used by permission of the
publisher, www.uncpress.unc.edu, and "We Owe It to Our Sex as Well
as Our Religion: The Sisters of Notre Dame de Namur, the Ladies
Auxiliary, and the Founding of Trinity College for Catholic Women,
Washington, D.C.," *American Catholic Studies* 115 (2004): 21–36.

13 12 11 10 09   5 4 3 2 1

for Thomas

Contents

Illustrations

Acknowledgments

Finishing this book brings with it the long-anticipated pleasure of thanking the many colleagues and friends who have helped and guided me along the way. I am grateful, above all, to everyone associated with the Cushwa Center for the Study of American Catholicism at the University of Notre Dame. Jay Dolan, Cushwa's founding director and my dissertation adviser, believed in this project from its inception. I admire Jay as a historian and teacher, and this project, as well as my academic career, would have foundered long ago had it not been for his encouragement and mentorship. Scott Appleby, Dolan's successor, hired me as Cushwa's associate director in August 2001, five weeks before September 11 and five months before news of the clergy sex-abuse scandal first hit the pages of the *Boston Globe*. Scott, an expert in both religious violence and American Catholicism, interpreted these events thoughtfully and judiciously to the broader public, and the opportunity to watch him in action truly was the silver lining in the clouds of those dark days. Scott sets a fine example as a scholar, teacher, and administrator, and I am grateful to him for his support and friendship. Scott's assistant, Barbara Lockwood, is a dear friend who never fails to lift my spirits and those of anyone lucky enough to be in her presence.

It would be difficult to overstate the debt I owe to the present staff of the Cushwa Center, especially its director, Timothy Matovina. Tim's generosity of spirit, careful scholarship, warm hospitality, and considerable organizational skills are a source of inspiration, and I am grateful to him for his support in this and all my scholarly endeavors over the past six years. Neither the Cushwa Center nor my life would run very smoothly were it not for the heroic contribution of Paula Brach, our accomplished and warm-hearted senior administrative assistant. Cushwa's graduate assistants Charles Strauss and, formerly, Justin Poché have made my job easier in a number of ways. This book also benefited from the assistance of several talented undergraduates, especially Amelia Schmidt, who translated the notes of the Council of Macon, and Elizabeth Stewart, who served as my research assistant during summer 2007. I could not have completed this book in a timely manner without her persistence and hard work. Having had Elizabeth as a student, I am pleased to wish her well as she begins her own teaching career. I would also like to thank the members of the Cushwa family, especially Bill and Anna Jean, for their ongoing generosity to all of us and to Notre Dame.

Cushwa remains the epicenter of an exceptionally thoughtful and magnanimous group of scholars. Without a doubt each person who has participated in our seminars and conferences has enriched my understanding of the history of American religion and U.S. Catholicism. Several, though, merit special mention for their guidance on this particular project. Among Cushwa's friends at Notre Dame I am most of all indebted to Suellen Hoy, a gifted historian and cherished friend, who read the entire manuscript, offered excellent suggestions, and reminded me that there were always "blue skies ahead." I depended on Walter Nugent's expertise in Progressivism when writing my introduction. Philip Gleason's careful reading of chapter 3 made the final draft more precise, and I remain grateful to him for the example he provides of meticulous scholarship. I presented drafts of both the second and third chapters to the Catholic History reading group, and I appreciated the perceptive comments of Brad Gregory; Paul Kollman, CSC; Tom Kselman; Tim Matovina; John McGreevy; Kevin Ostovich; Charles Strauss; Robert Sullivan; and Charlotte Ames, who has served as my own personal cheerleader on this project for the past decade. During her long tenure as Notre Dame's Catholic bibliographer, Charlotte was instrumental in building Hesburgh Library's rich and varied collection in American Catholic studies. I am grateful to Charlotte and her successor, my friend and colleague Jean McManus, for guiding me through these resources.

This book also benefited from the suggestions and advice offered by many of Cushwa's friends beyond Notre Dame. James McCartin's comments on the final draft helped fine-tune my writing and my argument. Joseph Chinnici, OFM, not only helped me track down the elusive Lahitton controversy but also clarified my thinking on the history of religious life at an early stage in the completion of the manuscript. Patricia McNeal's comments on my book proposal helped this project take shape. Martin E. Marty reminded me to "write, write, write." Mary Oates, CSJ, generously shared with me her extensive knowledge on the history of teaching sisters and has provided welcome companionship and diversion at more than one academic conference over the years. Paula Kane's pioneering scholarship on gender and Catholicism provided a model for my own. My first chapter benefited from Bill Portier's expertise on modernism. Christopher Kauffman not only published my first scholarly article but also put me in touch with Elaine Maisner, my editor at the University of North Carolina Press. Mel Piehl read a very early draft of this manuscript and gave me helpful suggestions about revising it. Ellen Skerrett helped me track down photographs and has always been on hand to commiserate or celebrate, whichever the occasion demanded. Ellen also put me in touch with Martha Curry, RSCJ, who shared her research on Margaret Buchanan Sullivan and introduced me to Sullivan's great-grand-nephew, Peter Buchanan. I am also grateful to Peter himself for providing the photograph of Sullivan.

Throughout this process I have been very fortunate to have been associated with Notre Dame's Department of History. John McGreevy, chair from 2002 to 2008, is a scholar whose work I admire deeply, and I have appreciated his advice and staunch support. Gail Bederman read an early draft of my proposal and encouraged me along the way. Steve Brady reminded me to keep a sense of humor. Dan Graff has been a supportive and good friend. A timely conversation with Patrick Griffin helped me gather the momentum to finish this project. Mark Noll provided a generous and thoughtful reading of the entire manuscript. Linda Przybyszewski's comments on chapter 3 helped sharpen my writing. Tom Slaughter, now at the University of Rochester, has been a valued senior colleague whose counsel and judgment proved particularly helpful over the past year. Tom Kselman's characteristically thoughtful questions improved this book immensely.

I also hold a concurrent appointment in the Department of Theology, and its chair, John Cavadini, has long supported my growth as a scholar and a teacher, perhaps most especially as the convener of the Lilly Faculty Seminar on Vocation in 2002–3. Special thanks also to other members of the Theology Department who have offered encouragement: Regina Coll, CSJ; Mary Rose D'Angelo; Mary Catherine Hilkert, OP; M. Cathleen Kaveny; Paul Kollman, CSC; Cyril O'Regan; Mark Poorman, CSC; Maura Ryan; and Robin Darling Young. My primary appointment in the Department of American Studies at Notre Dame is a recent and welcome development that has expanded my circle of conversation partners and broadened my intellectual horizons. I am grateful to all my colleagues there, especially our chair, Erika Doss. I am very grateful to Notre Dame's Institute for Scholarship in the Liberal Arts for its generous subvention grant in support of this book. Finally, I am indebted to the helpful and dedicated staff at Notre Dame's Hesburgh Library, especially those who work in Circulation, Document Delivery, and Inter-Library Loan.

Between 2005 and 2007 I had the privilege of participating in the Young Scholars in American Religion Program, sponsored by the Lilly Endowment and Indiana University–Purdue University Indianapolis (IUPUI). John Corrigan and Judith Weisenfeld were the best mentors our cohort could have hoped for, and they helped us all grow as teachers and scholars. Judith, in particular, went above and beyond, reading much of the manuscript and offering wise counsel at various stages. All participants in the seminar read this book's third chapter, and I am grateful to them not only for their comments but also for the fun and fellowship we shared in Indianapolis. I count two members of our cohort, Eve Sterne and Kristy Nabhan-Warren, among my best friends in the historical profession.

Equally important to my development as a scholar was my participation in a conference that Catherine A. Brekus organized at the University of Chicago in October 2003, "Women and American Religion: Reimagining the Past." Kathleen Conzen's perceptive comments on an early version of my second chapter improved it significantly. That conference also provided me with the occasion to meet and share my work with Julie Byrne, Emily Clark, and Amy Koehlinger, all thoughtful scholars on women and American Catholicism. By far the greatest result of my participation in that conference, however, was the opportunity to work with and learn from Catherine Brekus. I am grateful to Catherine for many things, not least of which is her insightful commentary on portions of this manuscript.

Catherine included a version of the second chapter in her edited collection, *Women and American Religion: Reimagining the Past* (North Carolina, 2007). An early version of chapter 1 was also published as "Not the New Woman: Irish American Women and the Creation of a Usable Past," in *U.S. Catholic Historian* 19 (Winter 2001): 37–52. Excerpts from chapter 2 appeared in " 'We Owe It to Our Sex as Well as Our Religion': The Sisters of Notre Dame de Namur, the Ladies Auxiliary, and the Founding of Trinity

College for Catholic Women, Washington, D.C.," published in *American Catholic Studies* 115 (Winter 2004): 21–36. I am grateful to Maggie McGuinness for encouraging me to publish that article, which I originally presented at the Sixth Triennial Conference on the History of Women Religious held in Atchison, Kansas, in June 2004. I am also indebted to Maggie for our conversations in Atchison, Milwaukee, New York, and especially at Casey's in Malvern at the end of a long day in the archives at Immaculata.

Historians depend heavily on archivists, and with gratitude and respect I acknowledge the sisters and archivists of the women's religious congregations that appear in this book: Sister Mary Hayes, SND, of Trinity College; Sister M. St. Michel, IHM, of the Sisters, Servants of the Immaculate Heart of Mary; Sister Patricia Annas, SSJ, of the Sisters of St. Joseph of Philadelphia; Sister Helen Jacobson, OSF, and Sister Marie Therese Carr, OSF, of the Archives of the Sisters of St. Francis of Philadelphia. I thank them not only for guiding my research but also as representatives of all their community members, who have performed "the wageless work of paradise" for my benefit and that of all Philadelphia Catholic school children for the past century and a half. Sister Connie Derby, RSM, of the Archives of the Diocese of Rochester, helped me locate sources on Katherine Conway, and Bonnie Weatherly of the Archives of the Daughters of Charity, Emmitsburg, Maryland, sent me references to Elizabeth Ann Seton's canonization in the Provincial Annals. Shawn Weldon of the Philadelphia Archdiocesan Historical Records Center guided my research in the McDevitt Collection. Finally, I will be forever indebted to the consummate professionals at the University of Notre Dame Archives, especially Kevin Cawley, Charles Lamb, and Sharon Sumpter.

I consider myself very fortunate to have worked with Elaine Maisner at the University of North Carolina Press. Since our first conversation in San Francisco in January 2002, Elaine has supported me every step of the way as we sought to bring this project to completion. I imagine that it would have been very easy to abandon this book had it not been for her constant encouragement. I am grateful to Tema Larter, editorial assistant at the press, and Paula Wald, associate managing editor, for their help in the final stages of preparation. Thanks also to Grace Carino for her careful copyediting. I am also grateful to the readers at the press. The late Peter D'Agostino read the proposal, and his comments pushed me to make a bolder and ultimately better argument. Leslie Tentler read both the proposal and the final draft and in both instances offered her characteristically wise and insightful comments. Indeed, Leslie has been a consistent supporter of my work since I first met her at the Cushwa Center's Engendering American Catholicism Conference in 1995. I am also grateful to the anonymous reader at the press, whose comments helped me clarify my argument and sharpen the final draft.

I am indebted to all my neighbors on and around Bronson Street. I treasure the friendship of Marie Harrer, Carl Loesch, Becky Reimbold, Bryon Thomas, Leanne Suarez, Lyn and Jay Caponigro, and all their children, especially my godson Patrick Loesch. Tami Schmitz, another key person in my neighborhood network who doubles as my running partner, helps me hold on to my sanity in the midst of daily life. Marie, Tami, and Lyn are also members of my book club, along with Sylvia Dillon, M. J. Adams Kocovski, Jenny Monahan, Melissa Paulsen, and members emeritus Mary Beth Borkowski and Colleen Knight Santoni. I am grateful to all these women for many reasons, including their decision to add this book to our nonfiction list in 2009. I am also grateful to Tami Barbour, Marty Hurt, Megan Jung-Zimmerman, Emily Pike, and Melinda Wesolowski for their generosity toward my children and for also serving as reminders that all parents need a broad network of support. In that vein I also thank the staff at St. Joseph Parish School in South Bend, Indiana, and indeed the entire parish community.

At various stages throughout this project I have depended on the moral support of a number of friends and colleagues, near and far: Dorothy Bass, Dominique Bernardo, Alan Bloom, Una Cadegan, Teresa Calkins, Jim Carroll, Annie Crew-Renzo, Jane Hannon, Meghan Harmon, Rebecca Huss, Nicole Gothelf, Nancy Johnson, Jody Vaccaro Lewis, Will McDowell, Cindy Mongrain, Maureen Mulholland, Kristy Nabhan-Warren, Elizabeth O'Reilly, Susan Poulson, Trish Powers, Dottie Pratt, Sheila Provencher, Kim Savage, Barbara Searle, Colleen Seguin, J. P. Shortall, E. Springs Steele, Eve Sterne, and Barbra Wall.

Finally, I have been sustained over the years by my family, whose love has shaped this project and its author in large and small ways. I am grateful to all members of the Sprows family, including my parents, Tom and Kathy; my sister, Marybeth; my brother, Tom; my sister-in-law, Mala; my niece and nephews, Lauren, Jonathan, and Evan; and my grandmother Helen, as well as the members of the Rodemer and Burke families. Joining the Cummings clan was in many respects the best thing that has ever happened to me, and I appreciate the support of my extended family, most especially my parents-in-law, Tom and Elaine Cummings.

My beautiful children are a blessing and a delight, and I am grateful to all three of them: to Margaret Grace, a young author herself, who wondered why it took me so long to complete this book, considering I was merely its author and not also its illustrator; to T.C., who will be disappointed not to find more battle scenes in these pages but who will be proud of me nonetheless; and to Anne Therese, whose impending arrival hastened the preparation of my final draft and whose smiles enchanted me throughout the revision process. Most of all, I am grateful to their father and my husband, Thomas Christopher Cummings III. Our conversation and partnership began more than a decade ago, and our journey together continually evolves in interesting and exciting directions. Thomas is my most loyal supporter, most perceptive critic, and best friend. Without him, this book would not have been completed, and to him it is dedicated, with all my love.

Introduction

In 1897, Right Reverend Patrick Ludden, the bishop of Syracuse, New York, shared his thoughts on the study of the past. "Too often," he observed, "it is *his story*, not *history*." At the time, the bishop was exhorting historians to maintain absolute objectivity, to refuse to allow their "ontological training, religious prejudices, social environment or political predilections" to influence their interpretation of past lives and events. This advice may appear quaintly naïve in a postmodern age. But the admonition of this nineteenth-century prelate still rings true in another context: historians of U.S. Catholicism continue to write "*his*" story, overlooking women as historical actors.[1]

Certainly progress has been made in this regard over the past four decades. Until the 1960s, the ecclesial focus of the field had obviously reduced the number of potential female subjects. Since then, reinterpretations of the church as the "people of God" after the Second Vatican Council (1962–65) and the influence of the "new social history" have prompted many historians to turn their attention to the women in the pews. The past decade has been particularly fruitful in this regard. Suellen Hoy, Carol Coburn and Martha Smith, and Diane Batts Morrow are among those scholars who have published excellent studies of Catholic women religious, while books written by Deirdre Moloney, Deborah Skok, and Dorothy Brown and Elizabeth McKeown have illuminated the social activism of Catholic laywomen.[2] Another valuable publication has been *Gender Identities in American Catholicism*, a primary source collection edited by Paula Kane, James Kenneally, and Karen Kennelly. All three editors had already made excellent individual contributions to the field; Kenneally and Kennelly published fine historical surveys of American Catholic women, and Kane's study of Boston Catholicism incorporated her pathbreaking research on women and gender.[3]

Yet these and other fine studies have had little impact on synthetic narratives, in which Catholic female subjects remain "in short supply as shapers of history."[4] This problem is not unique to historians of U.S. Catholicism. As Ann Braude noted a decade ago, women's stories do not easily fit into the frameworks that have traditionally structured American religious history.[5] More recently, Catherine A. Brekus has pointed out that most scholars of American religion "assume that women's stories are peripheral to their research topics, whether Puritan theology or church and state. They do not seem hostile to women's history as much as they are dismissive of it, treating it as a separate topic they can safely afford to ignore."[6]

Catholic women's historical invisibility is compounded by their virtual absence from narratives of American women's history. Because the field developed in tandem with the modern feminist movement, its early practitioners largely focused on the white, middle-class, native-born, Protestant women who either espoused or prefigured feminism. In recent decades, this history has been enriched and complicated by attention to differences of race, class, and ethnicity among American women. Yet few historians appreciate the extent to which religious identity also confounds traditional categories and questions. Perplexed as to where to place Catholics, authors of women's history texts have often been content to discuss laywomen only as "anti-s"—antisuffrage, as well as anti–birth control, antiabortion, and anti-ERA.[7] Scholars of U.S. women, in marked contrast to their counterparts in France, are even less inclined to view Catholic women religious as historical subjects.[8] Two notable recent exceptions to these trends are Anne M. Boylan's *Origins of Women's Activism*, which incorporates Catholic laywomen's organizations into the study of women and public life in antebellum America, and Maureen Fitzgerald's *Habits of Compassion*, which places Irish Catholic nuns at the center of historical scholarship on women, welfare, and social reform.[9] Ann Braude has praised both Boylan and Fitzgerald for "transcending the Protestant frameworks embedded in the field" and suggested that their work will prompt other women's historians "to include the impact of distinctive Catholic values, practices, and institutions."[10]

Still, while these recent publications may offer reason for optimism, they are likely to remain exceptional for reasons that Braude herself pointed out in her introduction to the second edition of *Radical Spirits*: women's historians continue to evince a "certain squeamishness" about religious faith. Braude herself, in writing about women and spiritualism, sought to overcome this barrier by choosing to explore "the religious motivations of historical actors who would appeal to contemporary readers." In contrast, many Catholic women of the past—celibate, seemingly subservient, often antisuffrage—are decidedly unappealing to modern women. Here again, this phenomenon applies not only to Catholic women but also to women in other religious traditions with conservative ideologies of gender.[11]

As more attention is paid to religious identity, women's historians will be forced to confront many difficult questions; among them is where to place women who were part of patriarchal traditions. In *Women's America*, Linda K. Kerber and Jane Sherron De Hart observe that the perspective of women's history has enriched our understanding of the American past by identifying sources of female power within male-dominated structures such as the state. Yet women's historians in general are reluctant to see that women could also have power within a patriarchal structure like the Catholic Church. Indeed, many current discussions of Catholicism might give the impression that Catholic women's only route to empowerment is out the church doors.

I suspect that historians of U.S. women are reluctant to search for sources of female power in the male-dominated church because they seriously doubt that they exist. Much of their skepticism derives, it seems, from a tendency to view the Catholic past through a Catholic present. Since the late 1960s, a Catholic woman in American society has had vastly more opportunities for education and meaningful work outside church structures than within them. But from the mid-nineteenth century until the late 1960s, quite the opposite was true. To get a sense of the breadth of Catholic women's activities in the early twentieth century, consider some statistics from Philadelphia, a city that this book's third chapter explores at some length: in 1925, there were 30 congregations of religious women in the city, with a total of 4,382 members. Religious women staffed 3 colleges, 17 private academies, more than 200 parish schools, 5 high schools, 8 hospitals, 13 orphan asylums, 11 day nurseries, 1 settlement house, 7 homes for the aged, 3 homes for the handicapped, 8 boardinghouses for working women, 5 homes for "unfortunate" women, and 3 visiting nurse associations. These figures, of course, do not include the indeterminate number of laywomen who worked under the auspices of the church as writers, educators, or social reformers.[12]

Women's religious leadership presents another area in which the realities of the present may be skewing our perception of the past. Today, American women have far more opportunities for leadership within Protestant denominations than they do within Catholicism. But another set of statistics demonstrates how different this picture looked less than a century ago. For one gauge, consider that only 685 women listed themselves as "clergy" on the U.S. Census of 1910 and that even by 1930 only 1,787 had done so. In contrast, the number of women who were members of Catholic religious communities far exceeded these totals. There were 61,944 sisters in 1910 and 134,339 twenty years later.[13]

By examining female power within Catholic religious communities and organizations, this study challenges the widespread assumption that women who were faithful members of a patriarchal church were largely incapable of genuine work on behalf of women. It is true that, at times, a sense of Catholic tribalism limited what was possible for women in arenas of education, work, and public life. But if Catholic identity was often marshaled in support of traditional gender roles, so too could it serve as a vehicle through which women contested and renegotiated the parameters of their experience.

This book explores these themes by highlighting the lives and work of four women: Margaret Buchanan Sullivan (1847–1903), a prolific Chicago writer who published in both the secular and Catholic press; Sister Julia (Susan) McGroarty, SND (1831–1901), American provincial superior of the Sisters of Notre Dame de Namur and founder of Trinity College for Catholic women; Sister Assisium (Catherine) McEvoy, SSJ (1843–1939), a Philadelphia educator who played a key role in consolidating Catholic education both locally and nationally; and Katherine Eleanor Conway (1852–1927), a Boston journalist, editor, and public figure.

Sullivan, McGroarty, McEvoy, and Conway lived "varied lives" that were nonetheless "produced within a common field."[14] With the exception of McGroarty, who was a generation older than the other three, all were born within a few years of one another in the mid-nineteenth century. Two were born in Ireland and immigrated to the United States as young children; two were born to Irish immigrant parents. Sullivan was married, Conway was single, and McGroarty and McEvoy were vowed members of religious communities. Two were writers by profession; two were educators. Three of them knew one another; all of them almost certainly knew *of* one another. They were all well educated. Based respectively in Chicago, Cincinnati and Washington, D.C., Philadelphia, and Boston, they were not only decidedly urban but also concentrated in the Northeast and Midwest. In this sense I make no claim that these four were representative of all U.S. Catholic women.

I do maintain, however, that Sullivan, McGroarty, McEvoy, and Conway are especially enlightening: each of them illuminates a particular arena of confluence between the articulation of Catholic identity and the redefinition of gender roles. These four women might be considered "extraordinary" in that they did not, as the majority of their sisters did, live and die in obscurity. But Sullivan, McGroarty, McEvoy, and Conway were emblematic of other Irish American Catholic women in their commitment to education, in their rootedness in a Catholic past, and, above all, in their belief that they were far more marginalized as Catholics than they were as women. Collectively, their stories show how impossible it is to separate the question of what it meant to be a woman in the church from the question of what it meant to be a Catholic in American society.

Sullivan, McGroarty, McEvoy, and Conway lived through a period of transformation for many middle-class American women, one marked by the increasing availability of higher education, the development of new opportunities for professional employment, and the revival and expansion of the woman suffrage movement. The emergence of the "New Woman," a symbol of these changes, signaled the disintegration of the ideology of domesticity that had shaped gender roles in the United States since the Victorian period.[15] As an identifiable and convenient symbol of the expansion of the female experience, the New Woman was embraced by proponents of gender role transformations and held in contempt by the much larger group of Americans who supported traditional and clearly defined roles for men and women. Roman Catholics figured prominently in this latter category. For Catholics of Irish background, ethnicity and class inspired much of the resistance to the New Woman. She was, for example, regularly caricatured in the weekly columns written by Chicago journalist Finley Peter Dunne. His portrayal of "Mollie's" ridiculous efforts to imitate the New Woman captured Irish Americans' collective uneasiness about assimilation and loss of ethnic identity, especially as they divided along gender lines.[16]

Religious concerns, however, proved even more decisive. The New Woman stood in stark contrast to the Catholic "True Woman," the model whom all Catholic women were supposed to emulate. According to the

Reverend Bernard O'Reilly in *The Mirror of True Womanhood* (which was published in seventeen editions between 1876 and 1892), God had created the True Woman to be more spiritual than her male counterpart. Her highest calling was to motherhood, if not in the physical sense, then at least in the spiritual one. The home was her "God-appointed sphere" and the place where she should remain except for attending church or performing acts of charity. Characterized by generosity, self-abnegation, and a penchant for self-sacrifice, the Catholic True Woman exercised power only through her influence over men. "Just as Mary gave the savior to the world," O'Reilly noted, "a true woman in every home is the saviour and sanctifier of man."[17]

This idealistic view of womanhood had not been invented by O'Reilly; nor was it original to Catholics in general. The distinction between "public man" and "private woman" emerged in the United States in the early nineteenth century, when the advent of industrialization increasingly divided home from work. The ideology of "separate spheres" supported the concept of the "ideal" woman, who was characterized by her piety, purity, domesticity, and submissiveness. In the second half of the nineteenth century, many Catholics appropriated this gender ideology as they joined the middle and upper classes. But while Catholic gender ideology resembles and is often intertwined with that of American society at large, there is no question that beliefs about women's divinely mandated subordination have historically proved more intractable within a patriarchal institution such as the Roman Catholic Church. In that sense it is by no means surprising to discover that the New Woman was routinely lambasted in the Catholic press as a threat to traditional womanhood and, consequently, the social order.

But Catholic responses to the New Woman were much more complex than they initially appear. The emergence of the New Woman coincided with a dynamic period in the history of U.S. Catholicism. Beginning in the late 1880s, American Catholics were prompted by both internal and external factors to reevaluate their place in American life. From without, the resurgence of anti-Catholic nativism forced many Catholics to defend the compatibility of their faith and their government. From within, increasing ethnic diversity in the church, the dominance of Irish and Irish Americans among the church hierarchy, and the ascension of many Irish Americans to the middle class led to an extensive conversation and many disagreements about what it meant to be both Catholic and American.

At the heart of this debate were a series of controversies grouped under the broad heading "Americanism." Americanism sharply divided the Catholic hierarchy between the convocation of the Third Plenary Council of Baltimore in 1884 and the appearance of Pope Leo XIII's *Testem Benevolentiae* in 1899. At issue was the question of how the church should relate to American culture and society. On one side of the debate stood liberals or "Americanists," who promoted greater Catholic integration into U.S. social and political culture. Seeking to "unite Church and age," Americanists advocated rapid assimilation of Catholic immigrants, more participation of Catholic laity in public life, and stronger cooperation between parochial and public schools. They also believed that the United States, with its constitutional protection of religious freedom, provided the ideal conditions for the flourishing of Catholicism. Members of the opposing group, called conservatives, generally supported a more insular Catholic community. Wary of the Americanists' exuberant patriotism, they believed that the American church should keep barriers intact to shield its members from the evils of the United States. Conservatives also advocated closer ties between the American church and the Vatican.[18]

In 1896, the controversy escalated when several European Americanists claimed that the church in the United States should serve as a model for the rest of the world. Three years later, Pope Leo XIII settled the conflict with an apostolic letter. *Testem Benevolentiae* condemned as heresy a series of propositions under the heading "Americanism," the most noteworthy of which was the claim that the American church was intrinsically different from the church universal. Though the pope had worded the document in such manner that allowed both sides to claim a victory, *Testem Benevolentiae* dampened Catholic liberals' public enthusiasm for the American experiment for years to come.

The controversy over Americanism has been considered one of the most significant episodes in U.S. Catholic history, and its underlying cause—disagreement over what it meant to be Catholic and American—might even be described as the central organizing principle of the discipline. While studies of intellectual debates and hierarchical conflict lend themselves quite easily to inclusion of powerful men in Rome and Baltimore, it is initially difficult to imagine how these developments might affect Catholic women. A closer look, however, reveals multiple arenas of intersection between the emergence of the New Woman and Catholics' struggle to define their place and purpose in American culture during the late nineteenth and early twentieth centuries.

The writing of Margaret Buchanan Sullivan, for example, offers an ideal starting point to explore how Catholics used their critiques of the New Woman to defend their claims to American citizenship. By calling attention to previously unknown Catholic women of the past, Sullivan sought to contrast the hapless New Woman with the stalwart daughters of the "Old Faith." Her efforts in this regard were widely imitated by other U.S. Catholics, both women and men, who relied on a range of female historical figures to support a number of contentions. Canadian missionary Marie de l'Incarnation, Mohawk convert Kateri Tekakwitha, and American nun Elizabeth Ann Seton were among those cited as evidence that Catholics had played a key role in the founding and preservation of the American nation. European female saints and scholars constituted another popular group of Catholic heroines. Though Saint Elizabeth of Hungary, Saint Jane de Chantal, and professors at the University of Bologna, Italy, had never set foot on the North American continent, U.S. Catholics also enlisted them and others in a national project. Pointing to the extraordinary accomplishments these women had compiled under church auspices, U.S. Catholics maintained that it was their church, not the contemporary American women's rights movement, that offered women the best chance for emancipation. This argument was often crafted in deliberate response to those people who, by making the opposite claim, implicitly impugned Catholics' suitability for participation in American democracy.

Catholics' repeated contrasts between the daughters of the Old Faith and the New Woman masked the profound influence that the latter exerted over women of the community. The expansion of higher education, one of the most significant hallmarks of New Womanhood, offers a case in point. By the early 1890s, the daughters of an emerging Catholic middle class expressed a growing desire for access to institutions of higher learning. Admitting women to existing Catholic men's colleges was not a viable option, as there was virtually unanimous opposition to coeducation among Catholics. Equally threatening, however, was the prospect of Catholic women enrolling at one of a growing number of women's colleges, as studying at these "Protestant or infidel" institutions would surely jeopardize their Catholic faith.

Sister Julia McGroarty, recognizing that "education was the cry of the age in America," set out in 1897 to establish Trinity College in Washington, D.C.[19] In doing so, however, she unwittingly landed in the middle of the Americanist conflict at nearby Catholic University, and her alleged alliance with the liberals elicited a protest from the Vatican. Even after she secured official permission from Rome to continue her work, Sister Julia encountered a variety of hurdles erected by people who had competing visions of how "American" Trinity should become. The story of how she navigated the tensions between competing constituencies—women versus men, religious versus lay, and American versus European—underscores the dangers inherent in renegotiating what was possible for women under church auspices. Trinity's founding also illustrates the complications that attended U.S. Catholics' efforts to define their place in American society during the Progressive Era.

Education was indeed the "cry of the age" in Progressive Era America, especially at the elementary level. As historian Maureen Flanagan recently noted in her history of the period, Progressives believed that "a democratic society absolutely required equal access to a good education for every child" and that "women's engagement with decision-making was absolutely essential for achieving this goal." As Suellen Hoy makes clear in *Good Hearts*, Catholic women religious are an important part of this story. Throughout the Progressive Era and beyond, they played a critical role in providing the children of America's working poor with access to education and social mobility.[20]

Here again, Progressive Era developments intersected with Catholics' attempts to articulate and defend their religious interests. Catholic education, and women's role in it, were shaped by the church's commitment to expanding and consolidating a parallel school system in the late nineteenth and early twentieth centuries. Although the "school question"—how Catholics should educate their children—had been fundamental to debates over Catholic identity since the 1840s, in 1884 American bishops mandated that every parish have a school attached within two years. While that goal was never attained, the Catholic parochial school system developed into the largest nonpublic school system in the world. None of this would have been possible had it not been for the subsidized labor supplied by Catholic sisters. Though women religious were not Catholic educators' first choice as instructors for parochial schools, they soon became the preferred option, in part because they were both less expensive and more easily controlled than were their male counterparts.

Staffing Catholic schools was not the only task that preoccupied Catholic teaching sisters in the early twentieth century. Their work in classrooms, like that of public school teachers, was shaped by the Progressive quest for uniformity, efficiency, professionalization, and centralization. Sister Assisium McEvoy was the person charged with teacher training in the Sisters of St. Joseph of Philadelphia, a large congregation in a city whose episcopal leaders were among the most enthusiastic supporters of parochial school expansion. As such, she provides an ideal gateway to explore how gender and Catholic identity intersected within and shaped Catholics' response to Progressive Era developments in American education. McEvoy was one of many Catholic sisters who collaborated with the Reverend Philip McDevitt, archdiocesan superintendent between 1899 and 1916, in efforts to improve Philadelphia's Catholic schools. Throughout this period they also increasingly aspired to meet state standards, sought more benefits from the state, and watched schools become more subject to state control. In light of this, McEvoy and McDevitt went to great lengths to emphasize how Catholic schools prepared children for dual citizenship, not only in the American Republic but also in the kingdom of heaven.

The final chapter of this book explores how Catholic identity shaped debates about women in public life. In many ways, this topic represents the most complex and least understood arena of intersection between the process of Catholic self-definition and expanding options for women in American society. Throughout the Gilded Age and Progressive Era, women increasingly carved out a public presence through their participation and leadership in organizations devoted to temperance, labor, or social reform. After 1890, the most obvious way that women sought public influence was through the suffrage movement. Between 1890 and the passage of the Nineteenth Amendment in 1920, American Catholics engaged in a spirited discussion of the "woman question," shorthand for both women's participation in public life in general and the suffrage question in particular. U.S. Catholics' opinions on suffrage were always more diverse than conventional wisdom and existing historical scholarship would suggest, and thus this chapter uses Katherine E. Conway, a prominent antisuffragist, as a springboard to explore how deeply the woman question became intertwined with larger questions of Catholic identity.

Conway's antisuffrage views, her repeated affirmations of Catholic gender ideology, and the inconsistency between her beliefs and her actions have been interpreted as evidence of Catholic women's inability to grasp how much their lives were circumscribed by the church. Conway, however, would have been surprised to see the church portrayed as an oppressor of women. It was the Old Faith, after all, that had provided her with education, meaningful work, and multiple opportunities for leadership. Though she herself believed otherwise, Conway was undoubtedly affected by the more pronounced "consciousness of womanhood" that characterized the Progressive Era, and it is indeed possible to interpret the gap between her rhetoric and reality as the space in which she sought to renegotiate women's role within the church. Still, the bonds of religion proved much stronger than the bonds of ethnicity, class, or gender. Moreover, as a woman who saw herself perpetually motivated by a desire to act with "implicit Catholicity," Conway would have found little reason to ally with suffragists, whose hostility to the Catholic Church was readily apparent.

Sullivan, McGroarty, McEvoy, and Conway are unlikely to receive more than token mention in histories of American Catholicism, and with the possible exception of Conway, who might be cited for her antisuffrage views, they would not surface in a survey of U.S. women's history. While adjusting the historical narrative to reflect previously unknown figures represents an important step in taking Catholic women's religious experience seriously, ultimately this measure alone is insufficient if one is to make a more convincing case that their stories matter to the study of American religion. As Brekus points out, "Recovering women's stories is certainly crucial, but it is not enough. Especially at this point in the evolution of women's history, when so much has been discovered about women's lives in the past, historians must try to answer difficult questions about historical significance."[21] How, in other words, does attending to what was said by and about women amplify our understanding of the past?

In terms of American Catholic history, the greater inclusion of women reveals above all the extraordinary energy U.S. Catholics poured into differentiating themselves from their fellow and sister citizens. Many Catholics in the Progressive Era translated changing gender roles in the following manner: whereas the New Woman's unabashed assaults against the social order clearly augured disaster, the daughters of the Old Faith were simply bringing ancient wisdom to bear on modern culture. Students at secular women's colleges were foolishly seeking to "reorganize the Universe"; the women of Trinity, in contrast, would simply be following through on a development that was "perfectly logical, religiously and socially." Public school teachers and other professional women were preoccupied with money and prestige, while teaching sisters performed "the wageless work of paradise" out of their love for children and desire for eternal life. The woman suffragist was trying to squeeze a few measly and meaningless rights from the state; Catholic women, meanwhile, derived their rights from a higher power, which left them not only happier and more fulfilled but also better prepared for life in the modern world.

U.S. Catholics' widespread reliance on gender as a differentiator calls into question assumptions about their place in Progressive Era America. The defeat of the Americanists in 1899, coupled with the more emphatic condemnation of modernism by Pope Pius X in 1907, has led to a historical understanding of Catholics as uniquely insulated from broad currents of Progressive reform that swept the United States in the early years of the twentieth century.[22] Historians often cite the American Bishops' Program of Social Reconstruction, issued in 1919, as the great, if short-lived, rapprochement between Catholicism and Progressivism. Until then, Joseph M. McShane contends, U.S. Catholics lacked the intellectual tools to develop a coherent response to the problems of industrialization and to reconcile their ethnic faith with American ideals.[23]

Sullivan, McGroarty, McEvoy, and Conway suggest otherwise. Progressivism undoubtedly shaped their lives and work, and long before 1919 they proved very deft at mediating between the tradition of the Old Faith and the exigencies of a new, industrialized nation. Sullivan sought, along with other Progressive Era journalists, to use the power of the press to educate American citizens. As she contemplated the woman of the twentieth century, however, Sullivan used historical examples of female scholars, physicians, and influential figures to argue that women's contemporary achievements in education, the professions, and public life were only "apparently new." Sister Julia, determined to "supply the wants of the age for American girls," established friendships with key secular women's educators such as M. Carey Thomas of Bryn Mawr College. While these relationships reflected an unprecedented level of Catholic engagement with broader American culture, Sister Julia was canny enough to maintain that in seeking to open a women's college, the Sisters of Notre Dame were not trying anything new and dangerous but merely "enlarging [their] lives to suit the times." Sister Assisium McEvoy's work in education—shaped by a more pronounced differentiation of roles, a drive for efficiency, increased bureaucratization, and higher levels of accountability to the state—indelibly bears the mark of Progressivism. Yet she translated these changes as a modern manifestation of her congregations' centuries-old commitment to balancing the life of contemplation with the active life of a religious, a task she often expressed in biblical language as the complementary calls of "Mary" and "Martha." Katherine Conway's ruminations on woman suffrage reflected the Progressive struggle to balance individual rights with the common good and to redraw the boundaries between public and private. In addition, like many of her contemporaries, Conway challenged gender prescriptions. In doing so, however, she insisted that she was motivated by "implicit Catholicity," rather than by a desire to imitate the New Woman.

Sullivan, McGroarty, McEvoy, and Conway were most certainly not New Women. Yet in recognizing and responding to the demands of a new century, they are inevitably part of the story of American Progressivism. Their rhetoric notwithstanding, these women did in fact arrive at modernity in the early twentieth century, though their path looked different from that traveled by Jane Addams and other figures who have captured far more historical attention. As Catholics became more like, rather than different from, their fellow citizens, they intensified the rhetoric of differentiation, often enlisting gender for this purpose. Jane Addams, in fact, loomed large in American Catholics' discussions of Progressive Era womanhood. Addams's charitable contribution, they argued, paled in comparison with the legacy of the legions of Catholic saints who antedated her by centuries. Neither did Addams's record stack up very well against that established by contemporary members of women's religious orders, who, as Catholics never tired of pointing out, far outnumbered settlement house workers. Furthermore, many Catholics took pride in the fact that nuns, unlike Addams and other New Women, were preternaturally adverse to self-aggrandizement. This rhetoric of differentiation obviously served a Catholic apologetic purpose. But it also allowed Catholic women to affirm their loyalty to the Old Faith, thereby establishing a distance from the New Woman that, conveniently, enabled them to emulate her in many respects.[24]

To claim that these women and other American Catholics shared more with Progressives than they liked to admit is not to overlook the fundamental differences that separated them from the majority of Progressive reformers. Perhaps the key one is this: if many Catholics shared the Progressive belief in the power of institutions to reform and transform American society, they parted ways with Progressives in dramatic fashion when it came to deciding *which* institution was best suited to this purpose. Most Catholics were deeply suspicious of Progressive attempts to extend the reach of federal and state governments, particularly because they perceived them, in many cases correctly, as motivated by antipathy toward Catholics. It was the Catholic Church, they maintained, that was best equipped to help its adherents respond to the demands of a new age.

Acknowledging U.S. Catholics' powerful devotion to and confidence in their church has significant implications for situating figures like Sullivan, McGroarty, McEvoy, and Conway in the history of American women. In the sixth edition of *Women's America*, Kerber and De Hart emphasize that the best recent scholarship in women's history not only accounts for differences of race, class, ethnicity, and sexual orientation but also analyzes the way these factors interact to shape, support, and ultimately obscure gender systems. Although other scholars have argued for the inclusion of religion in this matrix, most historians of U.S. women and gender continue to show "little interest in religion, leaving the field to those who identify themselves explicitly as religious historians."[25]

The stories of Sullivan, McGroarty, McEvoy, Conway, and their contemporaries suggest that inattentiveness to religion has caused women's historians to overlook a powerful source of women's meaning and identity. For many Catholic women in the Progressive Era, religious identity was not simply an important factor but the decisive one in determining how they ordered their world. Without recognizing how Catholic identity factored into the construction of gender, it is not possible to appreciate the choices women made. Neither is it possible to understand how religious identity interacted with variables of race, ethnicity, and class. At a time when the identity question was paramount, what it meant to be a woman in the Catholic Church largely depended on perceptions of what it meant to be a Catholic in American culture.

For many of the women in this book, in other words, religious identity was always present and therefore must always be considered. This argument paraphrases Deborah Gray White, who observed in *Too Heavy a Load* that "although it cannot be said that black women always chose race over other aspects of their identity, it can be said that race, *along with* gender and class, were variables *always* factored into whatever [African American women's] national organizations did."[26] In acknowledging my debt to scholars of African American women, I join both Maureen Fitzgerald, who drew a number of parallels between her analysis of Irish Catholic nuns and studies of women of color, and Ann Braude, who recently noted that "Protestantism often functions as an unmarked category in women's history because religion is not analyzed as a source of difference, just as whiteness disappears when the impact of race is only considered for non-whites."[27]

I realize, of course, that a comparison between the status of U.S. Catholics and that of African Americans extends only so far. By no means am I suggesting that levels of antipathy toward Catholics in American culture approached the degree of hostility experienced by African Americans or that Catholics had to overcome obstacles similar to those created by the legacy of slavery and racism. Nevertheless, there are similarities between the Progressive Era experience of women of color and Catholic women that are instructive. I see remarkable parallels between the black church that Evelyn Brooks Higginbotham describes in *Righteous Discontent* and the immigrant church to which many Catholic women belonged. If the black church provided African Americans with their "most effective vehicle" to combat the effects of racism and poverty, the Catholic Church offered its faithful a way to rally against a culture that considered them suspect. If, through women's activism, the black church "built schools, provided clothes and food to poor people, established old folks homes and orphanages, and made available a host of needed welfare services," Catholic women's labor also created a vast parallel network of schools, hospitals, colleges, and social service organizations that provided members of a beleaguered minority with succor and a path to upward mobility. And while "the cynical era of Jim Crow and the optimistic women's era stood entangled with each other," it is also true that this crucial period in American Catholic history coincided with and was shaped by this defining period in the history of U.S. women.[28]

Thanks to the work of scholars like White, Higginbotham, and others, historians of U.S. women understand that race often trumped gender in terms of categories of identity. What they have not yet fully considered, I would argue, is the power of religious alliances to overcome gender-based ones. For Sullivan, McGroarty, McEvoy, Conway, and others, Catholicism was indeed always present, though, like race, it never stood alone. Many of the women who appear in this book may have been united by gender and religion, but they were often divided by boundaries of class and ethnicity. And, of course, the way they defined religious identity privileged other identities—white, Irish American, and, for the most part, middle class—in ways that they themselves did not acknowledge or even recognize. Katherine Conway, for instance, believed—against considerable evidence to the contrary—that Irishness and Catholicism were "practically convertible terms" in the late nineteenth-century United States. This assumption blinded her to ethnic and class divisions. But her conviction that Catholics' loyalty to the Old Faith would supersede all their other allegiances is nonetheless essential for understanding her relationship with non-Catholic women.

While the stories of women like Sullivan, McGroarty, McEvoy, and Conway undoubtedly demonstrate how "women have challenged, or at least reshaped, their subordination in Christian religious traditions," their historical significance goes beyond judging whether they and their counterparts were primarily empowered or oppressed.[29] These women understood that they were far more marginalized as Catholics than they were as women, and this understanding explains why they and other women like them perennially allied themselves with men who shared their religious beliefs and why they remained largely unpersuaded by the emerging feminist movement and its immediate precursors. This is not to say that gender tensions did not exist; as we will see, they are inevitably part of the story of these women's lives. But those tensions were held in check by an overwhelming sense of solidarity as members of the Catholic Church. Though Catholic women of the early twentieth century were not entirely unaware of their own subordination in a patriarchal institution, the vast majority of them defined themselves in such a manner that made any identification with feminism far beyond their purview.

Religion would not always play such a decisive role within this particular cohort of American Catholics. Indeed, by the 1960s, the seeds of discontent buried under Catholic alliances would begin to sprout, watered by a number of theological and demographic shifts. Catholic women would respond very differently to the encounter with feminism in its second wave than they had done in its first.

CHAPTER ONE Chiefly among Women

THE OLD FAITH, THE NEW WOMAN,

AND THE CREATION OF A USABLE PAST

In 1875, "An American Woman" published an article in the *Catholic World* that represented an outraged response to a comment made by William Gladstone, the former (and future) prime minister of Great Britain. Speaking of the growth of the Catholic Church in England, Gladstone had observed that "the conquests have been chiefly, as might have been expected, among women." Across the Atlantic, "An American Woman" bristled at the insult, interpreting Gladstone's comment as "an indirect and ungraceful way of saying that the Catholic Church brings conviction more readily to weaker than to stronger intellects, and that because the 'conquests' are 'chiefly among women,' the progress of the church among the people is not substantial, general or permanent."[1]

"An American Woman" was the pseudonym of Margaret Buchanan Sullivan, an Irish-born Roman Catholic then in the early stages of a successful career as a journalist. An ardent Irish nationalist, Sullivan was poised to disagree with Gladstone on just about any subject, but she found his assumptions about Catholicism and women particularly agitating.[2] Marveling at the thoughtlessness that enabled him and other "well-read men" to misinterpret the place of women within the church, Sullivan turned Gladstone's insult on its head: nineteen centuries on, she argued, the Catholic Church was flourishing precisely because it had appealed so successfully to women. To support her case, Sullivan "offered in evidence" a litany of examples of accomplished women who professed the Catholic faith, ranging from the first-century apostle Thecla of Iconium, to the sixteenth-century French foundress Jane de Chantal, to the nineteenth-century

American nun Elizabeth Ann Seton. Noting that "religion alone supplied their motive," Sullivan asked whether any woman in "profane history" could equal the accomplishments of these and other daughters of Catholicism. For if the church owed its success to its women, the inverse was also true: only under church auspices could women develop their "heroic characteristics" to the fullest potential.[3]

There are many reasons why "Chiefly among Women" should have been altogether forgotten. It was an early work of Sullivan's, it was written anonymously, and it considered women in an age when female subjects rarely surfaced in Catholic publications. But far from fading into obscurity, "Chiefly among Women" would repeatedly receive new leases on life. Over the next four decades, it was cited, quoted, and reprinted, with the author's identity revealed at some point along the way. Jesuit George Tyrrell, for example, referred at length to "Chiefly among Women" in his 1897 essay "The Old Faith and the New Woman," which appeared in the *American Catholic Quarterly Review*. The "Old Faith" was Roman Catholicism, and Tyrrell, an Irish-born theologian, was one of many late nineteenth-century Catholic intellectuals who struggled to reconcile this ancient religion with modern rationality.[4]

Tyrrell's ruminations on the Old Faith and the New Woman suggest that there was a significant gender dimension to what R. Scott Appleby has described as Catholic modernists' "thoroughgoing commitment to preserving theological continuity with the fullness of the Catholic tradition as it had unfolded in history."[5] In contrast to the Old Faith, then a venerable nineteen centuries old, the New Woman was of far newer vintage, having arrived only recently on the American scene. Novelist Henry James had coined the phrase "New Woman" to describe wealthy widows living abroad. According to James, what made them "new" was their freedom from male control. In a variation on that theme, the American version of the New Woman derived both her newness and her freedom through her break with traditional domestic roles. By attending college, earning her own living, working in a settlement house, or otherwise participating in activities outside women's "sphere," she challenged the ideology of domesticity that had prevailed since the mid-nineteenth century. Financially independent from either a father or a husband, the New Woman "stood for self-development as contrasted to self-sacrifice or submergence within the family."[6]

Catholic writers routinely castigated the New Woman as the antithesis of the Catholic True Woman. Tyrrell criticized the New Woman's silly style of dress, her selfish disregard for family, and her pursuit of equality in marriage. Other Catholic writers agreed, accusing the New Woman of being "unpardonably ridiculous, for, unconsciously we trust, she launches forth her tiny javelin at the very corner-stone of the social edifice, which demands that for its preservation there always exist a suitable subordination of powers, the essential principle of all right order in heaven and earth."[7] Another writer compared the New Woman to Lady Macbeth and observed that outside the home "[a woman] is a foreign excrescence [sic] ugly to behold."[8] The New Woman's presumed alliance with proponents of woman suffrage earned her special condemnation. In a 1914 *Catholic Encyclopedia* article titled "Woman," Augustine Rössler observed that "it is difficult to unite the direct participation of woman in the political and parliamentary life of the present time with her predominant duty as a mother." According to Rössler, God and nature had designed the two sexes to complement each other, and "man is called by the Creator to [the] position of leader, as is shown by his entire bodily and intellectual makeup."[9]

These critiques were fairly run of the mill; most Americans, after all, despised the New Woman for her perceived assault on the social order, her implied sexual freedom, and her demand for public influence over matters and decisions best left to men's judgment. But among their perfunctory complaints, Tyrrell and others did raise a few distinctively Catholic objections. The New Woman was "an abomination to Catholic instincts" primarily because she was "animated by many false principles for which J. S. [John Stuart] Mill [was] largely responsible." Tracing her antecedents to the Protestant Reformation, Tyrrell accused the New Woman of representing a type of individualism that was "essentially uncatholic and anti-catholic."[10]

Tyrrell's linkage of the New Woman to both modern liberalism and the Protestant Reformation was telling. Among her many troubling characteristics, it was the New Woman's autonomy that proved most alarming to Catholics. It was not her financial independence from male relatives that especially concerned them. Indeed, thanks in part to enduring Irish patterns of gender segregation, unattached, wage-earning women occupied a respectable place in American Catholic culture. But because single Catholic women understood themselves to be, and were expected to be, intimately invested in the larger faith community, the New Woman's rootlessness and "disintegrating individualism" proved anathema to many Catholics of both

sexes. As the fourth chapter shows, this rootlessness was the most significant reason why many Catholic women turned a deaf ear to the cries of
woman suffragists. Allying with the leaders of that movement not only
would have meant rejecting the social group that claimed their primary
loyalty but also would have required them to look beyond the "organic
conception of society" that formed the basis of Catholics' worldview.[11]

The New Woman's detachment from tradition proved equally disturbing
to most Catholic commentators. Tyrrell, for example, harped on the New
Woman's very novelty: as a fleeting and inconsistent phenomenon, unmoored to any tradition, she marked an unfavorable contrast with the
resolute daughters of the Old Faith. It was in this context that Tyrrell
recycled "Chiefly among Women," citing Sullivan's meticulous "retrospect
of the past" to prove that "where the Church has her way, and is not
trammeled by local prejudices, she desires the fullest and possible mental
and moral development of women."[12] The "local prejudices" to which Tyrrell referred had a very particular meaning to readers of the *American
Catholic Quarterly Review*. The journal had been founded in 1876 as a vehicle
designed to mediate the uneasy relationship between Catholicism and another development that was, comparatively speaking, very novel: the
United States of America. According to Tyrrell, both the New Woman and
the young nation were inclined to jettison the past too easily, to their
mutual detriment. By bringing the wisdom of the ancient church to bear on
both of them, Tyrrell maintained that U.S. Catholics could position themselves as advocates of "sane progress" in a culture that apparently seemed to
value progress only for its own sake.

As U.S. Catholics grappled with the dissonance between old and new—
whether faiths, countries, or women—their conversations about the boundaries of True Womanhood intersected with debates over American Catholic
identity. In this context the strategy that Sullivan had implemented in
"Chiefly among Women" would be widely imitated. Indeed, in the late
nineteenth and early twentieth centuries, American Catholics called upon
an astonishing variety of female historical figures, most of whom had been
named by Sullivan, to defend and define the church in the United States.
Though Catholics' collective admiration for these daughters of the Old Faith
initially strikes a discordant note in an era defined by "progress," it is clear
that they used them to meet thoroughly modern ends. To better appreciate

those ends, it is important to understand Margaret Buchanan Sullivan and the larger American Catholic landscape of which she was a part.

MARGARET BUCHANAN SULLIVAN AND THE CATHOLIC ANSWER TO THE NEW WOMAN

Margaret Frances Buchanan was born in Drumquinn, County Tyrone, Ireland, in 1847, the ninth child of James and Susan Gorman Buchanan. Though her birth coincided with the worst of the famine years, it is unlikely that the family's finances suffered too much as a result of that national calamity. Of Ireland's four provinces, Ulster was the least affected by famine, and James's occupation as a manufacturer would have further protected them from its adverse consequences. Far more ominous for the Buchanan fortunes was James's death, which occurred soon after Margaret's birth. In 1851, Susan and her children immigrated to Michigan, where her two eldest sons had settled in the early 1840s.[13]

In Detroit the Buchanans attended Mass at Holy Trinity Parish, where Margaret received her first Communion.[14] She attended a Catholic academy run by the Society of the Sacred Heart, a French congregation that had been established in the United States since 1818. By the mid-nineteenth century Sacred Heart sisters had opened a number of girls' academies, many of which catered to daughters of the wealthier classes. Katherine Conway, a friend of Sullivan's whom we will focus on in the fourth chapter, was another Sacred Heart alumna who acknowledged that the congregation attracted not only upwardly mobile Irish American girls but also non-Catholic elites. Conway speculated that many Protestant mothers sent their daughters to the Sacred Heart so "that they might not be surpassed in ladylike gentleness and reserve by the Mary O'Connors and Nora McFarlands of the new stock."[15] Margaret Buchanan Sullivan also recognized the congregation's association with the upper class when she noted that the "accomplished women" associated with Sacred Heart possessed a "refined taste" that distinguished them "as heirs of the authentic tradition of true womanhood."[16]

After her graduation Margaret Buchanan became principal of one of Detroit's public high schools. But she had aspired to be a writer since she was a child, and in 1870 she moved to Chicago to begin a career as a

Margaret Buchanan Sullivan, circa 1870. Courtesy of Peter Buchanan, Berkley, Michigan.

journalist.[17] Buchanan's intrepid efforts to secure an editorial position later became the stuff of legend. Most accounts of her life include a variation of the following story: after she submitted a series of anonymous articles on the most pressing issues of the day, the editor of the *Chicago Evening Post* was so impressed with their quality that he offered the author a job before he was aware of her sex or her age.[18] In short order she became "the best man on the paper," but her sex would continue to be a liability.[19] In 1872 a feature in the *Woman's Journal* commended Buchanan for her habit of writing without a byline. By not identifying herself as a woman, the writer observed, Buchanan would "checkmate prejudice . . . without gratifying her own vanity or decreasing the force of her press by the signature of her name."[20]

During her early years in Chicago Buchanan lived at Sacred Heart's convent on Taylor Street. She was reportedly delighted to be "surrounded by a greater number of cultivated, pure, and intellectual women than [she] could possibly find elsewhere. In this convent woman's right to her own soul and body is realized and fulfilled."[21] Buchanan's congenial living quarters might explain why, according to an article that appeared in the *New York World* in 1872, she appeared to be "a girl who seems to have never yet seriously thought of marrying."[22]

However skeptical she might have been about the married state, in 1874 Buchanan married Alexander Sullivan, an Irish American lawyer with whom she had been acquainted in Detroit. The couple settled in Chicago, where they would remain for the rest of their lives, despite subsequent attempts to lure Margaret to bigger newspaper markets in Boston and New

York. But Sullivan had "cast her lot decisively with the great Western Metropolis," and she remained active in Chicago's civic life until her death in 1903.[23] She was also active in her local parish, Holy Name Cathedral.[24]

By all accounts the Sullivans were happy together. The Reverend Maurice Dorney, pastor of St. Gabriel's Parish on Chicago's South Side and a family friend, reportedly said that "if ever there was a woman who understood what Christian sacramental marriage is, it was Margaret Sullivan." The marriage produced no children. According to her friend, Katherine Conway, this was both a source of lifelong sorrow to Margaret and the very reason her career as a journalist continued to develop after her marriage.[25]

Alexander Sullivan was a volatile and ambitious man best remembered for his leadership of Clan-na-Gael, the Irish revolutionary organization that had been established in New York in 1867.[26] In 1876, his hot temper, ignited by anti-Catholic prejudice, precipitated what certainly was the most colorful incident of Margaret's life. At a meeting of the Chicago City Council, a letter was read that accused Margaret Sullivan of using her editorial influence to interfere with the affairs of the school board, implying that as a Catholic she had a vested interest in undermining the city's public schools. The author of the letter was Francis Hanford, principal of Chicago's North Side High School. Alexander Sullivan was present at the meeting and, outraged at the insult to his wife, called upon Hanford that evening to demand a retraction. The argument soon turned physical and ended when Alexander fatally shot Hanford with his pistol, reportedly in self-defense. After the first trial ended in a hung jury, Sullivan was acquitted in a second trial.[27] In 1889, Alexander was also implicated in the brutal murder of Patrick Henry Cronin, a member of a rival faction of Clan-na-Gael. Though he was considered a leading suspect, he was never charged.[28]

Like her husband, Margaret Sullivan believed passionately in Ireland's right to home rule, and she wrote prolifically about the subject.[29] Speaking of Sullivan's 1881 book, *Ireland of To-day*, nationalist hero Michael Davitt praised her for bringing "the salient facts of Ireland's history, with great literary skill, before the wide circle of her readers."[30] Sullivan was equally zealous in defense of her Catholic faith, and she was well aware that, in the eyes of many Americans, her Irishness and her Catholicism compromised her loyalty to the United States. But while Alexander Sullivan took up his pistol in response to ethnic and religious prejudice, Margaret's pen would become her fiercest weapon against anti-Catholicism.

After the publication of "Chiefly among Women" in 1875, Sullivan began to contribute more consciously to Catholic publications, even as she began to acquire more accolades in the field of secular journalism. Although she attributed her burgeoning interest in the Catholic press to the influence of her husband, more impersonal factors were also at work.[31] By the early 1880s, Catholics' collective increase in wealth, leisure, and religious consciousness created an audience to support a publishing industry, and so there were simply a wider array of magazines, journals, and newspapers from which to choose. By 1894 one priest compiled a list of more than four hundred Catholic publications, noting that while all were "not distinctively Catholic in purpose, [they] were yet, in general tone, more or less in marked and close sympathy with the Faith." Many of these "semi-Catholic" publications were Irish American.[32]

Another significant factor in Sullivan's growing interest in the Catholic press was her conviction that it could be used to counteract the persistent distortions or dismissals of Catholicism that appeared in print. In "Chiefly among Women," she had rebuked non-Catholic scholars for "reading too much on their own side of the line," and she believed that it was up to Catholic authors to balance the field with a sufficient amount of their own material.[33] It was with this purpose in mind that Sullivan joined other Catholic writers in contributing to the inaugural volume of the *American Catholic Quarterly Review* a year later. As its name implied, the *Review* aimed to be "not only Catholic, but American," and it aspired to reach "the large class of our non-Catholic countrymen . . . who dislike and condemn us, because they know us only, not as we are, but as we have been falsely presented to their view."[34] Sullivan's essay criticized a speech that had been delivered by "a prominent American statesman" entitled "The Republic: Will It Endure?" Charging that the lecture had contained "a curious . . . and wholly unaccountable attack upon the Catholic Church," she assiduously refuted the speaker's claim that Catholicism and republicanism had historically been at odds. Though she drew evidence from the sweep of world history to make her point, her essay was unmistakably national in its scope: Sullivan was determined to find evidence from the past that would underscore U.S. Catholics' patriotism and eligibility for responsible citizenship.[35]

By the early 1890s, the desire of Catholic writers to use their talents to defend the faith found concrete expression through the Apostolate of the Press, a loosely organized movement led by Walter Elliott, a Paulist priest.

Elliot urged members of the Apostolate to "adopt a spirit of intellectual aggressiveness" and to spread the "Catholic truth" through the medium of Catholic newspapers and magazines. With "we are right and we can prove it" as their motto, members of the Apostolate convened in New York City in 1892. A distinctive feature of the Apostolate was the number of female participants. Women delivered approximately one-quarter of the speeches at the 1892 convention, and according to Elliott, equality between the sexes was "so spontaneously felt" during the meeting "that allusion to it would have been superfluous."[36]

As Colleen McDannell has observed, many women writing for the Catholic press looked upon their work as a "spiritual vocation." Mary Browne, a Catholic from New York who would write as Marion Brunowe, spoke of a "certain pride in trying to build up a Catholic literature and show the non-Catholics that we can write as well & even better than they." Mary Meline, another aspiring writer, wanted to publish in Catholic journals for her "soul's sake."[37] Margaret Jordan, a Catholic writer from Portland, Maine, explained that while "others may write for intellects, I write to touch souls, and life holds few joys equal that of a brief glimpse into some soul helped in an hour of need by some thought of mine sent forth upon its mission on the wings of prayer."[38]

Though far more successful in the secular press than any of these women, Margaret Sullivan certainly viewed aspects of her work as a religious calling. She believed that Catholic writers were compelled to expose "the error which masquerades as truth in modern literature," and she dedicated herself to the task of "counteract[ing] the work of Protestant or agnostic historians and scientists."[39] Although Sullivan once described her profession as "the literary form of commerce that collects, corrupts and diffuses misinformation," she well understood the power that journalists had to educate. As she grew more accomplished in her field, she increasingly viewed her profession as way to "combat the anti-Catholic bigotry emanating from ignorance."[40]

In 1897 Mother Seraphine, an Ursuline sister, included Sullivan's profile in *Immortelles of Catholic Columbian Literature*, a compilation of the work of sixty-three Catholic women writers. Describing the book as "a fin-de-siecle offering to our Holy Mother, the Church," Mother Seraphine hoped that Catholic women of the twentieth century would read it and be inspired to follow in the footsteps of these writers.[41] Many of them did. By 1913 writing became such a reputable occupation for women that a Catholic priest would praise women's "prodigious literary output" and observe that "it is no longer necessary, in deference to public sentiment, for them to write under a pseudonym. . . . It is no longer considered unfeminine."[42]

The Apostolate of the Press not only facilitated a rise in the number of Catholic women authors but was also responsible for increasing the number of female *subjects* in the Catholic press. In this sense Sullivan's "Chiefly among Women" had been a harbinger of things to come. In 1875, articles about women were relatively rare in Catholic publications, with the exception of an occasional essay on the religious life of nuns or domestic servants. By the late 1880s, however, Catholic magazines and newspapers featured a variety of articles about women from a range of backgrounds.

In many cases author and subject were one and the same. This was certainly the case with Margaret Sullivan, as many Catholic publications boasted of her accomplishments. It was also true of Mary Austin Carroll, a Sister of Mercy. As Carroll's biographical sketch in *Immortelles* noted, her life was "given to America and Americans" even though she had been born in Ireland. After her 1854 arrival in the United States, she opened twenty convents and schools and established a respectable publishing record.[43] In the same year that *Immortelles* appeared, Henry Austin Adams, the editor of *Donahoe's Magazine*, devoted several of his opening editorials to Carroll's accomplishments. Adams complained that "woman, 'new' and otherwise, is being more discussed, written up, and 'organized,' in this last hour of the nineteenth century than she has ever been before since the world began." He claimed that Mary Austin Carroll's literary, scientific, and educational achievements "would have furnished a whole society of agitators with something to talk about for forty consecutive years." But as a nun who "does, and talks not," Mary Austin Carroll stood no "chance of notoriety." For this reason, Adams claimed, she presented a "withering and deadly answer to the New Woman."[44]

The question of why the New Woman merited such a devastating response is an interesting one, and the answer is explicitly tied to the objectives of the Apostolate of the Press. While the New Woman was attracting all the attention, Adams grumbled, Mother Austin Carroll and other daughters of the church were quietly going about their work. In Adams's view, the problem of Catholic women's invisibility would not be solved by persuading Mother Carroll and other Catholic women to modify their habits of "modest retirement" or "womanly reserve," which were understood to be both immutable and worthy of praise. Instead, it was incumbent upon the members of the Apostolate of the Press to highlight Catholic women's activities, to show that they at the very least rivaled, and probably surpassed, those of American Protestant women.

Donahoe's "Women's Page" had been instituted in 1893 for exactly that purpose. The editors argued that Catholic women's natural reticence had obscured their contributions to American society and, as a result, had damaged the "Catholic cause" in the United States. The editors felt this was especially true with regard to women's charitable work. While the public spotlight focused on Protestant women in the settlement house movement, Catholic nuns and laywomen served the poor in secret. The editors claimed that it was their duty to show "that men and women fitted for any position demanding qualifications of brain, heart, and soul could be found in the Catholic Church."[45] Writing in another Catholic publication, Lily Alice Toomy offered biblical reasoning for this greater recognition. In the past lay Catholic women, like vowed religious, had performed charitable works in secret, abiding by the exhortation to "let not thy right hand know what thy left hand doeth." Although this standard suited the old world, Toomy reasoned, the modern age demanded that U.S. Catholics adopt a new guiding principle: "let your light shine before men so that they may see your good works."[46] Once again, it was the people *writing* about Catholic women's actions, rather than the actors themselves, who were charged with shining that light.

If other Catholic writers were more oblique than Adams, they were no less deliberate in supplying their readers with alternatives to the New Woman. More often than not, these responses constituted the New Woman's literal opposite: women of the past. One thing the New Woman could never compete with was the weight of tradition, and as always, Catholics played to their strengths. As Margaret Sullivan had done in "Chiefly among Women," Catholic writers supplied an astonishing variety of Catholic heroines that could inspire and guide their modern counterparts. In addition to shoring up Catholic womanhood in the face of contemporary assaults against it, these examples were also used to articulate and defend a distinctive American Catholic identity. By examining the kind of women Catholic writers chose to feature, it is possible to more fully understand their preoccupations and concerns as they tried to define a place for members of the Old Faith in a new and industrializing nation.

Catholic writers supplied heroines of at least three types, all of which had been included in Margaret Sullivan's "Chiefly among Women." The first of these were women who could be said to have contributed in some fashion to the founding and the preservation of the American nation. Descriptions of these national heroines merged with broader patterns of Catholic hagiography and eventually shaped the quest for the first American canonized saint. Writers stretched farther back in history to recover a second type of Catholic woman, female figures from the Middle Ages through the seventeenth century who had compiled significant records of achievement under church auspices. Though these women predated the establishment of the United States, they also served a national purpose for U.S. Catholics in the late nineteenth and early twentieth centuries. Faced with repeated accusations that their church served as a historical and ongoing oppressor of women, American Catholics used these examples to argue that the opposite was true.

The third and final type of Catholic heroine was distinguished in this sense: while the first two types were routinely employed by Catholics of both sexes, the third type proved most expedient to women who were seeking to expand the boundaries of true Catholic womanhood. Using the strategy Margaret Sullivan had implemented in "Chiefly among Women," many women would rely on a Catholic past to mediate between the proscriptions of the Old Faith and the possibilities of New Womanhood.

THE OLD FAITH AND THE NEW LAND

In "Chiefly among Women," Margaret Buchanan Sullivan had listed Mary of the Incarnation as one of the daughters of the Catholic faith with whom Protestant historians should acquaint themselves. Mary of the Incarnation was the Americanized name of Marie de l'Incarnation, a French Ursuline who served as a missionary to Quebec in the mid-seventeenth century. Born Marie Guyart in France in 1599, she had been a widowed mother when she entered the Ursulines at the age of thirty-two. It was only "love of the Faith," Sullivan observed, that could have enabled Marie to set forth from her beloved France in 1639, "with certain expectation never to return, and equally certain that in the new land [she] would encounter an almost perpetual winter" and other perils. According to Sullivan, Marie de l'Incarnation inaugurated an American tradition of sending "pioneers of religion to the frontiers of civilization, equipping hospitals, asylums and schools wherever and whenever called." Her bravery and achievements were unparalleled outside Catholic circles. "What stately woman's figure," Sullivan wondered, "rises in profane history to the height of Mary of the Incarnation?"[47]

Sullivan's inclusion of Marie and other North American women on her list of luminous daughters of the faith hints at the national implications of an argument she would make more explicit elsewhere. Convinced that the "religious predilections" or "incomplete reading" of most American historians had prompted them to overlook Catholics, Sullivan was determined to reveal a history unknown to most American citizens. Historian John Gilmary Shea agreed. Writing in the nation's centennial year, Shea insisted that Catholics must be more consciously included in accounts of the nation's past. Eight years later, Shea would be instrumental in organizing the American Catholic Historical Society. Members of this group committed themselves to collecting, researching, and maintaining a history of Catholic contributions to American culture, so as to show that "from the beginning of our history, Catholics have been instrumental in adding to the forward progress of our nation."[48]

Over the next few decades, Margaret Sullivan and others would join Shea in compiling "a grand record of heroic deeds for the Old Faith and the New Land." In the process they created a Catholic version of American history that would, courtesy of a thriving Catholic publishing industry, receive wide circulation.[49] As historian Joseph Moreau points out, this Catholic interpretation of the national narrative would also be disseminated to Catholic children in parochial schools and, like the history presented to white schoolchildren in the segregated South, would coexist with the dominant accounts of the American past until the 1940s.[50]

The "ideal retelling of America's stories," primarily intended to foster both religious and civic pride, was also used to reinforce gender distinctions.[51] Indeed, while most of the nominees for inclusion in "the Catholic pages of American history" were men, there was room for a few women, especially if their stories could be used to affirm the feminine characteristics that the church defined as ideal. The historical figures of Christopher Columbus and his patron, Queen Isabella, demonstrate this confluence of gender and religious identity.

Although Columbus's story had long been a staple in U.S. history texts, in the hands of Catholic authors the daring adventurer was reinvented as a devout Catholic. Sadlier's *History*, published in 1879 for use in parochial schools, described the discovery of America as "pre-eminently a Catholic enterprise," noting that "Protestantism did not yet exist" as of 1492.[52] In 1882, the Knights of Columbus, a Catholic fraternal organization, was organized in the discoverer's honor, to restore "the records of Catholic achievements on this continent."[53] In 1889, recognizing the centennial of the first U.S. diocese, John Gilmary Shea declared unequivocally that Columbus "belonged" to American Catholics.[54] At the Catholic Centenary Conference that same year, one enthusiastic participant staked an even greater proprietary claim, insisting that "without Catholic Columbus, America would never have been discovered."[55] Though this was an unlikely proposition, it served the larger purpose of reinterpreting the American past through a Catholic lens.[56]

Queen Isabella added an important female dimension to Catholics' widespread appropriation of Columbus. Biographical accounts of the Spanish queen, like those about Columbus, exaggerated her contribution to the American nation. Eliza Allen Starr and other ladies of the Queen Isabella Association, inspired by "patriotic, religious and womanly honor," championed Isabella as "the co-discoverer of the New World." Catholic novelist Eleanor C. Donnelly observed that "it was the genius of a woman, the generosity of a woman, that first made possible the discovery of America."[57] Eliza O'Brien Lummis, founder of Filiae Fidei (Daughters of the Faith), suggested that the influence of Isabella's "self-sacrificing spirit" had lent Columbus the encouragement to continue when his energy was flagging.[58]

Admirers of Isabella extolled her as a True Woman. Exceeding Columbus "in beauty, in personal dignity, in acuteness of genius and in grandeur of soul," Isabella combined "the active and resolute qualities of man with the softer side of woman."[59] At the 1893 World Columbian Exposition in Chicago, Mary J. Onahan, the daughter of William Onahan, chair of the exposition's Catholic Congress, hailed Isabella as the "true queen and true woman." Though Isabella was long dead, the ideal of womanhood she represented continued to be held up by the "Church of which she was so valiant a daughter." Observing that "the Catholic Church is not ashamed of the ideal in womanhood that it presents—an ideal that it has upheld for centuries," Onahan argued that, by honoring Isabella, U.S. Catholics could both uphold that ideal and honor "the religion that made Isabella possible—the religion of the future."[60]

As they had done with Columbus, Catholic writers suggested that Isabella's contribution to the fledgling American nation should remind Catholics of their patriotic heritage. But Isabella's usefulness for the Catholic pages of American history was obviously limited by the fact that she had never actually traveled to North America. It made much more sense for Catholic chroniclers of the American experience to concentrate, as Margaret Sullivan did, on European Catholics like Marie de l'Incarnation who had served as missionaries to the New World. Marie's reputation for holiness gave her an added advantage over the Spanish queen in terms of her appeal to nineteenth-century North American Catholics: while even the most ardent of Isabella's supporters had not suggested she was a candidate for canonization (at least, not by this point), Pope Pius IX had declared Marie de l'Incarnation to be "Venerable" in 1877, thus placing her well along the path to official sainthood.[61]

Marie de l'Incarnation had left behind a twelve-year-old son when she entered the Ursuline convent. Although this was unfortunate for the boy himself—at one point he wailed outside the convent wall, beseeching the nuns to "give me back my mother"—it has proved fortuitous for posterity, as Marie's letters to him would later be published. Not only would these missives inspire other young women to travel as missionaries to the New World, but they would also form the basis for Marie's hagiography.[62] Like all stories of saintly lives, Marie's was "fundamentally a discourse about gender" that displayed cultural ideals about male and female religiosity.[63] Along with the other females who surfaced in Catholic narratives of American history, Marie de l'Incarnation was also used to buttress Catholic understandings of traditional womanhood from the perceived assaults against it. Sadlier's *History* listed "chastened piety, genius and good judgment" as Marie's saintly qualities.[64] One of her biographers noted that by guiding students in the continent's "pioneer female academy," Marie presented a refreshing contrast with women of the late nineteenth century who were tempted "to try the ridiculous experiment of studying everything—a sure route to the mastery of nothing."[65]

Marie's contribution to nation building was emphasized along with her feminine saintliness. Catholic school children learned of pioneering efforts on behalf of the education of native children.[66] In a lengthy biographical sketch of Marie, Anna Sadlier emphasized how this "marvelously gifted woman" had helped establish civilization in the Canadian wilderness.

Echoing Margaret Sullivan, Sadlier described Marie as an "inspired proph-etess," who forecast to future generations the work Catholic women would accomplish on the American continent. Sadlier insisted that while it re-mained for children of the church to revere Marie for proclaiming the faith "amid the forests, the hills, the streams . . . with giant strength," all North American "people of culture" owed her a debt of gratitude.[67]

Marie de l'Incarnation's Quebecois roots made her a daughter of Canada rather than of the United States, but like other Catholic writers, Sullivan and Sadlier effectively blurred this northern border by fusing Canadian and U.S. history in the colonial period. Nevertheless, it was another saintly group of French Ursulines who were awarded pride of place in national narratives by virtue of their status as the first Catholic sisters to arrive in territory that would later become the United States. In a series of articles in the *American Catholic Quarterly Review*, "M.A.C." chronicled the work of Mother Marie Auguste Tranchepain and the eleven French Ursulines who accompanied her to Louisiana in 1727. "M.A.C." was shorthand for none other than Mother Austin Carroll of the Sisters of Mercy, the daughter of the church who would later become Henry Austin Adams's "withering and deadly answer" to the New Woman. Meanwhile, however, Carroll formu-lated her own response, holding up the "nun of the past" as a much more pleasing companion than the "tiresome votary of fashion, or the soulless worshipper of wealth, in which our age is so fertile."[68]

Like many other historical studies of American Catholics, Mother Austin Carroll's history of the Ursulines had been inspired by frustration. A group of historical essays published by the Louisiana Education Society had over-looked the Ursulines entirely, assuming, Carroll speculated, that education had begun only with the advent of "godless schools." Carroll intended to render a "tardy justice" to the days of old by illuminating the history of Louisiana's first teachers, a distinction that subsequent chroniclers of the Ursulines would often repeat.[69] As one of them pointed out, the congrega-tion had established free schools in New Orleans in 1727, "a considerable period, as even the most prejudiced must admit, before the Declaration of Independence."[70]

In addition to their traditional feminine characteristics, Carroll's Ur-sulines displayed in abundance the patriotism commonly ascribed to sub-jects in American Catholic history. A boon to any government fortunate to harbor them, the congregation had maintained a consistent presence in Louisiana even as the colony shifted from French to Spanish control and back again. According to Carroll, the Ursulines' capacity for loyal citizenship would not be fully realized until 1803, when New Orleans became a part of the United States. Initially unaware of the "genius of the American government," they worried that leaders of the new regime might confiscate their property and halt their educational work. Secretary of State James Madison and President Thomas Jefferson soon assuaged these fears in letters that Carroll reproduced in her essays. Even the "infidel" Jefferson, she noted, deemed the sisters worthy of his respect and devotion. She also noted that a future American president, Andrew Jackson, would remain ever grateful to the congregation for their "prayers and vows on his behalf" during the Battle of New Orleans in 1815.[71] Carroll's history of the Ursulines presented them as first among equals, merely the pioneer dispensers of education and health care that scores of other European congregations, including her own Sisters of Mercy, were destined to imitate. Other historians celebrated the Ursulines as "the first nuns to set foot upon America's soil." Writing in the official journal of the American Catholic Historical Society, Ettie Madeline Vogel described Mother Marie Tranchepain as a woman who embodied the "beautiful type of saintly womanhood" and had labored along with other members of her community to convert New Orleans from a "spongy swamp" into an elegant city. Again the author underscored the congregation's contribution to both church and nation, noting that the "results of their labors are no less gratifying to the Ursulines than to the citizens of the State."[72]

The Ursulines of Quebec and New Orleans were simply the best known of a number of daughters of New France who, by virtue of both their femininity and their contribution to the American past, were deemed eligible for inclusion in national narratives.[73] Catholic historians were a bit more hard pressed to find similarly distinguished females in the former English colonies. Even colonial Maryland, which yielded a number of promising male candidates for the Catholic pages of American history (notably Charles Carroll, the only Catholic signer of the Declaration of Independence, and his cousin, the future Archbishop John Carroll, who led a diplomatic mission to Canada in 1776), produced few Catholic heroines.[74] Sadlier's *History* mentioned only one, the daughter of patriot Ethan Allen, who had joined a convent of Hospital Sisters in Montreal and whose "saintly death" provided a source of inspiration even to the non-Catholic doctor who attended her.[75] As she had done with Marie de l'Incarnation, Anna Sadlier provided a fuller biographical sketch of Fanny Allen, holding her up as an example of a Catholic woman who blended faith and patriotism in the Revolutionary era. Describing Fanny's vows, Sadlier contrasted "the liberty for which her father fought and bled, which belongs of right to every child of free America," with "the liberty of the Children of God." It was Fanny, not her agnostic father, who "offered the American character under its noblest and most ideal aspect." Sadlier argued that Fanny's life, like the lives of other daughters of the church, "made manifest to the outer world the marvelous efficacy of the Church's teaching."[76]

Anna Sadlier may have touted Fanny Allen as "the first American nun," but it was Sadlier's cousin Agnes who published a biography of another female convert to the Old Faith who could lay special claim to that distinction: Elizabeth Seton, the founder of the Sisters of Charity, the first congregation indigenous to the United States. Born in 1774 to a wealthy Episcopalian family, Seton had been a widowed mother of five when she converted to Catholicism in 1801. Sadlier portrayed the young Elizabeth as a woman especially "chosen by God to do a great work in a new country," suggesting that Seton's conversion left her uniquely poised "to repair to the Church the losses inflicted upon her by the schism of the sixteenth-century."[77] Others hagiographers also emphasized that Seton's own status as a convert helped to attract to the congregation other candidates whose souls had been left bereft by the Protestant Reformation. One story circulated about a Methodist girl who wondered: "Luther is Luther, Calvin is Calvin, Wesley is Wesley; but where is the Church of the Apostles?" She found her answer upon meeting Seton and soon joined the Sisters of Charity.[78]

While Seton's life was undoubtedly used to underscore religious differences, it was also used to affirm Catholics' patriotism. One priest, noting the synchronicity between the growth of Seton's congregation and the expansion of the young nation, pointed out that the Sisters of Charity had opened their first mission just as Francis Scott Key was composing "The Star-Spangled Banner" in the Baltimore harbor during the War of 1812: each in their own way, Seton and Key were helping to preserve the Republic.[79] Another writer cited Seton's imposition of an even more rigid economy on her congregation during the War of 1812, as well as her readiness to respond to the yellow fever epidemic in Philadelphia in 1814, as proof that she was a "Catholic heroine of America."[80] Another woman emphasized the contribution Seton's Sisters of Charity had made to their fellow Americans, though she noted that, like other Catholic sister-nurses, the congregation was habitually overlooked in an age when secular nurses captured the limelight.[81]

Although Seton was widely celebrated as a "Catholic heroine of America," her Old World connections were duly emphasized in efforts to describe her suitability as "the model of American Catholic womanhood."[82] In "Chiefly among Women," Margaret Sullivan placed Mother Seton in the long tradition of Jane de Chantal, a sixteenth-century saint who, like Marie de l'Incarnation, had been a widowed mother before her entrance into religious life. Paulist Walter Elliott noted that while Seton's Sisters of Charity were canonically an independent congregation, their rule was closely modeled on that of the Daughters of Charity in France, a congregation founded by Saint Vincent de Paul in 1633. According to Elliott, Seton's ties to Saint Vincent established her as a perfect model for modern Catholic women. "We hear much in our day of the elevation of the female sex, and we hear it very gladly," Elliott wrote. But while contemporary endeavors to improve women's condition were often misguided, Catholic daughters of the faith had before them Vincent de Paul, who continued to lead the world "in the true advancement of the sex, always safe and yet wonderfully progressive." Seton, anchored firmly to this tradition, was far more worthy of imitation than were imprudent modern reformers.[83]

Mary Browne, a Catholic writer who had been educated by the Sisters of Charity, agreed, noting that it was Seton who planted "a branch of Vincent's wondrous tree . . . upon the virgin soil of a New World." Browne also touted Seton's achievements as an educator. In a time "when error and bigotry were rampant," she observed, Seton's Sisters of Charity opened parochial schools, "wherein young girls were thoroughly grounded in the principles of the Faith."[84] A member of the Sisters of Charity noted that while the Ursulines of New Orleans often received credit for establishing the first American Catholic school, it rightfully belonged to Seton, since New Orleans was not part of the original territory of the United States.[85] Indeed, as the number of Catholic schools multiplied, Seton would often be proclaimed "the founder of the parochial school system," though in reality nothing approaching a school "system" existed until long after her death in 1821. But as the U.S. Catholic hierarchy accelerated its commitment to the establishment of a parallel educational system in the late nineteenth century, Seton's early efforts to establish Catholic schools increasingly appeared to be prescient.

In addition to her educational work, the presence of several of Seton's descendants among the American clergy and hierarchy helps account for her popularity during the second half of the nineteenth century.[86] She received even more attention when the hagiography surrounding her merged with the national quest for a patron saint. By the 1880s, the fact that the United States had not yet produced a saint had become a source of increasing consternation. An 1885 article in the *Catholic World* bemoaned the lack of American saints, asking, "What is a nation without patrons or shrines?" Acknowledging that "the church, in her wise and well-disposed economies, is slow and cautious in such matters," the author nevertheless insisted that the time had come to canonize a person from the United States: "Yes, America has her saints, and now we ask that they, too, may receive the homage paid to the servants of God."[87] The politics of canonization explain the delay in large part. In addition to a reputation for holiness, candidates also needed wealthy and influential backers in order to secure official recognition of their sanctity. Whereas a country such as Peru had a sufficient number of such people to lobby successfully for Saint Rose of Lima's canonization as early as 1679, there were few nineteenth-century U.S. Catholics who could act in a similar capacity for one of their own.[88]

Seton's dual credentials as a true daughter of the church and a loyal U.S. citizen made her an appealing candidate for a national patron. Securing an American saint was clearly on the mind of Archbishop James Gibbons when he visited Seton's congregation, now called the Daughters of Charity, in Emmitsburg, Maryland, in 1882. He praised Seton's reputation for holiness and proposed that the congregation initiate procedures for her canonization. Realizing that the sisters did "not like notoriety," Gibbons understood that they might be "loathe to open the process." He volunteered to "gladly take the initiative, if I had any encouragement from here; the first movement must naturally begin here." When Gibbons assured the sisters that having "in your Community a canonized Saint would be productive of the best results," he was thinking not only of the congregation but also of American Catholics in general. In urging Seton's sisters to initiate her cause, Gibbons reminded them that "American canonized saints are very rare birds."[89] Acquiring an American saint would boost Catholics' estimation in the eyes of two very different audiences: for their non-Catholic fellow citizens, it would help to root the "foreign" religion more firmly in U.S. soil, and for Vatican officials, it would also affirm U.S. Catholics' loyalty to the Roman Church during a time when some were beginning to consider it suspect.

Because the Vatican required extensive documentation for canonization, a flurry of biographies of Seton and histories of her congregation would be produced after paperwork on her cause was officially submitted to the Vatican in 1911.[90] Seton's 1774 birth meant that she had technically been born a "British subject," and she was occasionally identified as such.[91] Saint seekers discovered a more unambiguously American candidate in Tekakwitha, a Mohawk Indian born in 1656 who was baptized in the name of Catherine of Siena in her teenage years. Though Tekakwitha died in 1680, her potential as an American saint was not realized until more than two centuries later, when her birthplace was discovered in upstate New York. As historian Allan Greer has explained, Tekakwitha's "post-mortem naturalization" as a U.S. citizen was largely owed to the efforts of the Reverend Clarence Walworth, a priest from the Diocese of Albany, New York, and his niece Ellen "Nelly" Walworth. While Clarence traveled far and wide promoting her cause, Ellen produced a biography of Tekakwitha that completed her Americanization not only by reshaping her story into a drama about "the thoroughly modern quest for personal autonomy" but also by rechristening her "Kateri," which Ellen claimed was "the Iroquois form of the Christian name of Catherine." Greer notes the irony: "Nelly Walworth, anxious to eliminate the blatantly European 'Catherine' from her title, was using a Mohawk mispronunciation of an Italian saint's name . . . to clothe her heroine in an identity designed to look immaculately aboriginal. The gambit was a complete success, and ever since Tekakwitha/Catherine has been known around the world as Kateri Tekakwitha."[92]

Kateri emerged as an attractive candidate for sainthood because, as an aboriginal innocent, she represented "the perfect antidote" to nativist perceptions of the church as foreign, industrial, urban, and radical. As the "virgin par excellence," Kateri also represented the perfect fusion of religion, nationality, and femininity.[93] Ellen Walworth contrasted the life Tekakwitha chose for herself with contemporary understandings of freedom, noting that on the day she consecrated herself to perpetual virginity, the "Lily of the Mohawks" felt "a feeling of freedom rather than thralldom. . . . At last she had an acknowledged right to live her life in her own way."[94]

Kateri's official cause for canonization would languish until the mid-twentieth century. It was Elizabeth Seton who would in fact become the first American-born saint, though not until 1975, more than a century after Gibbons made his initial appeal to the Daughters of Charity.[95] Though their quest for a canonized compatriot would continue to prove elusive for quite some time, American Catholics in the Progressive Era could nevertheless draw inspiration from the number of existing female saints, many of whom were used to send other messages. While Catholics were generally defensive about their suitability for American citizenship, they were particularly touchy about how their record on women's issues compared with that of Protestants. Here again, they would mine a Catholic past for evidence that would present them in a favorable light.

HAVE WOMEN SOULS?:
THE CONTESTED LIBERATION OF WOMEN

In January 1906, more than three decades after its original publication, Margaret Sullivan's "Chiefly among Women" reappeared in pamphlet form in Philadelphia under the heading "Boards of Education and Historical Truth." Just as Sullivan had originally produced the essay as a rejoinder to William Gladstone, it was reissued in response to another slight directed against the church. Henry Edmunds, the president of Philadelphia's board of education, had made a deprecating remark at the commencement ceremony for Philadelphia Girls' High School the previous June: "Woman has always been unfairly discriminated against by man," Edmunds observed. "Even as late as the fifteenth century there was held in the south of France a council of learned prelates who for two days discussed the question of whether woman had a soul or not."[96]

Surprised to hear this, Catholic members of the audience appealed to Edmunds to name the council and to produce a source. After some equivocation, he cited *Sketches on the Old Road through France to Florence*, a book that had been published a year earlier by the artist A. H. Hallam Murray. According to Murray, the debate had actually taken place in the sixth century, during the Council at Mâcon in the south of France: "The question before the Council was whether women had souls. That point was left open, but the subsidiary dogma was fixed forever, and since that Council in the middle of the sixth century it has been quite possible to remain a good Catholic and yet to doubt . . . that women are practically of the same species as ourselves."[97]

This reference did little to placate the Reverend Philip McDevitt, the superintendent of schools for the Archdiocese of Philadelphia. As we will see in the third chapter, McDevitt played a central role in consolidating the U.S. Catholic educational system in the first two decades of the twentieth century. But in addition to staffing, improving, and defining Catholic schools in Philadelphia, McDevitt moonlighted as an indefatigable Catholic apologist. Subjecting the official decrees of Mâcon to careful scrutiny, McDevitt found no references to the alleged debate. He did discover in the notes to the council an account of a quibble over terminology that he believed was "the only possible thing that could be distorted into the calumny" Murray reported. McDevitt explained it in detail: "The note states that there was at the Council a certain bishop who said that 'woman' could not be called 'man': *Extit enim in hac synodo, quidam ex episcopis, qui dicebat mulierem hominem non posse vocari*."[98] It was likely, McDevitt explained, "that the bishop's knowledge of Latin was limited and that he did not know that *homo*, the generic term, could be applied to *mulier*, 'woman,' as well as to *vir*, 'man.'" Subsequent chroniclers of Mâcon, determined to present the church in a bad light, had transformed confusion over grammar into a debate over dogma. "From this trifling incident," McDevitt noted, "occasioned by one bishop not unduly equipped with a knowledge of Latin terms, the Council of Mâcon is made to discuss for two days whether woman had a soul."[99]

According to McDevitt, this "gross distortion" was all too typical when Protestants reported "facts" about the Catholic Church. "Nothing," he lamented, "is too small or improbable for people with preconceived antipathies to represent the Catholic Church as issuing palpably absurd pronouncements."[100] In this case, this misrepresentation was particularly insulting, considering that it completely "contradicted the belief and practice of the Catholic Church in regard to women." McDevitt offered Sullivan's "Chiefly among Women" as evidence: the history Sullivan presented, he maintained, proved beyond a doubt that "woman owes her elevation in the social and intellectual as well as moral order to Catholic teaching and practice."[101]

Whether or not the Philadelphia pamphlet elicited a mea culpa from Edmunds is unknown, but he undoubtedly could have deflected much of the blame for his error by pointing to a number of other sources that corroborated Murray's account. In 1879, August Bebel had described in *Woman and Socialism* how the bishops of Mâcon "indulged in a serious discussion as to whether woman had a soul, and finally decided in her favor by a majority of one." The Council of Mâcon, Bebel argued, "disproves the claim that Christianity was favorable to woman."[102] In 1893, Matilda Joslyn Gage cited the meeting at Mâcon as evidence of the misogyny of the church in her critique of patriarchal religion, *Woman, Church and State*.[103] Given her belief that "the repression of women . . . was one of the principal *functions* of churches," it is hardly surprising that Gage repeated the fabled account of Mâcon.[104] But it also surfaced within mainstream Christian denominations. Writing in the *Gospel Advocate* in 1896, Mrs. T. P. Holman wondered: "Is there a New Woman, and if so, What Causes Led to Her Creation?" To consider the question properly, Holman maintained, it was necessary to consider how women were treated in the remote past: "The position of woman in the past ages has been a low one," she declared. "In A.D. 585, a solemn ecclesiastical council was held at Mâcon for the purpose of determining whether or not women had a soul."[105]

McDevitt's rebuttal and recirculation of "Chiefly among Women" hardly laid the legend of Mâcon to rest. Later that year, a Cornell professor repeated the account during a public lecture on the education of women in France, noting that "one of the Church councils had even discussed the question as to whether women had souls or not and had arrived at a negative conclusion." Writing in the *North American Review* in 1915, Lawrence Gilman praised the recent progress of "woman—once despised—woman—to whom at the Council of Mâcon a soul had been denied." Also in 1915, a writer in the *Atlantic Monthly* cited the debate at "an ecumenical council of the Middle Ages" as an example of men's tendency to deny women's intellect. The alleged challenge to women's souls at Mâcon would appear elsewhere, although the council in question was alternately identified as Nicea, Trent, or an unspecified ecumenical council of the Middle Ages.[106]

The periodic surfacing of the Mâcon myth, and Catholics' vigorous attempts to dispel it, provide important context for understanding how American Catholics relied on a gendered past to define and defend themselves in the late nineteenth and early twentieth centuries. Many Catholics interpreted the Mâcon accounts as part of a broader American plot to paint their church as a historical oppressor of women, and as historian Justin Nordstrom makes clear in his recent study of anti-Catholicism during the Progressive Era, they were not being entirely paranoid. One representative article observed that within the Catholic Church "the idea of inferiority of women and their unfitness for rule is naturally carried over from Church to State. Women should not, in their [Catholic priests'] view, have more or very different privileges from what they now have,—especially nothing that would make them equal to men in power."[107]

The author of this article was referring specifically to the Catholic Church's institutional opposition to suffrage, which, as the fourth chapter shows, was also apocryphal. But there is no question that most Catholics were suspicious of the "woman suffragist" and her sidekick, the New Woman, believing that it was they who were the architects of the conspiracy against Catholics, with an obvious vested interest in its success. If suffragists could show that the church had oppressed women in the past, they could make a reasonable case that it was likely to do so in the future and could thereby persuade Catholic women to join them in their foolish crusades.

Catholics defended themselves by insisting that, contrary to the New Woman's claims, the church had actually emancipated women. Often these assertions were made through simple declarative statements, as if the proposition was so evident that specifics were unnecessary. Catholic school children, for example, learned from Sadlier's *History* that indigenous North Americans viewed a woman as "a degraded being, in fact, a slave. Here, as elsewhere, Christianity first raised woman to her rightful position." Promotional materials for the 1893 Catholic Summer School in Plattsburgh, New York, noted that "to the Catholic Church woman owes her emancipation from the ancient trammels of inferiority and servitude." The same year, speaking at the World Columbian Exposition, Mary Onahan had referenced a Catholic past to show that "the age of woman dates not from the nineteenth century, but from the first; it is due not to modern civilization, not to modern progress, but to something grander than either—the mainspring of both—the religion of Christ and his Church." One priest dedicated a sermon to the way "the religion of Jesus Christ has lifted up and ennobled women."[108]

Elaborations on the claim that Christianity emancipated women inevitably made mention of the past, for if "some suffragist, impatient of Romish conservatism," could whisper the account of Mâcon into "guileless ears," Catholics could respond in kind.[109] Following Margaret Sullivan's cues, they could retrieve counterevidence that, unlike Mâcon, had the benefit of authenticity to prove that Christianity had liberated women in the past and would continue to do so in the future. Mary, the first woman of Christianity, was most often cited as the one who had "loosened the shackles of women and made her what she is to-day—or better still, what she will yet be."[110] Observing that Christianity had "raised womanhood from the slough of paganism," Anna Sadlier noted that no accurate history of women in the church could ignore "the omnipresent and almost omnipotent influence of Mary, the Mother of God."[111]

In his 1886 article "Relative Condition of Woman under Pagan and Christian Civilization," James Cardinal Gibbons observed that some writers tended to "lay undue stress on the amiable and tender qualities of Mary." Gibbons was himself guilty of this on more than one occasion, but in this instance he discussed the "strong and robust" points of her character and concluded that Mary proved the enduring wisdom of the church when it came to its daughters.[112] Like the Catholic heroines of America, Mary also doubled as an answer to the New Woman. One contributor to *Donahoe's Magazine* urged Catholic women to imitate Mary, rather than follow the "new woman, with all her inconsistencies and discords."[113] Another priest observed that it was only through devotion to Mary that the Catholic woman of the twentieth century would become "the New Woman after God's own Heart."[114]

Jane de Chantal was another daughter of the Old Faith who was often cited both as affirmation of the church's positive track record on women and as a more appealing alternative to the New Woman. Born in Burgundy, France, in 1572, Chantal was a widowed mother of four when she became a spiritual student of Francis De Sales. In 1610, she founded the Order of the Visitation of Our Lady, and before her death in 1641 she had established sixty-nine convents. In 1903 the Reverend Joseph McSorely identified Chantal as the "perfect type of Christian womanhood" and emphasized her relevance for modern Catholic women, who stood upon "the threshold of a new civilization" with regard to the new opportunities open to them. "Never before," he observed, "has woman occupied so great a place in the public eye or appropriated so large a share of public concern as now." It was therefore imperative that women choose the right models, namely, "the valiant women of history in whom the perfect Christian character stands forth personified."[115]

McSorely and others interpreted Chantal's sixteenth-century appearance in history as particularly auspicious. As one of the many pious women "who graced the Church in the first hundred years after the birth of Protestantism," Chantal underscored an important corollary to the proposition that Christianity liberated women: it was Catholics, not Protestants, who had emerged from the Reformation divide as the proper heirs to Christianity's historical role as the protector of women's rights.[116] Margaret Sullivan had made this a prominent theme of "Chiefly among Women," using the example of Chantal and other Catholic founders to highlight "the undeniable fact that Protestantism has never been able permanently to maintain a single community of women." This failure, she argued, "proves that the *Catholic Church alone* is the sphere in which woman's religious zeal finds its fullest and most complete expression; that it is *the Catholic faith alone* which thoroughly arouses and solidly supports the enthusiasm of her nature, and embodies her ardor into a useful and enduring form."[117] Essayist Agnes Repplier made a similar argument about Marie l'Incarnation. Though faced with daunting obstacles, Marie "stamped herself firmly upon the history of the Church. . . . She did not destroy what she undertook to reform, which is always an easy thing to do."[118]

Many Catholic men made similar claims about Catholics, Protestants, and their relative commitment to women's rights. In his comparison of the rights of pagan and Christian women, Gibbons had begun by speaking of the liberating nature of Christianity more generally, but he concluded with the observation that "every impartial student of history is forced to admit that woman is indebted to the *Catholic* religion for the elevated station she enjoys to-day."[119] The Reverend John T. Murphy, writing in the *American Catholic Quarterly Review* in 1898, observed that "the Church, being the guardian of Christianity, is bound to regard herself in a particular manner as the guardian and champion of the rights and privileges of womanhood."[120] Thomas Carrigan intimated that the church's desire to safeguard women's "inalienable rights" had actually precipitated the Reformation, at least in England: "Mother Church has always insisted that those rights shall be respected, regardless of the cost. She lost a nation once sooner than concede that the marriage-tie could be set aside even for a king."[121] Others even suggested that the Protestant Reformation had retarded women's advancement. Thomas Shields, for example, blamed the Reformation and its suppression of convents for "the setback given to the higher education of women in England and Germany."[122]

Shields had found most of his evidence for this argument in *Woman in Science*, a book published in 1913 by H. J. Mozans. "H. J. Mozans" was the anagrammatic pen name of the Reverend John A. Zahm, CSC, a Holy Cross priest and professor of chemistry and physics at the University of Notre Dame. As the most prominent among a handful of Catholic priest-scientists at the end of the nineteenth century, Zahm was "uniquely situated to contribute significantly to the process by which the American Catholic community came to know the modern world."[123] Zahm is best remembered for his progressive views on evolution, which eventually caused him to become entangled in the modernist controversy. Far less familiar are his views on women. In *Woman in Science*, Zahm contrasted the openness of ancient Catholic universities at Salerno and Bologna toward women as students and professors with "the brutal opposition which women in our own country encountered when but a few decades ago, they applied for admittance to the medical schools of New York and Philadelphia." In his assessment, the Protestant Reformation in England and Germany had left "the masses of women . . . in a worse condition than they had been in the Dark Ages." According to Zahm, Martin Luther himself believed that "the intellectual aspirations of women were not only an absurdity, but were also a positive peril."[124]

Zahm expected that his review of the past would provide a definitive "answer to those who insist on a women's incapacity for scientific pursuits." He predicted that "women's long struggle for complete intellectual freedom is almost ended and certain victory is already in sight." While this optimism admittedly seems misplaced almost a century later, *Woman in Science* remains remarkable in many respects. As historian Cynthia Russett observes in her preface to the 1991 edition, Zahm exhibited a "startling absence of concern for the possible abnegation on the part of learned women of their domestic responsibilities."[125] Zahm's general pride in Catholic women's past intellectual accomplishments is less exceptional, as many of his contemporaries used the same examples to argue that the Catholic Church had for centuries been more enlightened than their modern American counterparts when it came to the education of women.

John Augustine Zahm, CSC, author of *Woman in Science*. Courtesy of the
Archives of the University of Notre Dame, GNEG 2E-32.

Noting that "this ancient Church of ours has been in education for over
nineteen hundred years," Thomas Carrigan claimed that Catholics had
actually anticipated many of the "supposedly new discoveries in pedagogy,"
especially those that related to the education of women. Catholics had
already accumulated eighteen centuries of experience in this enterprise, he
noted, before "the Liberty Bell first pealed forth its messages" in Philadelphia.[126] James J. Walsh, a medical doctor and professor at Fordham
University, was the early twentieth century's reigning expert on "the
Church and feminine education," writing and lecturing often on the subject. Walsh believed that most Americans were both "quite sure" that the
first serious development of women's opportunities came in our time and
equally certain that the church objected to the education of females. Even a
"short resume of feminine achievement of the past," Walsh maintained,
could prove these assumptions wrong. Like Margaret Sullivan, Zahm, and
others, Walsh included Saint Catherine of Siena, Saint Catherine of Alex-

andria, Saint Jane de Chantal, and Saint Teresa on his list, claiming that anyone familiar with the history would understand that daughters of the Catholic faith had long ago foretold supposedly American innovations.[127]

Walsh's expertise in the history of "feminine education" and the church derived in large measure from his position as "the outstanding American Catholic contributor to the tradition of popular medievalism" in the early twentieth century. Historian Philip Gleason has observed that while Walsh's boasts about the Middle Ages were animated primarily by apologetical tendencies, several other prominent motifs shaped his admiration for the medieval period. Among them was the theme of social critique. Walsh and other American Catholics relied upon "an idealized version of the Middle Ages as an alternative social model against which the defects of the modern world could be contrasted."[128]

The social-critique motif undergirded Walsh's observations about medieval women. Noting that "it is usually considered an almost self-evident proposition that it is only in our times, that women have come to exert anything like the influence that they should have in life," Walsh claimed that one of the factors that made the thirteenth "the greatest of centuries" was "that the women of the time were not behind the men in achievement." His heroines of that period rivaled the New Woman in their ability to expand women's opportunities. The lifework of Saint Clare of Assisi, for example, was nothing short of "the making of a new vocation for women." But like other daughters of the church, Saint Clare was invariably happier, more peaceful, and more worthy of admiration than any modern woman influenced by "any feministic movement."[129]

Both apologetic and social-critique motifs were also behind Walsh's characterization of Elizabeth of Hungary, who was, next to Saint Clare, "the best known woman of the thirteenth century." Explaining how Elizabeth habitually left the shelter of her castle to assist the suffering poor around her, Walsh insisted that "the serious historian recognizes that she was the first settlement worker of history."[130] His readers would not have missed the implication. No other New Woman of the late nineteenth century attracted more attention than Jane Addams, the founder of Hull House, the first settlement in the United States. Many Catholics were exasperated by the publicity Addams received. Echoing the claim that educated Catholic daughters of the faith had long anticipated their twentieth-century counterparts, Walsh suggested that Saint Elizabeth had prefigured Jane Addams by more than six hundred years. Others made similar claims. Chicagoan Mary Onahan made an implicit contrast with Addams when she noted that Catholic charity was dispensed "not by a few scattered individuals, but thousands of them." In Chicago alone, Onahan observed, "there are not less than one thousand nuns" who relieved "the state of many of its burdens" and "stepped in when all others failed." Catholic charitable workers were distinguished both by greater numbers and by superior motives: they had "no salaried officers, and they toil[ed] not for earthly reward or earthly glory, but for God and for eternity." Above all, they were anchored to a long Catholic tradition against which women of "modern enlightenment" could not hold a candle.[131] The editors of the *New World* (Chicago) agreed, asking: "But really, is Hull House the chief agency in diffusing culture and teaching civilization in Chicago? The Catholic Church is building civilization here after a manner which Hull House does not understand and cannot appreciate."[132]

Chicago Catholics were not the only ones to make these types of claims. Philadelphia's Jane Campbell noted that the birth of Christianity was responsible for "genuine widespread charity," largely dispensed through monasteries and convents. Pointing out that "almshouses were unknown in England until the reign of Henry VIII," Campbell blamed the upheavals of the Reformation for the temporary interruption of the church's efforts to provide succor to the poor. But she noted that, while monks and nuns had long ago resumed their "works of mercy," "no American institution could lay claim to any very venerable antiquity."[133] As Catholic social work developed as a professional field in the early twentieth century, leaders would continue to differentiate themselves from their secular counterparts, pointing to the Catholic saints who held the "key note of *real* charity."[134]

James Walsh would continue to promote Saint Elizabeth as a Catholic answer to Jane Addams. In 1911, her name was one of the first on a list he sent to Philip McDevitt, the Philadelphia superintendent of schools who had so energetically disputed Henry Edmunds's account of Mâcon six years before. McDevitt was preparing to open Philadelphia Catholic Girls' High School, the nation's first secondary school for girls under diocesan auspices. He wanted to decorate the foyer of the new building with panels bearing names of Catholic women of history, so as to remind students of the glorious tradition of femininity of which they were a part. It was for this reason that he contacted Walsh, who suggested that "Saint Elizabeth of Hungary, the friend of the poor," be included, along with "Isabella of Castile, friend of Columbus," and "Kateri Tekakwitha, Lily of the Mohawks."[135]

As for the legendary debate over women's souls, McDevitt was still laboring mightily, though in vain, to lay the myth to rest. One of his contemporaries had predicted that the apocryphal accounts of Mâcon would never die because "the story is too good and will go on developing. The controversialist, the evolutionist, the after-dinner wit, the educational reformer, the woman suffragist, all will appeal to some mythical Church council, deliberating for weeks or months in any century before Luther and liberty."[136] Indeed, the specter of Mâcon haunts Roman Catholics to this day, even though the myth has since been debunked in far greater detail than McDevitt did a century ago.[137] Although some would attribute its persistence to the lingering presence of anti-Catholicism in the United States, there is perhaps a more precise and more convincing explanation: then and now, the deliberations at Mâcon simply do not appear as implausible to outsiders as defenders of the church would like to believe. While there is no question that exaggeration and misunderstanding have exacerbated the problem, the Catholic Church became the bête noire of the "woman suffragist" and the contemporary secular feminist for good reason. As one early twentieth-century subscriber to the Mâcon myth mused, it had "never occurred to the Council to discuss whether man had a soul, possibly because all its members were men."[138] Given the church's patriarchal structure and intransigence on positions especially important to women, it is not exactly beyond the pale to believe that some of its leaders could once have questioned women's soulful humanity.

In fact, the Catholic Church has never denied women a soul. But it has perpetuated an ideology of gender that reinforces women's status as inferior to men. Consider, for example, James Walsh's observation that "whenever a great work for the uplift of the people occurs in the Catholic Church, the invitation to it is usually shared by a man and a woman: Before St. Patrick stands St. Brigid, beside St. Benedict stands his sister St. Scholastica, beside St. Francis is St. Clare; beside St. Francis de Sales is St. Jane de Chantal." Only in one instance did he reverse the order of the sexes: "Beside St. Teresa, for here woman is the leader, stands St. John of the Cross."[139] This was Catholic gender ideology at work: in all but the rarest of cases, even the most illustrious of Catholic women were destined to be "helpers" to men.

Even Walsh, a self-proclaimed champion of women's rights, was not above using the past to control and contain. The presence of this ideology of gender does not mean, however, that women were completely without power in a male-dominated institution, for if some men used the past to circumscribe women, certain women would put it to opposite use. While a Catholic past was often marshaled in support of traditional gender roles, it could also serve as a vehicle through which women contested and renegotiated the parameters of their experience.

THE PAST AS CHALLENGE

In 1889, Margaret Sullivan traveled to France as a representative of the Associated Press, assigned to cover the Paris Exposition. Unable to obtain a pass that would permit her to attend the opening-day festivities, she eventually petitioned the French president, Marie François Sadi Carnot. Explaining why it would not be possible for Sullivan to receive press credentials, Carnot admitted that "the French Republic has never given official recognition to a lady." "Your excellency," Sullivan replied, "it is time the French Republic created a precedent." Without further protest, Carnot allowed her to attend.[140]

There is a great deal of irony in the pride American Catholics took in repeating Sullivan's exchange with Carnot. If her ability to create precedent in France caused her to be so widely admired, it was her success in *finding* precedent that accounts for her enduring popularity closer to home. In "Chiefly among Women," Margaret Sullivan had listed many dangers arising from the general ignorance about the history of women in the church. Among them was delusion: unaware that Catholic female saints and heroines had anticipated them by centuries, modern women would wrongly think of themselves as the authors of a "new, an unwritten, chapter in the culture of the sex."[141] The claim that daughters of the Old Faith had long been more enlightened than their modern counterparts pervaded Catholic apologetics: it was heard in James Walsh's description of a thirteenth-century saint as history's first settlement worker; it was implied in John Zahm's assertion that the women of twelfth-century Bologna fared comparatively better than did the nineteenth-century female pioneers at medical schools; and it was declared unambiguously by Mary Onahan, who observed that "the nineteenth century has hugged itself to many delusions, but it has never hugged a vainer one than when it claimed to have discovered woman."[142] Catholic women's past accomplishments simply provided more proof of the Catholic Church's prescience and wisdom when compared with upstart people (or nations) unmoored to tradition. This premise was unmistakable in Sullivan's observation about a Harvard researcher who in 1903 made what he claimed to be an astonishing discovery about Catholic scholarship: "Facts and phenomena familiar to centuries," she noted, "seem quite new to those who come upon them for the first time, confusing their own recent arrival in the field with the age of the field itself."[143]

But if Sullivan often shouted in the voice of a Catholic apologist, she occasionally whispered as an advocate for the female sex. In "Chiefly among Women" she had referred to women's "increasing demand" for more education, professionalism, and public life and advised that the best way to secure these advancements was not by looking "forward to that which they have never had, but backward to what they have lost or abandoned."[144] Interpreting the achievements of women in the past as justification for expanding opportunities in the present, Sullivan would do so even more assertively in the decades after she wrote "Chiefly among Women," as women's demand for more opportunities in all these areas continued to accelerate. In an 1893 essay describing the coming twentieth-century woman, Sullivan allowed herself a few provocative predictions (she intimated, for example, that that wives and daughters of the future would receive material compensation for the work they performed in the household, a proposition that would still be considered radical more than a century later). Most of her prophecies about the woman of the future, however, were designed to soothe and comfort other Catholics who interpreted women's recent behavior as augurs of disaster: "The woman of the twentieth century," she reassured, would be "essentially like the nineteenth century woman," who was, in turn, "essentially like the woman the world has known since Christianity established the ideal of womanhood." Only those people who were "little acquainted with the past" could possibly be alarmed by changing gender roles. Repeating many of the names she had included in "Chiefly among Women," Sullivan supplied historical examples of female physicians, scholars, and influential figures to show that Catholic women's advancements in the professions, institutes of higher learning, and public life were only "apparently new."[145]

Sullivan's assessment of these developments as only "apparently new" would be echoed by other Catholic women who attempted to anchor themselves to a Catholic past during an otherwise confusing time. Mary Blanche O'Sullivan, editor of *Donahoe's* "Women's Page," celebrated the lives of "women saints and women warriors; women of song and story; heroines of history," suggesting that the lives of "Catholic women of long ago" could guide and inspire their modern counterparts.[146] Echoing Margaret Sullivan, convert Emma Forbes Cary "appealed to history" to comfort those people concerned about the impact of women's changing role. With Mary as their inspiration, Cary urged Catholic women to join her "at the threshold of the twentieth century and muse on the future that it holds . . . we have no thought of losing courage. . . . We claim all that is highest, and unite ourselves to the traditions of the past."[147]

Catholic women's desire to unite themselves to the traditions of the past provides important context for understanding how the New Woman functioned as a foil for those of them who chafed against the boundaries of True Womanhood. Catholic women criticized the New Woman as vociferously as most Americans did, and many echoed their male counterparts in complaining about her rashness, her rootlessness, her threat to the social order, and her selfish lack of regard for ties to family and community. Amid the standard rants about the New Woman, however, it was possible to find Catholic women who combined a critique of the symbol with a tacit endorsement of the symbolized.

In 1896, for example, six Irish American women addressed the fortieth convention of the Ancient Order of Hibernians (AOH) in Detroit. These women represented the Ladies Auxiliary of the AOH, an organization that had been officially established two years earlier. Petitioning the board for national recognition and a uniform constitution, the women emphasized that they were "not the new women," despite their belief in the equality between the sexes.[148] In an article that appeared in the *Catholic World* a year later, Marguerite Moore described the remarkable accomplishment of Mrs. Morrogh-Bernard.[149] According to Moore, Morrogh-Bernard's energetic work in industrial reform had transformed the western Irish town of Foxford from a depressed village into a thriving mill town. Moore was careful to remind her readers that the subject of her essay, despite her accomplishments, was quite different from a "new woman."[150] Also in 1897, *Donahoe's Magazine* quoted Miss Emma Hemingway in its Women's Department. In her valedictory speech at the Woman's College of Baltimore, Hemingway had spoken for her classmates when she declared, "It is not the new woman we emulate, but the true woman."[151]

Despite their disclaimers, all the women in these examples were emulating America's new women in at least some respects. The six women who represented the Ladies Auxiliary of the AOH had taken a very public stance to demand national recognition. Marguerite Moore, the author of the *Catholic World* feature on Mrs. Morrogh-Bernard, was an Irish American who became a leader in the Irish nationalist movement. Along with Fanny and Anna Parnell (the sisters of famed national leader Charles), Moore had organized an American branch of the Ladies Land League in 1880. In 1920, she would lead British sailors and New York City longshoremen on a three-and-a-half-week strike to protest the arrest of two Irish nationalists.[152] Clearly, Moore did not live up to the ideal of the true Catholic woman. For that matter, neither did her heroine, Mrs. Morrogh-Bernard, who had single-handedly revitalized an Irish village. In a similar way, attending college marked a departure from the proscriptions of True Womanhood. Yet those people who read excerpts of Emma Hemingway's speech in *Donahoe's Magazine* were assured that she, too, eschewed New Womanhood.

What made these women's disavowals of New Womanhood so credible was the connection they claimed to a Catholic past. As Margaret Sullivan had used precedent to comfort people who worried that "Catholic women shall do something that Catholic women never did before," these women could point to women of the past as proof that their new ventures were simply resurrections of past ones. For the Ladies Auxiliary of the AOH, it was ancient Irish heroines; for Miss Hemingway, it was a long tradition of intellectual Catholic women. Marguerite Moore chose a more recent prototype, reassuring her readers that "there is no such thing as the new woman; she is just the same one you have known all along since she first sang you to rest."[153] By drawing on a panoply of identities—as mothers, woman saints, and heroines of history—Catholic women could recast themselves as daughters of the Old Faith, thus establishing a necessary distance from the New Woman that, ironically, allowed them to emulate her in significant ways.

Equally ironic was the fact that many of the female figures Catholic women employed to disassociate themselves from the New Woman were the very same people who had been publicized by Catholic men in service of other purposes. Among the most popular of these were "saintly scholars" such as Catherine of Alexandria and Teresa of Avila, both of whom had been cited by James Walsh and others as evidence of Catholicism's rich feminine intellectual heritage. But while Walsh depended on Catherine and Teresa to defend the church, women would use them to support their arguments in favor of expanding women's educational opportunities. Katherine Tynan, for example, was an Irish poet and novelist whose work was familiar to Irish Catholics on both sides of the Atlantic. In her 1893 proposal for a Catholic women's college, Tynan insisted that scholarly endeavors had enhanced, rather than inhibited, the saintly qualities of both Catherine of Alexandria and Catherine of Siena. Tynan also suggested that advanced study could lead modern Catholic women down the path to sainthood, and she claimed that highly educated women were more even tempered and more charitable than their less academic sisters.[154] Two years later, a female contributor to *Donahoe*'s Women's Page wrote with wistfulness about Catholic women's scholarship in ages past and encouraged her contemporaries to compensate for "time lost since the middle of the sixteenth century."[155] In 1902, Marie Donegan Walsh wrote about twelfth-century female scholars at the University of Bologna, marveling at their beauty, femininity, and intellect. "In an atmosphere of self-congratulation upon Women's colleges and universities," she mused, "can it come as anything but a revelation to find oneself face to face with a city of learned women of long centuries past?"[156]

Establishing these precedents helped pave the way for the development of Catholic women's colleges in the late 1890s, a subject that the next chapter explores in greater detail. But the claim that "there was nothing new under the sun" also helped insulate Catholic women from accusations that they were imitating the New Woman. According to Mary Onahan, the idea that a woman had a "fundamental right and duty . . . to work out the best that was in her" was not a modern principle; on the contrary, it had been taught by the Catholic Church since it "raised Catherine of Alexandria to the dignity of a Doctor of the Church."[157] Mary Nixon, another Catholic writer who supported women's education, advised the " 'New Woman,' who is striving for the higher education and greater prominence of her sex, to read the life of St. Catherine. To this day she is known as the patroness of schools, colleges, learning, elocution, philosophy, scientists. . . . She commanded the highest worldly position, riches and honor; yet with all she was the most lovely of women."[158]

Nixon also touted Catherine of Alexandria's confidence in occupying "a public place, the observed of all observers." A year later, Mary Elizabeth Blake celebrated the public life of another Saint Catherine, this time of Siena. In 1377 Catherine had persuaded Pope Gregory XI to abandon his outpost in Avignon and return to the papal states, thereby resolving a crisis in the church. Blake argued that Catherine's diplomatic success in Avignon should inspire modern Catholic women to seek new opportunities for public activism, presuming the full support of their church. Catherine, after all, provided "enduring testimony of the large wisdom and broad views of the Church, which in such an age threw open such exceptional opportunities for usefulness and action to a woman."[159]

Isabel M. O'Reilly, a Catholic writer who participated in the effort to script the Catholic pages of American history, made a similar argument about Joan of Arc, a fifteenth-century French woman who had helped Charles VII reclaim the French throne in 1430. Betrayed and accused of heresy, Joan was burned at the stake in 1431 in Rouen, France. She was officially exonerated twenty years later, but the ultimate vindication came with her beatification in 1905 and canonization fifteen years later.[160] As her case for sainthood gathered momentum in the 1890s, Joan played an important and elastic role in the development of French national identity in the late nineteenth century.[161] American supporters like O'Reilly also tried to incorporate Joan into the American Catholic national story by citing her example as proof that "an unselfish patriotism has the full sanction of heaven." O'Reilly also adopted her as the "patron saint of New Womanhood," observing that "no woman of the present time who steps into the arena of public life" could equal Joan's accomplishment. Here again, O'Reilly made the key differentiation: the "Holy independence" and "self-sacrificing spirit" of the Maid of Orleans was much more appealing than the "self-glorification of the 'Woman's Rights' party."[162]

Irish national heroines proved equal to their French sisters when it came to legitimating public life for Catholic women. Katharine O'Keeffe O'Mahoney, an Irish American teacher and writer from Lawrence, Massachusetts, illustrates the significant Irish dimension to the Catholic fascination with the past. Like other Catholics, O'Mahoney lamented that most Americans, inhabiting a new country, had little appreciation of history. Members of the Irish race, by contrast, knew that this "remarkable antiquity, this noble past, is rather something to glory in, to be proud of, to respond to, to be a source of noblest and highest inspiration."[163] In 1907, O'Mahoney published *Famous Irishwomen*, a collective biography of a number of women intended to inspire their descendants. Among them was Margaret O'Carroll, a fifteenth-century Irish woman who had successfully defended her hometown of Offaly against invaders. O'Mahoney emphasized that while O'Carroll did "go forth in a public capacity," she was inspired to do so by her "true woman's heart."[164] O'Mahoney's characterization of O'Carroll appears particularly propitious in the light of her own public activities on Ireland's behalf. She was one of a number of Irish American women who began to participate more vigorously in the Irish nationalist movement in the late nineteenth century.[165] Lecturing often on the cause, O'Mahoney was reputed to have been the first Catholic woman to speak from a public platform in New England. She also participated in the organizational life of the nationalist movement, eventually becoming a leader of the Ladies Auxiliary of the AOH in her home state of Massachusetts. By claiming O'Carroll as their model, O'Mahoney and other Catholic women protected themselves against charges that they were imitating the New Woman.[166]

Catholic women also employed American heroines in their efforts to subvert gender expectations. Philadelphian Agnes Repplier, who referred to her Catholic faith as "the most vital thing in life," was one of many Catholic women who found "few things more wearisome" than the monotonous repetition of the "new woman" by people who had "apparently forgotten all about" women such as Saint Theresa, Jeanne d'Arc, and Christine de Pisan.[167] In her biography of Marie de l'Incarnation, Repplier joined other Catholic writers in highlighting Marie's role in shaping "a new country." But Repplier was also determined to show the possibilities Marie's example held out to modern women for a "life of adventure." She complained that it was the "habit of hagiographers to exclude from their narratives any circumstance which might possibly link them with life, to deny to the subjects of their pious memoirs any characteristic which savors too strongly of humanity. In their desire to be edifying, they seek to be convincing."[168] Repplier applauded Marie's freedom "to fulfill her heart's desire"—entering an Ursuline convent—even at the cost of abandoning her son. In a thinly veiled critique of the prevailing ideology of motherhood, Repplier praised Marie's wisdom in entrusting her son's care to a religious community of men, noting that "the Seventeenth Century, unlike the Twentieth, did not regard youth as the personal property of his mother."[169]

If Repplier's "independence of mind was not in the least compromised by the conservatism of the Catholic Church," the same was true of Jane Campbell, another Philadelphia Catholic woman whose sense of connection to a Catholic past prompted her to make what would otherwise seem startling claims about women's future.[170] In 1894 Campbell became an officer of the American Catholic Historical Association, and she served on its Historical Research Committee.[171] In addition to compiling material for the Catholic version of American history, Campbell would also retrieve stories about "the enlightened scholar nuns of the Middle Ages." These women, she argued, proved "the important fact that a woman was not considered incapable by reason of sex of exercising authority over great institutions made up of both men and women."[172] Unfortunately, according to Campbell, the modern age was not so enlightened, given that women were considered "incapable by reason of sex" of exercising political authority over the American nation. In her arguments in support of woman suffrage, Campbell pointed to the legions of Christian women who ruled nations in the past. Using her knowledge of American history, she cited the early history of New Jersey, when women property holders had held the franchise, as proof that "it was not even a new thing to vote in the United States."[173] In her journal, *Women's Progress in Literature, Science, Education and Art*, Campbell combined clarion calls for political equality with short essays about Catholic women's past achievements in education and charitable work.[174]

Though most Catholic women did not extend the arguments as far as Campbell did in support of woman suffrage, many used the lessons of the past to endorse the New Woman in theory, if not in name. Pointing to Joan of Arc, Jane de Chantal, Catherine of Alexandria, and Saint Teresa as "models given to us to copy," Eliza O'Brien Lummis organized Catholic women into a group called Filiae Fidei, or Daughters of the Faith. Yet Lummis also hoped the Daughters of the Faith would collectively inspire a Catholic version of the New Woman. She predicted that as Catholic daughters began to meet the needs of the twentieth century by taking a more activist role in American society, "the 'new woman' may yet outgrow the prejudice that coined the title."[175]

Pope Pius X approved Filiae Fidei in 1907, an auspicious year in church history. It is the same year in which he issued *Pascendi Dominici Gregis*, an encyclical that condemned modernism. *Pascendi* prompted a doctrinal and disciplinary crisis in the church. George Tyrrell, the Jesuit theologian who had written "The Old Faith and New Woman," was excommunicated, and the condemnation of modernism dealt a severe blow to Catholic intellectual life. Like Tyrrell, the major players in the modernist crisis were European. But the condemnation of modernism also had a chilling effect on Catholic intellectual life in the United States. It had come on the heels of the condemnation of Americanism, another crisis that had dampened Catholics' enthusiasm for the modern world.

A century later, *Pascendi*'s meaning and impact remain the subject of debate, which is invariably made more acrimonious by the ideological positions adopted by people on its opposing sides. While it is beyond the scope of this chapter to interpret those meanings, it is clear that though *Pascendi* effectively silenced theological modernists, the efforts to reconcile the Old Faith with the modern world continued in other venues, including gender roles.[176] Eliza O'Brien Lummis, for example, had strategically aligned Filiae Fidei against the forces of modernism. Echoing Pius, Lummis described naturalism as "the underlying cause of widely prevalent social evils," and the constitution of the Filiae Fidei stated that "the spirit of Naturalism must be cast out and its teachings counteracted by the restoration of the true Christian life, the revival of the Catholic spirit, and the close profession of the teachings of the Church."[177] Lummis's positioning of the Daughters of the Faith as the enemy of modernism, and her corresponding endorsement of expanding roles for Catholic women, suggest that the conversation over gender roles remained an important way to negotiate the dissonance between old and new long after the theological modernists had been silenced.

THOUGH MARGARET BUCHANAN SULLIVAN died in 1903, her "Chiefly among Women" would continue to be reprinted and referenced for quite some time.[178] In the original version Sullivan herself had provided a clue as to why her essay would prove so enduring: "Women's power in the present and the future," she wrote, "is reasonably deducible from her past."[179] In this observation Sullivan was being nothing short of prophetic: "Chiefly among Women" remained popular, and was so widely mimicked, because for Sullivan and other American Catholics, the record of women in the past helped translate what was happening to them in the increasingly complicated present.

Contained in the multiple conversations about the New Woman and the Old Faith are the prevailing themes that characterized the overlapping relationship between gender and American Catholic identity in the late nineteenth and early twentieth centuries. Catholics relied on gender not only to affirm their suitability for citizenship but also to underscore the essential differences between them and other American citizens, a task that took on particular significance at a time when some of the less fundamental differences seemed to be disappearing. Catholic women's energetic dis-avowals of the New Woman were just one sign that they believed whole-heartedly what they had so often been told: the Catholic Church alone secured their rights, not only in the next world but in this one. Yet, con-vinced as they were of the church's wisdom, they could also, on occasion, manipulate gender to justify endeavors that would otherwise seem beyond the boundaries of True Womanhood.

These patterns were reinforced in the other arenas of intersection be-tween gender and American Catholic identity. New developments in higher education, more urgent calls for professionalization, and expanding opportunities in public life signaled great changes, but Catholic women would interpret and accept these developments as daughters of the Old Faith, not as New Women. As these changes intersected with debates about American Catholic identity, gender would continue to be used to differenti-ate U.S. Catholics from their fellow citizens; Catholic women would over-whelmingly align themselves with the men who shared their religious beliefs rather than with the women who did not; and some Catholic women would display the same tacit endorsement of "feministic movements" de-spite their professed aversion to them.

CHAPTER TWO Enlarging Our Lives

HIGHER EDUCATION, AMERICANISM,

AND TRINITY COLLEGE FOR CATHOLIC WOMEN

In November 1900, Sister Julia McGroarty presided over the opening of Trinity College for Catholic women in Washington, D.C. McGroarty, the American provincial superior of the Sisters of Notre Dame de Namur (SND), had by that point dedicated more than fifty years of her life to educating Catholic young women and girls. The success of her final and most ambitious venture had depended in large part on her ability to underscore the essential differences between the future Trinity student and the threatening New Woman. Early publicity for the college had emphasized that "while the New Woman, with her head full of vagaries, is reconstructing the Universe, Trinity College will offer to her Catholic sisters an opportunity to accrue knowledge which, though adapting itself to all rightful demands of the period, is firmly wedded to that unchanging faith which has lifted women of all ages to her true position."[1] As we have seen, American Catholics would have been very familiar with the two propositions contained in this statement: the contrast between the foolishness of the Progressive New Woman and the steadfastness of daughters of the Old Faith, and the assertion that Roman Catholicism alone provided women with the means to their true emancipation.

Trinity's supporters invariably connected the new project to a Catholic past in order to distinguish its students from the New Woman. In 1899, journalist and author Katherine Conway traveled to Namur, Belgium, where the motherhouse of the Sisters of Notre Dame was located. Reflecting on a century of the congregation's history, Conway insisted that founding a Catholic women's college would signify continuity rather than change.

"In working for Heaven we always plant better than we know," she mused, "and the evolution of the work of the Sisterhood of Notre Dame from the poor schools of France to the State schools of Belgium, the normal schools of England, and Trinity College of America is perfectly logical, religiously and socially."[2] Back in the United States, William Seton, a grandson of Mother Elizabeth Seton, urged the New Woman to chasten her relentless ambition by looking toward Trinity College, where Catholic women could pursue the "highest scholarship" while following safely in the footsteps of their foremothers.[3] Katharine O'Keeffe O'Mahoney, the Irish American nationalist who modeled herself on the fifteenth-century Margaret O'Carroll, emphasized that Trinity represented "no new departure in that Ever-Living Church that is ready to meet the needs of all places and all times."[4] For her part, Sister Julia claimed that by expanding educational opportunities for American Catholic girls, the Sisters of Notre Dame were merely "follow[ing] our old tradition, enlarging our lives to suit the times."[5]

Trinity and other pioneer Catholic women's colleges offer a clear example of how U.S. Catholic women "enlarged their lives" during the Progressive Era. Although an elaborate system of higher education for Catholic men was in place by 1890, including the newly established Catholic University, no Catholic women's colleges existed as of that date.[6] Since the 1870s, a few Catholic girls' academies had offered select students the opportunity to pursue collegiate instruction through private tutoring.[7] It was not until 1895, however, that the School Sisters of Notre Dame (an order distinct from the Sisters of Notre Dame de Namur) altered the curriculum of their Baltimore Institute to incorporate a structured four-year course of study that would result in the conferring of the baccalaureate.[8] The College of Notre Dame of Maryland officially became the first American Catholic women's college when the state legislature awarded the institute the power to grant the baccalaureate on April 2, 1896.[9] By 1918, fourteen colleges for women appeared on the Catholic Educational Association's approved list of accredited institutions.[10]

Unique among the early Catholic women's colleges, Trinity did not evolve from a preexisting academy, a circumstance that presented its founders with an array of challenges.[11] Some of these were logistical. The College of Notre Dame and other pioneer institutions were transformed into colleges through a change in charter and an adjustment of curriculum; Sister Julia, realizing that Trinity must, "like Minerva, spring forth fully armed Cap a Píe," set out to purchase land, design buildings, recruit students, train faculty, and raise money. It was this last task that she found most daunting. "I have seventy years' experience," she wrote, "[and] have erected through the assistance of my able sisters three large institutions, so why should we fear to fail? Simply because one element of success is wanting—the money." Though she was very proud of her congregation's self-sufficiency, noting that she had never employed a "man of business," she recognized the challenge of fund-raising as a formidable one.[12]

Opening Trinity without the benefit of a preexisting academy also introduced strategic challenges. First of all, it deprived its founders of the luxury of unobtrusiveness. Most early Catholic women's colleges made inconspicuous transitions from academy to college. In 1895, the School Sisters of Notre Dame turned their Baltimore Institute into the College of Notre Dame without fanfare or celebration. The *Chronicle*, a record of the institute, did not even mention the transition until September 1897, two years after the first college students had been admitted. At Saint Mary's in Notre Dame, Indiana, the Sisters of the Holy Cross paid scant attention to either the implementation of a college course in 1903 or the official separation between academy and college three years later. The Ursuline Sisters greeted the conversion of their boarding school in New Rochelle, New York, into the College of St. Angela (later the College of New Rochelle) with similar nonchalance.[13]

In one sense, this quiet evolution from girls' academy to women's college is not at all remarkable, given that most Catholic men's colleges had developed in a similar manner. As Philip Gleason has shown, Catholic institutions usually did not make the sharp distinctions between secondary and college education that secular counterparts did.[14] Yet, as the case of Trinity demonstrates, the founders of Catholic women's colleges had important incentives to use discretion. Trinity attracted far more attention than did the other pioneer Catholic women's colleges, and its founders were left much more susceptible to criticism as a result.

Geography further complicated Trinity's founding. The college was located one-third of a mile away from Catholic University, the epicenter of the controversy over Americanism. In their quest to open a Catholic women's college, the Sisters of Notre Dame unwittingly landed in the middle of that conflict, and for a brief period their alleged alliance with the Americanists placed the entire endeavor in jeopardy. Trinity's relationship to the Americanist controversy shows how dangerous it could be for Catholic women to be perceived as imitating New Women and illustrates how closely the debate over gender roles was linked to discussions about Catholic identity in American society. By founding a Catholic women's college, in other words, Sister Julia was not only redrawing the boundaries of what was possible for women within the church but was also participating in Catholics' broader effort to define the relationship of their religion to American culture.

Trinity's founding has not attracted widespread historical attention for several reasons. On the one hand is the long-standing lack of interest in Catholic women as subjects. Trinity's historical invisibility has also resulted from the characteristic humility and self-effacement that was part and parcel of Catholic women's religious life.[15] In 1901, Sister Julia had passed along to her community the advice of the Reverend Phillip Garrigan, the vice-rector of nearby Catholic University. Garrigan had reminded her that "like the dear Blessed Mother, the Sisters were chosen to do great things and like her too, they should be satisfied that he alone be witness of their cooperation with His grace. The Blessed Virgin did not publish her history to the world; neither should we be concerned whether people know what we do or not."[16] Not surprisingly, it would be Garrigan who proved to be the beneficiary of his own advice. Replicating a familiar pattern in Catholic women's history, he and other clergy at Catholic University are often described as the prime movers in Trinity's founding.[17]

There were other consequences. Several years after Trinity opened, Katharine O'Keeffe O'Mahoney included a profile of the Irish-born Mc-Groarty in *Famous Irishwomen*. Interviewing an unidentified Sister of Notre Dame about Sister Julia's efforts in founding Trinity, O'Mahoney had received this response: "Sister Superior prayed and Trinity was started."[18] If either Sister Julia or this anonymous nun had been encouraged to "publish her history to the world," the result would be far more interesting and illuminating than this astonishingly abbreviated account. Indeed, Trinity offers an excellent vantage point from which to view the complex territory in which Sister Julia and other Catholic women operated as the twentieth century dawned. By undertaking new initiatives, she and her sisters poised themselves between a host of dueling identities: male and female, religious and lay, Old World and New, Roman and American, and past and present.

SISTER JULIA MCGROARTY AND TRINITY'S EARLY DAYS

The future Sister Julia had been born Susan McGroarty in Donegal, Ireland, in 1827, the third child of Neil and Catherine Bonner McGroarty. In 1831, the family decided to join Catherine's three brothers, sister, and mother, who had immigrated to Cincinnati, Ohio, several years before. The Mc-Groarty family, which now included five children, set off in a lumber ship on a harrowing journey to Quebec, Canada. Although no one in the small traveling party would have been able to predict it, this was the first of fifteen Atlantic crossings the then four-year-old Susie would make in her lifetime. As a member of the Sisters of the Notre Dame de Namur, Susan McGroarty would make seven visits to the congregation's motherhouse in Belgium.[19]

From Quebec the McGroartys traveled by steamboat down the St. Lawrence River to Buffalo, New York, and across Lake Erie to Cleveland, Ohio.

From Cleveland they traveled by wagon to Cincinnati, where they were reunited with their extended family. Soon after their arrival, Neil purchased a farm in nearby Fayetteville, where over the course of six happy years he and Catherine welcomed five more children. In addition to farming, Neil also worked as a contractor for railroads and turnpikes, a lucrative endeavor during a period of rapid expansion and construction. By 1837, the area around Fayetteville had grown too crowded to sustain the farm, so the family moved back to Cincinnati, where they were surrounded by Bonners: Catherine's mother, with whom the vivacious and active Susie became a particular favorite; Catherine's brothers Hugh and Stephen, both successful physicians; Stephen's wife and children; another brother, John; and Catherine's sister Letitia Bonner, who was well known for her piety and for her almsgiving throughout Cincinnati.

Letitia Bonner's charitable work often led her to interact with the religious community she would eventually join, the Sisters of Charity, a branch of Elizabeth Seton's congregation that had been established there in 1829. In October 1840, the Sisters of Charity hosted a newly arrived European congregation: the Sisters of Notre Dame of Namur, Belgium. In 1804, Julie Billiart had founded the Sisters of Notre Dame in Amiens, France. Dedicating the congregation to the education of poor children, she pledged to send her sisters wherever they were most needed. When the bishop of Amiens interfered with this objective by attempting to restrict the nuns to his own diocese, Mother Julie moved the convent to Namur. Eventually the Sisters of Notre Dame established elementary schools and teacher training institutes throughout Belgium and England. The eight sisters who arrived in Cincinnati in 1840 had traveled to the United States at the request of John Purcell, archbishop of Cinncinati. After boarding with the Sisters of Charity for several weeks, the Sisters of Notre Dame moved into their own convent on Sycamore Street. By January 1841 they were operating a school with three divisions: boarding school, day school, and a free school.[20]

Accompanying her aunt Letitia on a visit to the new convent, young Susan was greeted by Sister Louise Van der Shrieck, a Dutch-born, newly professed sister whose fluency in English had led her to be chosen for the American mission. Beguiled by Susie's dark eyes, Sister Louise asked the young girl what she intended to do when she grew up. When she replied that she wanted to become a Sister of Charity, Sister Louise replied, "We shall see." Sure enough, within a few days Susan enrolled at Notre Dame's day school, and not long after her graduation in 1845, she entered the congregation. Sister Louise, now the American superior, wrote to the motherhouse at Namur of the community's first postulant: "Her coming has caused a great sensation in the city, as she is known to be of a very lively disposition, and the world cannot understand how she could decide to immure herself in a convent. Our boarders, who see how happy and contented she is, are struck with this example." After a three-month postulancy, or period of preparation, Susan became Notre Dame's first American novice in April 1846. She was assigned "Julia" as her religious name, a selection that did not please her at first. But when she realized it was the Anglicized name of Notre Dame's founder, Julie Billiart, she understood what a great honor she had received.[21]

On August 3, 1848, Sister Julia professed her religious vows. In addition to pledging herself to a life of poverty, chastity, and obedience, she promised as a Sister of Notre Dame "to devote herself to the instruction of young girls in the Company of Our Lady." McGroarty's life as a professed sister paralleled the expansion of the congregation in the United States. She taught at schools in Cincinnati until 1854, when she departed for Roxbury, Massachusetts, where Notre Dame had recently established a foundation. In 1860, she was appointed the superior in Philadelphia, where four years earlier the congregation had been summoned by Bishop John N. Neumann to teach in the city's parish schools. The expansion of parochial education prompted the Sisters of Notre Dame to make an exception to the provision in their rule that prevented them from teaching boys. In 1854, Sister Superior Louise had permitted sisters to teach boys until they reached the second grade.

Sister Julia remained the superior in Philadelphia for twenty-five years. During that time she supervised the establishment of a large academy, a parish school for African American children, and other parochial schools. In 1885, she was called back to Cincinnati to become the assistant to Sister Louise. Upon Louise's death a year later, McGroarty was elected her successor as provincial superior, and she would remain in that position until her own death in 1901.[22]

Congregations of American women religious grew rapidly at the end of the nineteenth century, and Notre Dame was no exception. Over Sister Julia's term as superior, the membership of the congregation increased from 720 to 1,139 sisters. Significantly, the majority of this growth came from

American vocations. The number of Belgian missionary sisters steadily decreased in the second half of the nineteenth century and stopped entirely in the 1890s.[23] Many of the American recruits, like Sister Julia, had Irish roots. As was the case with many other women's religious communities with origins on the Continent, the Sisters of Notre Dame would increasingly attract Irish American daughters. This phenomenon was partially owed to the presence and example of large numbers of nuns from Ireland, many of whom had emigrated in response to pleas from superiors of American communities who wished to swell their ranks. High rates of nonmarriage in Irish America also contributed to the "greening" of women's religious life; as Hasia Diner notes, an Irish American girl's desire to enter religious life did not break with accepted expectations in the way it would for other immigrant daughters.[24] In any case, as will become clear, the Americanization of the Sisters of Notre Dame would be one source of tension between the sisters at Namur and those in the United States.

Standardization and organization were other hallmarks of Sister Julia's administration. Between 1889 and 1895, she developed a uniform course of study based on the one designed at Namur. She appointed congregational supervisors of teaching in each city and increased formal teacher preparation for all the sisters. These measures were intended to establish consistency among schools in the United States as well as to maintain close links with Namur. Sister Julia kept a close eye on Notre Dame's schools overseas, and as a result she predicted in 1893 that Catholic sisters would eventually need state diplomas in the United States, as they did in Belgium and England.[25] (As it happened, Catholic sisters in the United States would eventually be required to have state certificates rather than state diplomas, but that is a subject for the next chapter to explore.)

In addition to watching developments in Europe, Sister Julia paid close attention to the expansion of women's educational opportunities in the United States. By the time she became Notre Dame's provincial superior, American women had a variety of options to pursue a college degree under secular auspices. Oberlin College in Ohio had admitted women since 1833, and eight state universities had become coeducational during the Civil War years. The founding of all-female Vassar College in 1865 initiated another trend. Other women's colleges followed: Wellesley in 1870, Smith in 1871, Bryn Mawr in 1885, and Mount Holyoke in 1888. In the early 1890s, Radcliffe and Barnard College opened as affiliated institutions of Harvard and

Columbia, respectively, providing a third type of American women's college. These early women's colleges are collectively known as the Seven Sisters.[26]

By the early 1890s, Sister Julia recognized that daughters of middle-class Catholics would need college degrees to compete with other American women for access to professional occupations. This realization provided her with another motive for redesigning the curriculum and instituting other improvements. Her efforts to prepare Notre Dame's students to study at the college level suggest that she viewed opening a Catholic women's college as simply the logical next step in meeting their needs. Whether she took the initiative in this regard, however, or whether the opportunity was presented to her remains a matter of some dispute.

The most detailed account of Trinity's founding years is provided by Sister Mary Euphrasia Taylor, the superior of Notre Dame's convent in Washington throughout this period. Born Ella Osmonia Taylor, she had been raised as an Episcopalian in Richmond, Virginia.[27] All final decisions regarding Trinity would fall to Sister Julia in her capacity as head of the American province, but because she was based in Cincinnati and traveled frequently, Sister Julia often designated Sister Mary Euphrasia as her representative in the capital. Although private correspondence between these two women reveals clearly that they both appreciated the significance and magnitude of their undertaking, they often denied taking any initiative. "We did not seek the work," Sister Julia maintained; "it came to us from a Higher Authority."[28] While she was undoubtedly referring to a divine mandate, one practical result of this statement and others like it is that Trinity's founding has usually been ascribed to a *temporal* higher authority. According to most historical accounts, it was the Reverend Phillip Garrigan, the vice-rector of Catholic University, who encouraged the sisters to open a college rather than an academy. Trinity's first historian, Sister Mary Patricia Butler, SND, wrote that Garrigan and Thomas Conaty, the rector of Catholic University, "entered into the project with such zest and wisdom as wholly to change and exalt the nature of the enterprise. They pointed out clearly and with excellent reasoning that what was needed was not an academy but a college for women."[29] Modern historical studies also credit the rectors of Catholic University with convincing the sisters to set their sights on a higher goal.[30]

Sister Mary Euphrasia told a slightly different version of the story. She recorded the initial conversation regarding Trinity as having taken place a full two weeks before her conversation with Garrigan. During a visit to Cincinnati, she, Sister Julia, and several other sisters discussed opening a "first class institution" in the vicinity of Catholic University. According to Sister Mary Euphrasia, it was Sister Julia who proposed that this institution be an actual college, a suggestion to which the others responded enthusiastically. Sister Mary Euphrasia claimed, therefore, that it was she who approached Garrigan with the plan to open a women's college.[31] Nuns' inveterate self-effacement probably explains this discrepancy in part. But it is also likely that attributing the idea to Garrigan contained an element of calculation, as it undoubtedly served the sisters' purpose to say that the idea originated with a prelate rather than themselves. Whether Garrigan or the sisters took the first step is, of course, a moot point. It is clear that Sister Julia had compelling reasons for "seeking the work" and that she had been preparing for it for almost a decade.

Congregational pride offered the sisters another important incentive to open a college. In 1897, the Sisters of Notre Dame de Namur taught at only one parish school in Washington, D.C. Sister Mary Euphrasia argued that because the capital was becoming the educational center of the country, and because the area around Catholic University was attracting many "dignitaries of the Church," it was imperative that the Sisters of Notre Dame increase their visibility in the city. Otherwise, she feared that visitors would receive the inaccurate impression that parochial schools were "the principal work of our society, for which *alone* the sisters were *fitted*." A superior Catholic women's college, she argued, would more adequately represent Notre Dame's mission in Washington. To emphasize the need for decisive action in this regard, she pointed out that Eckington College, a Protestant institution, had recently opened near the university.[32]

According to Sister Mary Euphrasia, Garrigan received the sisters' proposal with the "warmest and most cordial approbation." He explained why. Two years before, Catholic University had announced plans to allow women to attend lectures as "special students." Bishop John Keane, then the rector, declared that the university had no plans to admit women as regular students. Undeterred, twenty women applied to the university in the fall of 1895. Although these applications were rejected, they testified to a growing desire for higher education among Catholic women. Garrigan went on to speculate that those twenty female applicants, once rebuffed from Catholic University, had enrolled in "Protestant or infidel" institutions of higher learning.[33]

Garrigan's reasoning highlighted the two most compelling arguments in favor of Catholic women's colleges. The twenty female applicants to Catholic University contributed to increasing anxiety in the Catholic community over the prospect of coeducation. Among Catholics, there was virtually unanimous agreement that men and women be educated separately. Any Catholic women's college would need to avoid even the suggestion of coeducation if it were to succeed. According to Garrigan, that taint had already thwarted two other proposals. He reported that the Ladies of the Sacred Heart and the Sisters of the Holy Cross had each contemplated building "a women's annexe [sic]" to Catholic University. Francis Cardinal Satolli, the apostolic delegate in Washington at the time, had vetoed both plans because they had seemed perilously close to coeducation.[34]

As Garrigan's second comment indicated, providing an alternative to "Protestant or infidel" schools was also of paramount concern. Although Catholics were not expressly prohibited from attending non-Catholic institutions, they were discouraged from doing so because of widespread fear about the potential damage to their faith. It is not exactly clear how many Catholic women were attending secular schools at the time of Trinity's founding. The most reliable statistic comes from a 1907 survey conducted by the Reverend John Farrell, the Catholic chaplain at Harvard, who reported that 1,557 Catholic women were attending secular colleges.[35] There was no shortage of anecdotal examples, such as the following ones supplied by Archbishop Patrick Ryan of Philadelphia in a letter to Sister Julia in 1897: "I know two young ladies who graduated at Radcliffe to have lost their faith there," he reported. "We certainly need such a college as Trinity."[36]

Anxiety about Catholic women attending secular women's colleges was often intensified by the belief that women were more susceptible to Protestant proselytizing than were Catholic men. Austin O'Malley, a medical doctor and professor of literature at Notre Dame, explained why secular education would put the souls of Catholic females in greater jeopardy: "The life in a non-Catholic women's college, where attention to the 'evils of Popery' is more absorbing than in colleges for boys, is not the best atmosphere in the world for the growth of a Catholic girl's faith. . . . The girl in the non-Catholic college is exposed to stronger temptations than those experienced by a Catholic boy in a similar position, because the emotional preacher is more potent in the girls' college than in the boys."[37]

O'Malley claimed that "Catholic girls in large and increasing numbers are flocking to non-Catholic colleges, to the injury of loss of faith." Since Catholic men's colleges were taboo—he described coeducation as an "abomination"—he argued that the only remedy was to open Catholic colleges for women. Lest some worry that Catholic girls had the capacity to pursue a college education, O'Malley reassured his readers: "Up to the graduate degree, at least, she is equal to man except in original work." After all, he noted, college "required no genius to penetrate its abysses."[38] By the late 1890s, many Catholics who would otherwise oppose higher education for women agreed with O'Malley: Catholic women's colleges were a necessary defense against coeducation and mass apostasy.

Sisters Julia and Mary Euphrasia viewed the matter quite differently. Though they understood both of these arguments, neither had formed their primary rationale. Though the Sisters of Notre Dame were vigorously committed to single-sex education—in 1888 Sister Julia would only reluctantly permit the teaching of boys until the fourth grade—the dangers of coeducation never surfaced in their discussions about Trinity. While they were keenly aware that Catholic women had the option to attend secular schools, their students' potential loss of faith did not seem to be a leading concern. Sister Mary Euphrasia's uneasiness over the proximity of Eckington College, at least, stemmed from her fears that Notre Dame's prestige would suffer by comparison. She may have also worried about the implications that the competition for students would have on the SND's financial viability. After this conversation with Garrigan, however, both she and Sister Julia recognized that the twin goals of preventing coeducation and loss of faith constituted the most persuasive—and, not coincidentally, the least controversial—arguments in favor of establishing a Catholic women's college. From that point on, these objectives would figure more prominently in subsequent arguments that the sisters would make on Trinity's behalf.

Before she could proceed, Sister Julia needed permission from James Cardinal Gibbons, archbishop of Baltimore, under whose jurisdiction Trinity would fall. At their mid-March meeting, Garrigan had encouraged Sister Mary Euphrasia to present the plan to Gibbons as soon as possible. He cautioned her to emphasize that while Trinity would be loosely affiliated with Catholic University, it would be an entirely separate institution. He also suggested that she stress it would be a boarding school; otherwise, he felt, Cardinal Gibbons would worry that Trinity might siphon students away from existing academies. Sister Mary Euphrasia followed this advice when she met with Gibbons a few days later. The cardinal tentatively endorsed the idea but asked for time to reflect and to consult with the administrators of Catholic University. As Garrigan had anticipated, Gibbons stipulated that Trinity must not interfere with the work of the sisters at Georgetown Visitation.[39]

The Reverend Thomas Conaty, who had succeeded John Keane as rector of Catholic University in 1896, greeted the proposal with enthusiasm. He told Sister Mary Euphrasia that he had asked both the Sisters of Mercy and the Ladies of the Holy Cross to consider opening a college, but he was overjoyed at Notre Dame's interest: "Although Notre Dame is of all other orders the one I would desire to undertake such a work," Conaty reportedly said, "I would have never dared ask you. If only I had known that Notre Dame would undertake it, I would have asked no others."[40] Conaty's flattery on this occasion, though possibly sincere, was no doubt also intended to use the competition among congregations to advance his own goals. As we will see, this was a tactic that he and other Catholic educators would frequently employ.

The project also required sanction from Mother Aimee de Jesus Dullaert, the superior general at Namur. Mother Aimee cabled her consent on April 1: "Approve, hoping you can find means and subjects."[41] Less than a week later, the nuns received official authorization from Gibbons; his council voted in favor of an institution for women that "worked in union with though entirely independently of the Catholic University." Gibbons admitted in a later letter that he was delighted because Trinity's founding would "relieve the University authorities from the embarrassment of refusing women admission."[42] Although the project did not require official approval from Rome, Gibbons advised Sister Mary Euphrasia to visit Archbishop Sebastian Martinelli, Satolli's replacement as apostolic delegate, to keep him informed of the plans. She called on Martinelli on April 25, and they had an amiable conversation. The wisdom of this consultation would not be apparent until several months later.[43]

After canvassing the Washington suburbs for appropriate sites for the new college, the sisters purchased twenty acres at the intersection of Michigan and Lincoln avenues in the northeastern suburb of Brookland. This plot was located approximately one-third of a mile from Catholic University. The sale would not be final until later that summer, and the nuns had agreed to postpone a public announcement until then. Because Sister Julia knew that "everything would depend on the first impression," she wanted time to carefully formulate a statement that would include Gibbons's official letter of endorsement. She lost the opportunity to control the nature of the revelation in mid-June, when someone involved in the purchase leaked the news to the press. The newspapers sensationalized the story and misrepresented some of the facts. Some reported that the college was slated to open in 1898, when the actual target date was two years later. The *New York Times* erroneously described Trinity as "connected" to Catholic University. Sister Julia sent news releases to secular and religious newspapers to correct these exaggerations and misstatements.[44]

Sister Julia had anticipated that the sisters' proposal to begin a college would anger traditional opponents of higher education for Catholic women, who predicted disaster for the family and the church in general should Trinity open. But by 1897, the twin specters of secular education or coeducation had significantly undermined this resistance. Although there was by no means universal support, most agreed that Catholic women's colleges should be established as a matter of expediency. What Sister Julia had not foreseen was that far more menacing attacks on the college would emerge from a debate over Catholic identity instead of one about gender roles. The most dangerous threat to Trinity came from Catholic prelates and intellectuals who viewed the problem of higher education for women as symptomatic of a more egregious sin: Catholic capitulation to American culture.

NOTRE DAME AND THE WAR OF 1897

In mid-July 1897 Archbishop John Ireland of St. Paul, Minnesota, wrote a letter to Sister Julia in which he congratulated her on her work but warned that difficulties might lie ahead: "I am afraid," Ireland cautioned, "things will not go as smoothly as you expect."[45] It was fitting that this prophetic warning came from Ireland, the unofficial leader of the "Americanists" who had coined its slogan, "Church and Age Unite!" This group also included Cardinal Gibbons; John J. Keane, the first rector of Catholic University; Thomas Conaty, Keane's successor; Denis O'Connell, the rector of the North American College in Rome; and John Lancaster Spalding, bishop of Peoria and the brightest intellectual among the American hierarchy. Archbishop Michael Corrigan of New York and Bishop Bernard McQuaid of Rochester led the opposing group of conservatives. This group also included many German American priests and bishops who were suspicious of Irish American dominance among the American hierarchy.

Disagreements about Catholic education from the elementary through the college level exacerbated tensions between the two groups. Catholic University, which opened in 1889, was intertwined with the Americanist controversy in several ways. Early discussions about the institution had helped divide liberals and conservatives. Quarrels did not necessarily emanate from ideological differences; Archbishops Corrigan and McQuaid, favoring a New York location for the university, resented the eventual choice of Washington. The conservatives were further alienated by the close involvement of several key Americanists in the planning process. John Keane, bishop of Richmond, Virginia, was designated the first rector of the university; Ireland served on its organizing committee; and it was located in Gibbons's jurisdiction. John Lancaster Spalding's progressive talk at the cornerstone-laying ceremony further irritated conservatives by explicitly identifying the university with the liberal group.[46]

Monsignor Joseph Schroeder, a German-born professor of dogmatic theology, was the leading conservative at Catholic University and an outspoken enemy of the Americanists there. He led a faction of German American Catholics based primarily in the Midwest and attacked the Americanists through the St. Louis–based paper *Das Herold des Glaubens* (The Herald of Faith). Schroeder had disproportionate influence in Rome through his friendship with Francis Cardinal Satolli, the former apostolic delegate to the United States (who had earlier, according to Garrigan, vetoed proposals to incorporate a "women's annexe" to Catholic University). When Satolli arrived in the United States in 1892, he initially allied himself with the Americanists. But by the time he returned to Rome four years later, he had moved into the conservative camp. With help from Schroeder, Satolli began to undermine Keane at the Vatican, criticizing the rector for his liberal views and his close association with American Protestants. In September 1896, Satolli used his influence with the pope to orchestrate the dismissal of Keane as rector of Catholic University. Keane's departure represented a stunning defeat for the liberals.[47]

Early discussions of Trinity came on the heels of this particularly bitter episode in the Americanist debate. Both sides recognized the proposed women's college as a potential weapon. For the Americanists, Trinity demonstrated the promise of Catholic acculturation to American society. Ireland's enthusiastic support, for example, stemmed from what he perceived as the need for college-trained teachers in parochial schools. In his own diocese, he would support his sister, Mother Seraphine Ireland of the Sisters of St. Joseph, in her efforts to open the College of St. Catherine in 1905.[48]

Other Americanists praised Trinity. Spalding of Peoria became one of its staunchest supporters. In a lecture about the college, he affirmed one of Americanism's central tenets, the belief that the United States provided the most favorable conditions for moral perfection. Spalding described the new opportunities open to women as the "chief glory" of the nineteenth century. While Christianity had liberated woman from being man's "drudge, his slave, his chattel," the United States had provided for the higher education of women "with an energy and a generosity unequalled by any other country." Attributing the widespread lack of religion among men in France to "the very imperfect mental culture of their mothers and wives," Spalding argued that Catholic women's higher education was essential to save Catholicism in the United States from the same fate it had encountered in Europe.[49]

Although it was Spalding who molded Trinity most perfectly to the Americanist argument, others would make a similar case. Cardinal Gibbons described the college as a "blessing to our country" and a "glory to our Church."[50] Conaty emphasized Trinity's "utmost importance to Church and state . . . the age demands scholarship, and women's responsibilities urge that intellectual and moral development unite in fitting her to do her full duty to society."[51] The Reverend Edward Pace, a Catholic University professor of philosophy, agreed that Catholic women's colleges were needed because the American "democratic spirit" had given Catholic women in the United States more potential for achievement.[52]

For Americanists, then, Trinity symbolized all the good that would result from a union between church and age; for Schroeder and his supporters, the college represented the perils of such an alliance. As early as mid-April, before the sisters had even chosen a site, Schroeder had, through Satolli, reported to the Vatican that the Sisters of Notre Dame had purchased property near Catholic University and that they planned to have the same teachers and the same classes that the male students had. Just before his late April meeting with Sister Mary Euphrasia, Archbishop Martinelli received a letter from Pope Leo XIII in which he asked for clarification about these rumors. After hearing more about the plans for Trinity, the apostolic delegate had denied that the nuns planned to sponsor coeducation. He did not even mention the correspondence to Sister Mary Euphrasia, thinking that he had heard "the end of it."[53]

The Sisters of Notre Dame did not learn about negative rumors until Schroeder and his supporters publicly attacked them through *Das Herold des Glaubens* in late summer. Editor John Enzleberger wrote one of the most damaging critiques, entitled "The 'New Woman' at the 'University.'" The word choice was provocative. As we have seen, association with the New Woman was potentially lethal, and by invoking her in relation to Notre Dame, Enzleberger was suggesting that the sisters "wanted to imitate Protestants and unbelievers." His use of the term "University," which raised the specter of coeducation, presented equal cause for alarm. Describing Trinity as a "wing" of Catholic University, Enzleberger contended that the nuns did not care about the danger that higher learning would pose to the students' faith. As evidence of Trinity's blatant disregard of Catholicism, he pointed out that its admission requirements did not include religion. Enzleberger described Trinity as a nondenominational institution masquerading as a Catholic one and concluded that the college had only served to strengthen his "old-fashioned conviction that, for the present, man's world should stand at the pinnacle of learning."[54]

Sister Mary Euphrasia responded to the accusations in a letter to the editor of *Das Herold des Glaubens*. She emphasized that Trinity would be no "annex or wing" of Catholic University. Although she admitted that Trinity did not stipulate religion as an entrance requirement, she caustically reminded the editors that such a prerequisite would exclude the very students that Catholic colleges hoped to benefit, those who had attended secular secondary schools. She did assure the editors that the curriculum would have a number of religion requirements.[55] Her rejoinder came too late, however, to repair the damage that had already been done. By the time these attacks were made public, Schroeder and his cohort had succeeded, with the help of Satolli, in convincing Pope Leo XIII that something was amiss at Trinity.

On August 15, Satolli wrote to Gibbons: "I have learned also of the project of a University for the weaker sex . . . ; this affair, as mentioned in the newspapers, has made a disagreeable impression here, particularly so because it was described that it would be a dangerous addition and amalgamation of Institutions, for the teaching of students of both sexes."[56] A week later,

Martinelli informed Gibbons that the Holy Father had heard of the matter "from sources unknown to me." He suggested that the Sisters of Notre Dame seek approval from the Holy See before they continued their plans.[57]

This development brought an immediate halt to progress on Trinity. Cardinal Gibbons summoned Sister Mary Euphrasia to Baltimore and, blaming "the German element in the West," told her that she and Sister Julia must stop work on Trinity until the matter was resolved. With characteristic aplomb, Sister Mary Euphrasia assured the cardinal that she would not lose heart and that she had "every confidence that God would himself carry through a work in which his Hand had been visible from the beginning." Later, in recounting this exchange in a letter to her superior, she reflected on the humor of "giving what seemed to be a lecture on confidence in God to the Cardinal Archbishop of Baltimore." In an attempt to hearten Sister Julia, she compared this setback to Mother Julie Billiart's trials with the bishop of Amiens during the congregation's early days.[58]

After the news had leaked that Schroeder had succeeded in thwarting the sisters' plans, reporters descended on the Notre Dame convent on North Capitol Street.[59] In what one sister later described as an "impromptu press conference," Sister Mary Euphrasia attempted to correct those reports by explaining the purpose and plan of Trinity.[60] On the advice of Cardinal Gibbons, she decided to pay a personal visit to the apostolic delegate to convince him to intercede on Trinity's behalf. She arrived at Martinelli's Washington residence only to discover that he was vacationing in Atlantic City. Undaunted, she visited him at the ocean resort a few days later, traveling half a day for an audience that lasted a little more than an hour.

It was during this meeting that Martinelli told her about the papal letter he had received prior to their April conversation. He promised to tell the Vatican, once again, that the Sisters of Notre Dame were not promoting coeducation. Martinelli also explained the exact nature of the prohibition on the college, which involved the distinction between a college and a university. Whereas a university would require papal consent, a college needed only the permission of the local bishop. Martinelli did tell her, though, that Gibbons was unlikely to approve of any plan discountenanced by the Holy Father.[61] In saying this, Martinelli was being somewhat disingenuous in that he himself was the one who had advised Gibbons to stop the sisters until they resolved matters with Rome.

Sister Julia was in Cincinnati when the trouble began but was kept apprised of developments through frequent correspondence. She was initially cheerful. In an early letter to Sister Mary Euphrasia, she claimed to be "not in the least troubled. . . . I would much rather have the storm before we begin than a breeze later which might insure a feeling of distrust and thus injure the work."[62] But her frustration increased as she recognized the assault as a thinly veiled attack on the Americanists. Understanding that the sisters were "obviously a figurehead," she knew that the accusations against the college were unwarranted, yet she had little recourse to defend herself. In early September, she decided that the matter had become grave enough to necessitate her presence "on the spot," so she left the motherhouse and went to Washington, D.C.[63] Sister Agnes Loretto, a young nun who accompanied Sister Julia on her travels and acted as her secretary, reported that her patience was wearing thin. At one point, Sister Julia lamented the inaction to which her sex confined her, vowing that "if she was a man, she could put on her hat and go off to see the pope."[64]

Unable to "go off to see the pope," Sisters Julia and Mary Euphrasia pleaded Trinity's case through written correspondence. Soon after her meeting with Gibbons, Sister Mary Euphrasia had written to Cardinal Satolli. Upon learning how closely Schroeder was allied with Satolli, the sisters decided any appeal to him would ultimately be fruitless. Instead, they wrote to three men who they hoped would be able to restore their favor with Rome: Dominic Cardinal Ferrata, the cardinal protector of the Sisters of Notre Dame de Namur; Mariano Cardinal Rampolla, the cardinal secretary of state; and Gaetano Cardinal Aloisi-Masella, pro-datary of the pope. Gibbons encouraged the sisters to compose their own letters, but he offered to read them before they were sent. Sister Mary Euphrasia brought drafts of these letters to Baltimore in early September, showed them to the cardinal, and copied them in the episcopal library.

In drafting the letters the sisters received shrewd advice from Dr. Frederick Rooker, one of Archbishop Martinelli's aides. Reading an early version of several of them, he chided the sisters for mincing words. He urged them not to be sentimental: "Remember, it is business not charity you have to write!" He reminded them that they had nothing to lose by stating their case strongly and everything to lose if they did not act decisively; if Trinity was not approved, he speculated, the work and the prestige of the congregation would be set back twenty years. He also advised them to assure the cardinals that they had the full support of Mother Aimee in Belgium and to send copies of their letters to her.[65]

Though Sister Julia signed her letters "your obedient child," her arguments were anything but submissive. First and foremost, she dismissed out of hand the erroneous reports about coeducation. She attributed these rumors to "the spirit of opposition in the Western Churches," insisting that "anyone who knows the order [Notre Dame] will recognize [the rumors about coeducation] as gratuitous."[66] Indeed, it was not until 1914 that the Sisters of Notre Dame would agree to teach boys up until the eighth grade. Given this, the idea that they would countenance coeducation at the college level appeared ridiculous.[67]

Sister Julia also emphasized the need to prevent a loss of faith should Catholic women enroll at secular colleges. In the United States, after all, education was the "cry of the age," and "if the Church does not supply the want of the age for American girls [they] will continue to frequent godless schools." She claimed that there were a dozen Protestant, anti-Catholic women's colleges in the United States; in those institutions, the "anti-Catholic interpretation in Science, Philosophy, History, and the Arts" caused its Catholic students widespread moral injury.[68] In her own letter to Cardinal Satolli, Sister Mary Euphrasia had dramatized the impending disaster by reporting that, over the past four years, eleven Catholic students had "lost the faith" at Colombian University (later George Washington University), a Baptist University in Washington, D.C.[69]

As Rooker had advised her to do, Sister Julia also intimated that jealously of other congregations had generated some of the ill will against Trinity; she wrote that there was "an unfriendly feeling towards the College, on the part of some who consider the success of this project a drawback to their own work; whereas it is intended to be a help to all." Also acting on a suggestion from Rooker, Sister Julia emphasized how damaging a "public rebuke" from Rome would be, both to the Sisters of Notre Dame and to the Catholic religion in the United States. She also made clear that she "possessed the entire approval and encouragement of our Superior General" at Namur.[70]

Finally, the sisters employed an argument commonly used by Catholic women who were accused of leaving their proper "sphere": they disassociated themselves with modern women by emphasizing their ties to the past. In the midst of the controversy the sisters had read and admired both

George Tyrrell's "The Old Faith and New Woman" and Margaret Buchanan Sullivan's "Chiefly among Women," and they, too, invoked a connection between their new initiatives and a luminous Catholic past.[71] Sister Mary Euphrasia reminded Satolli that religious teaching had long been the "alpha and omega" of Notre Dame's philosophy of education.[72] Sister Julia assured Rampolla that "the memory of Italy's renown in its women saints and scholars" would be "the law and guide" of Trinity College.[73] Establishing this connection to a Catholic past not only differentiated Trinity from its secular counterparts but also refuted any suggestion that the nuns were behaving like America's New Women.

Meanwhile Gibbons defended the SNDs. He promised Martinelli that the college would have "no official or organic connection whatever with the Catholic University," since they were separated by one-third of a mile. Georgetown College and the Visitation Convent were even closer to each other, he noted, "yet no inconvenience has resulted though they have been in existence there for a hundred years." And Gibbons assured Satolli that "the reports which have reached Rome with regard to a new female school of higher studies are utterly false or greatly exaggerated, and are the off-spring of ignorance and malice."[74]

The Paulists, a religious order of men who shared Americanist views, published an "authoritative statement" about Trinity College in the September issue of the *Catholic World*. Attempting to correct reports about the college that had been "prematurely circulated," the author testified to the impeccable credentials of the Sisters of Notre Dame de Namur, both in matters of faith and in teaching ability. Emphasizing that the project had been approved by Gibbons and Conaty, he argued that Trinity would "offer to its students all the advantages of the best American colleges, and will have, in addition, those benefits that come from education given under the direction of experienced religious teachers." Proximity to Catholic University would help Trinity's students achieve academic excellence by giving them the benefit of the university's public lecture courses. Finally, he argued that by seeking "friendship" with the university, the sisters were not challenging Catholic teaching; on the contrary, they were showing their "desire to be in close touch with the bishops of the Church."[75]

The nuns put their plans on indefinite hold for several months, during which Sister Agnes Loretto observed that "waiting is more tiresome than work."[76] Good news arrived in November, when Rampolla wrote to Martinelli in the name of the pope: "His Holiness, after having considered the matter well, thinks that there should be nothing more said considering the difficulties in the way of the project of the erection of an Institution for females in the vicinity of the Catholic University."[77] Three days later, Gibbons summoned Sister Mary Euphrasia to Baltimore to dictate a translation of this letter.[78] Conaty, also present at the meeting, advised the sisters not to gloat over their victory: "Do not exult too loud, but proceed joyfully in secret, grateful that this great difficulty has been so happily overcome."[79] The nuns did rejoice privately: "Glory be to God in all things!" Sister Agnes Loretto wrote. "We can build our college as soon as we have money enough, and go right on without minding what anyone says to us."[80]

What led to the Vatican's reversal? The SND's lobbying efforts undoubtedly helped, as did the support of influential prelates such as Martinelli and Gibbons. But it is unclear whether these measures alone would have sufficed. What was probably the most significant factor in the decision was Schroeder's rapidly declining influence at Catholic University and in Rome. In what Archbishop Ireland dubbed the "War of 1897," the Americanist contingent at Catholic University launched an offensive against Schroeder and collected witnesses who testified that he regularly stayed out until dawn, frequenting disreputable saloons. In October, they presented this evidence to the Vatican, and the university's board of trustees voted for dismissal. At the request of the pope, Schroeder was permitted to resign.[81] Rampolla had specifically linked Schroeder's fall from grace to the Trinity question in a letter to Gibbons. Quoting the letter to the sisters, Gibbons reported that "the University would receive no further annoyance" from Schroeder and that the pope would no longer listen to "disadvantageous reports" about Trinity.[82]

In retrospect, it is clear that the Sisters of Notre Dame de Namur were not in league with the Americanists; in fact, Sister Julia once claimed to never even have heard of Americanism until she was accused of it.[83] Given their proximity to Catholic University, and their timing, it was unlikely that the sisters would have remained completely insulated from the conflict. But that Trinity became intertwined with the controversy to such a great extent is significant because it demonstrates how easily gender could be manipulated to serve other purposes. Members on both sides of the debate used gender to either impugn or defend the Americanist position. Supporters of the Sisters of Notre Dame exalted them as True Women; opponents assailed them as New Women. This remarkable affair shows how vulnerable Catholic women became when they attempted to renegotiate gender boundaries within the church.

But the Sisters of Notre Dame were never mere pawns in a larger power struggle, and their story represents much more than an interesting footnote in the tangled history of Americanist politics. Trinity's founders experienced the same tensions that had prompted the debate over Americanism, and long after the "War of 1897" ended, the challenge of adapting Old World Catholicism to American culture awaited them. Responding to this challenge often involved negotiating between religious and national identities that competed against each other in a variety of ways.

TRANSATLANTIC AND LOCAL TENSIONS, 1898–1899

Like most American Catholic women, Sister Julia went to great lengths to emphasize that her new endeavors were adaptations of tradition rather than radical departures from the past. In a letter she wrote to the American SNDs on the eve of Trinity's founding, she explained how recent changes in the curriculum did not constitute any great change from the rule that had guided the congregation since it had received papal approval in 1845.[84] As she proceeded with plans to open Trinity College after the Vatican lifted its prohibition, however, Sister Julia's work was complicated by people who had different interpretations of how far she should go in modifying tradition to "suit the times." On the one side was Mother Aimee de Jesus Dullaret, the superior general in Namur, who eventually judged that Sister Julia had gone too far. Taking the opposite view were Trinity's clerical and lay supporters in Washington, D.C., who believed that Sister Julia's close ties to Namur prevented her from going far enough.

Methods of financing the college proved to be the source of most of the disagreements. As noted previously, Sister Julia had regarded this task with no small amount of trepidation. Trinity's first fund-raising campaign must have confirmed all her worst fears; the venture alienated supporters on both sides of the Atlantic and, in the end, did not raise a penny. The "Belgian plan" had been devised by Countess of Lichtervelde, the wife of the Belgian minister to the United States and a good friend of Sister Mary Euphrasia Taylor's, the superior of Notre Dame's convent in Washington. In early 1898, the countess learned that Prince Albert, Count of Flanders and heir apparent to the Belgian throne, was planning a visit to the United States. She suggested that the sisters use this as an opportunity to launch a fund-raising drive. The countess and Sister Mary Euphrasia persuaded Sister Julia to write a letter to the prince's mother, explaining the purpose of Trinity and requesting a formal statement of support from the prince. In return for his endorsement, the first building of the college would be named in honor of Albert. The names of donors to the building fund would be inscribed in an album that would be presented to the prince at the end of his American tour.[85]

According to custom, Sister Julia should have forwarded this missive to Mother Aimee at Namur, who would have then presented it formally to the Countess of Flanders. In the interest of time, however, Sister Julia decided to write directly to the countess and smooth matters over with Mother Aimee during her trip to Belgium that summer. But the superior general, who heard of the plan long before the visit, resented both the lack of protocol and the interference of the Countess of Lichtervelde. According to one source, Mother Aimee criticized Sister Mary Euphrasia for becoming "impregnated with the spirit of the world and losing the spirit of simplicity that should characterize a Sister of Notre Dame." Sister Julia abandoned the project immediately.[86]

Underlying this particular episode were much broader issues regarding the relationship between the American Sisters of Notre Dame and their superiors at Namur. As previously noted, the percentage of American-born members increased over the nineteenth century, and by the early 1890s, the influx of Belgian sisters had ceased. As fewer members of the congregation had little or no connection to European motherhouses, a strain in the relationship was certainly understandable and perhaps inevitable, but Trinity's founding undoubtedly accentuated this transatlantic tension.

Throughout the founding process, Sister Julia repeatedly tried to balance her loyalty to Namur with the realities of the American context. Early on, she recognized that her progressive supporters in the American hierarchy would find European interference troubling, especially if it came from Namur, as the conservatism of Belgian Catholicism was well known.[87] Indeed, Gibbons, Garrigan, and Rooker had all raised concerns about this issue. Although Sister Julia assured them that the American sisters had been "singularly free from European influence" since their foundation in the United States fifty-seven years earlier, these prelates continued to suspect that Namur retained too much control over the fledgling college.[88] For her part, Sister Julia did her best to minimize Namur's influence on Trinity. She emphasized that the college would fall under the direct supervision of her office rather than the superior general's authority.[89] Acknowledging that Notre Dame's normal schools in England provided a logical recruiting ground for Trinity professors, she resolved to hire only those candidates who "have been selected by their special talents and who have been rigidly trained in American educational methods."[90]

At the same time, there was no question that Sister Julia would act in solidarity with Namur. The American and Belgian members of the congregation were bound by the same rule, and Sister Julia understood them to be a group of individuals who worked together as one entity: "Notre Dame is made up of individual members, who, if all right, work like the fingers of a hand," she wrote. "If anything is the matter, even with the little finger, the whole body suffers."[91] One of Sister Julia's motivations in standardizing the curricula of Notre Dame's academies was to achieve consistency with institutions both in the United States and overseas. Sister Julia traveled to Namur seven times between 1868 and 1898, relishing her time at "the dear *Maison Mère.*" Her pleasure in these visits increased after 1888, when Mother Aimee was elected superior general. The two women had previously met at one of Notre Dame's training schools in England, and the knowledge that they had professed their vows the same year deepened their friendship. Sister Julia told the American Sisters of Notre Dame that "our well-beloved mother is the true sunshine of house and of hearts."[92]

Trinity's founding permanently strained the friendship between Mother Aimee and Sister Julia. Reports of the U.S. sisters' alleged alliance with the Americanists had reached Mother Aimee and dampened her initial enthusiasm for the project. Her distrust of Sister Julia was increased by the latter's clear violation of the chain of command. In her September 1897 appeal to Notre Dame's cardinal protector, Cardinal Ferrata, Sister Julia had addressed the letter directly to him instead of sending it to Namur to be forwarded to the Vatican. She had confessed in her correspondence that the "motive of expedition alone prevents our having recourse to you through the ordinary channel of communication."[93] In the Prince Albert debacle the following spring, Sister Julia would again avoid using Mother Aimee as an intermediary, a decision that increased the superior's displeasure.

Even aside from issues of protocol, however, a general disagreement over fund-raising tactics widened the wedge between the two women. Mother Aimee advised Sister Julia to act prudently by delaying actual construction of the college until she had accumulated sufficient funds. Cardinal Gibbons, on the other hand, pressed the sisters to start building immediately after they received clearance from the Vatican. When construction had not begun by April 1898, Gibbons guessed that Namur was behind the delay, and he threatened to remove his support for Trinity as a result. In a letter to Garrigan, Sister Julia had defended her desire to act with caution, insisting that the principle of "being guided by my purse . . . has saved us from embarrassment thus far and will do so in the future."[94]

The suspicions of Garrigan and Gibbons, combined with the gathering distance from Namur, convinced Sister Julia that it was necessary to solicit financial support from U.S. Catholics. In this context she was particularly receptive to a suggestion made by Maurice Francis Egan, a professor of English at Catholic University, in spring 1898. He urged the Sisters of Notre Dame to call upon prominent laywomen to assist them in raising the necessary funds. After initiating private conversations with several such women in Washington, the sisters hosted the first official meeting of the Ladies Auxiliary Board at Notre Dame's convent on March 31, 1898. At this meeting, the women rejected a proposal to solicit donations from distinguished foreign sources and resolved to appeal only to Americans for aid, a decision that vexed Sister Mary Euphrasia, who would continue to solicit foreign donors. Throughout the founding process, the board members would consistently emphasize Trinity's "American" character.[95]

The auxiliary devoted the next several weeks to determining the membership and structure of its board. According the constitution, the board was organized with the purpose of "assisting and equipping Trinity College." Its core members, called regents, were women who spent at least part of the year in Washington but had close ties to another state. Ellen Carter, the wife of Senator Thomas Carter, became the state regent from Montana. Olive Risley Seward, the niece and adopted daughter of Lincoln's secretary of state, became the regent from New York. Ella Lorraine Dorsey, the daughter of Catholic novelist Anna Hanson Dorsey, represented Maryland. Mrs. Maurice Francis Egan, the wife of an English professor at Catholic University, served as regent from Pennsylvania. Elizabeth Sherman, the daughter of General William and Ellen Ewing Sherman, represented Ohio. Molly Elliot Seawell, a prominent Catholic convert and a grand-niece of President Tyler, served as the regent from Virginia. In total, thirteen states and the District of Colombia were represented on the Ladies Auxiliary Board.[96]

Each regent would appoint a vice-regent from major cities in her home state. Vice-regents would then organize committees, called associate boards, to coordinate fund-raising efforts from their respective cities.[97] As for governance, the constitution stipulated that all officers would be elected annually, with the exception of the "sister-in-charge," who would serve as treasurer. Olive Risley Seward was elected the board's first president, and Sister Mary Euphrasia was designated the sister-in-charge. This pairing would prove volatile.[98]

The board's first members appealed to common bonds of womanhood and Catholicism in a letter written to prospective supporters: "We, the undersigned, feel that we owe it to our sex as well as to our religion, to give our active co-operation" to the Sisters of Notre Dame, who, though "eminently fitted for educational work," were "debarred by their habit from going about to solicit patronage and assistance."[99] For the most part, a shared gender and religious identity did enable the board members and the sisters to work together in financing and publicizing the new college. One early observer pointed out that the alliance between the sisters and the Ladies Auxiliary meant that Trinity truly represented "the work of women for women."[100] As is often the case, however, the relationship between the two groups was much more complex than public statements would suggest. They were indeed united as women and as Catholics, and unlike Mother Aimee and the American SNDs, they were not separated by national and geographic boundaries. But other barriers divided them. Roman Catholics differentiated sharply between lay and religious and understood vowed life to be spiritually superior to life "in the world." This would hold true until the Second Vatican Council (1962–65), and it compromised, to say the least, the ability of lay and religious women to work together. In the case of Trinity, the lay-religious divide certainly placed limits on the collaboration between the sisters and their lay supporters.

The first signs of friction between the Ladies Auxiliary and the SNDs appeared the following autumn. Olive Risley Seward, like most of the regents, had spent the summer away from Washington. Upon her return, she was chagrined to discover that the sisters had not made more progress on Trinity. Part of the delay was explained by the onset of the Spanish-American War and Sister Julia's trip to Belgium, but Seward and other board members grew increasingly frustrated by what they perceived to be excessive caution on Sister Julia's part. In early November, Seward and Ellen Carter visited the Reverend Thomas Conaty, the rector of Catholic University, to express their concern. At the next meeting of the Ladies Auxiliary Board, they reported that Conaty shared their disappointment at the delay. Conaty told them that other supporters at the university were "losing interest" in the project and were prepared to turn to "other Sisters" if Notre Dame did not begin construction immediately. He encouraged the women to ask McGroarty for an explanation.[101] Conaty was using a two-tiered divide-and-conquer strategy here. By encouraging the Ladies Auxiliary to act more assertively, he was hoping to exacerbate the tension between lay and religious women to achieve quicker results, and by raising the threat of "other Sisters," he was hoping to exploit the competition between religious congregations to his own advantage.

Not surprisingly, Sister Mary Euphrasia was disturbed to hear of the appeal to Conaty, and she was further irritated that Seward and Carter planned to override her function as representative of the congregation by writing directly to the superior. In a journal that she kept of the founding years, she also reported that the Ladies Auxiliary delivered an ultimatum to the sisters at this meeting (there is no record of this in the minutes), threatening to dissolve themselves unless work began at once. Privately, she worried that "it is more talk than work with them."[102] A diplomatic intervention from Sister Julia diffused the tension within the next month. As she had told Garrigan and Gibbons the previous spring, she was unwilling to begin construction until she felt more confident that funds were forthcoming. Now, she reassured the auxiliary that while she did not intend to wait until the entire sum had been raised, she refused to begin the process "hampered by debt." The minutes of the board meeting describe her letter as a "decided and reasonable statement of the policy of the Sisters."[103]

The auxiliary members turned their attention to planning their first fundraiser, a benefit lecture by John Lancaster Spalding, bishop of Peoria, entitled "Women and the Higher Education."[104] Spalding's lecture, delivered in January 1899, was widely praised by Conaty and other Catholic University faculty members. One woman in the audience complimented both the speaker and the speech: "Spalding was handsome and buoyant, and treated his subject with common sense and wholesome humor, very refreshing after the stock arguments and platitudes commonly used to defend a position no longer assailed."[105] The event itself generated a great deal of publicity, and, at Spalding's suggestion, Sister Mary Euphrasia reproduced the speech in pamphlet form and arranged for copies to be circulated among Catholic reading circles and sodalities throughout the United States.[106]

Though the lecture raised more awareness than money, it represented an important turning point in the founding process. Sister Julia authorized the building to begin a few days after Spalding's lecture. She did so in a letter that, coincidentally, bore the same date as *Testem Benevolentiae*, Pope Leo XIII's apostolic letter that condemned as heresy a series of propositions under the heading "Americanism."[107] The decision created more dissension with Namur. By deciding it would be more effective to work and raise money simultaneously, Sister Julia clearly was acting contrary to her superior's advice. As one Sister of Notre Dame explained, this method "was the American way, not readily understood by foreigners."[108] Although Mother Aimee never retracted her official endorsement of the project, her friendship with Sister Julia permanently soured. Even the personal visit between the two women in the summer of 1898, which Sister Julia had hoped would provide an opportunity for reconciliation, did not diminish Mother Aimee's suspicion. Both nuns celebrated their golden jubilees that year, and a poignant statement in Sister Julia's biography reports that not even "the combined gold of the two jubilees had succeeded in restoring things to what they once had been."[109]

Ground was broken in June, and the cornerstone was laid on December 8, 1899. A "simple ceremony" marked each of these milestones, reflecting Sister Julia's desire to "go on quietly with everything."[110] Meanwhile, the members of the Ladies Auxiliary Board began in earnest to organize a national network of Trinity supporters among their own acquaintances, alumnae of Notre Dame's academies, and other friends of the sisters. Of the many enthusiastic responses they received to their requests for help, perhaps the most eager came from Emma Forbes Cary, a prominent convert to Catholicism and the sister of Radcliffe's president. Invited to serve as Trinity's vice-regent from Boston, Cary answered, "If Sr. Superior Julia asked for my head, I should try to unscrew it."[111] Boston's associate board flourished under Cary's leadership. One representative event featured a lecture by the Reverend Thomas Gasson, SJ, entitled "Women and the Higher Intellectual Life," in which Gasson urged his listeners to support the Sisters of Notre Dame. He contended that the college would "spread before Catholic women the highest culture of which the age is capable, and so temper knowledge with heavenly wisdom as to make Catholic maidens the rivals of an illustrious past, the glory of the science-bearing present, and the heralds of a renowned future."[112]

Within the next several years most of the regents had organized associate boards, usually with the endorsement of local bishops. When two members of the Ladies Auxiliary traveled to New York City to ask Archbishop Michael Corrigan for permission to recruit Catholic women, Corrigan registered his approval of the project, saying that "such an institution would have in its power for good the country at large, having as it did a national character."[113]

By the time Trinity opened, associate boards in St. Louis, Chicago, and Providence had each donated scholarships, and other boards would do the same within the next five years. Between them, Montana's three associate boards—in Helena, Anaconda, and Butte—pledged three scholarships and a laboratory. Annie Leary of New York donated money for a chapel; Boston contributed to a fund for the library. Throughout this period associate boards would continue to provide monetary support for Trinity. At the high point in 1911, the college had twenty-one boards, and their cumulative donation totaled $120,000. After 1911, associate boards gradually disappeared, having either been replaced by alumnae chapters, abandoned by regents, or, in some cases, disbanded by local bishops who wanted women to concentrate on diocesan efforts. Membership on the Board of Regents itself remained steady by comparison.[114]

In addition to monetary contributions, regents supported Trinity's cause in other ways. Several women provided Sister Julia with letters of introduction to prominent educators such as Agnes Irwin at Radcliffe and M. Carey Thomas at Bryn Mawr.[115] Through the influence of her senator husband, Ellen Carter played a critical role in gaining congressional approval for the extension of Michigan Avenue to the college and for Trinity's access to the city's water supply.[116] Yet Ella Lorraine Dorsey stands out as Trinity's most zealous advocate during these early years. Taking an extended leave of absence from her job at the U.S. Patent Office, Dorsey devoted more than eight weeks to publicizing Trinity in Cleveland, Cincinnati, Chicago, Milwaukee, St. Paul, Butte, and the Catholic Summer School in Plattsburgh, New York.[117] These visits, as well as the efforts of other regents to recruit students from their home states, undoubtedly contributed to the geo-

Ellen Carter, Ladies Auxiliary Board, Trinity College. Courtesy of Trinity College Archives.

graphic diversity of Trinity's pioneer class, which consisted of twenty-two students representing eighteen different states.[118]

Olive Risely Seward's leadership of the auxiliary was not destined to last. Within the first year of the board's existence, she emerged as the ringleader of a "number of strong women" and established a pattern of overstepping her authority. In the summer of 1899, for example, she visited Notre Dame's training school in England and reported to the Ladies Auxiliary Board that she was satisfied "that the Sisters of Notre Dame were capable of doing all they promised."[119] Repeatedly described as "indomitable," Seward often clashed with Sister Mary Euphrasia, who possessed a similarly strong personality. Their mutual struggle for control is symbolized by the rotating venues for board meetings between Seward's home and Notre Dame's convent.[120] Their skirmishes prompted several crises during Trinity's early years, which culminated in Seward's abrupt resignation in 1902. Ten other members resigned as well, and for a brief period the board was suspended. By this time, Sister Julia had died, so there was no chance for her to intervene as she had done in the past.[121]

In the wake of Seward's departure, Ella Lorraine Dorsey would join Ellen Carter as the leader of the Auxiliary Board, and both women remained active supporters of the college until their deaths some thirty years later.[122] The contrast in style between Dorsey and Seward is telling. Dorsey, well aware of the "conditions and restrictions of [the Ladies Auxiliary Board's] existence," never interfered in matters beyond the bounds of her authority. Her deference to the sisters is readily apparent. In response to an expression of gratitude for the work she had done, Dorsey assured Sister Julia that it was she who was grateful to have been selected "out of all the women of our faith in America" to serve on the Auxiliary Board.[123] Years later, Dorsey minimized her own contribution to the effort: "When I think of you [unclear] Founders, you valiant women, you heroic pioneers, and you learned teachers, I feel like a penny whistle that tried to pipe the beauty and glory of a symphony orchestra, but I do thank God if my little squeak woke the right note in the hearts of certain hearers."[124] Dorsey often closed her letters to the community at Trinity with a note to send her love to "all *my* sisters."[125] It is clear, though, that "sisterhood" between lay and vowed Catholic women had its limits.

What of the relationship between the American Sisters of Notre Dame and their Belgian counterparts? In 1901, Mother Aimee removed California from Sister Julia's jurisdiction as provincial superior. Although this decision was officially attributed to her advanced age, Sister Julia interpreted it as evidence of the superior general's distrust.[126] Her close friends in the community attest that being under a "cloud of suspicion" caused her deep sorrow. It is important to emphasize, however, that Mother Aimee had never ordered Sister Julia to withdraw from the project. Instead, she was put in the unenviable position of "having permission but not support . . . such a way is a lonely road for a Religious to travel," observed another Sister of Notre Dame.[127]

Despite the obstacles and the opposition, Sister Julia never appears to have considered abandoning the project. Her persistence is undoubtedly explained by her belief that failure would not only hurt the congregation but also damage—perhaps irrevocably—the cause of Catholic women's higher education in the United States. "For the sake of the work we must not fail," she had written in 1897, "or it will put it back twenty years or kill it."[128] As her biographer suggested, the success of the project may have afforded her a "gladness of heart bearing some proportion to her previous weight of sorrow."[129]

REALITY AND RHETORIC IN THE
AMERICANIZATION OF TRINITY COLLEGE

By fall 1900 Trinity College was at last coming to fruition. The sisters who were to teach at the college moved into an unfinished building on October 25, 1900, and the first students arrived a few days later. Classes began on November 8, and Sister Julia reported that the college was "in full blast." The official dedication ceremony took place on November 22. Members of the Ladies Auxiliary Board played a prominent, though clearly secondary, role in the festivities. The sisters planned the breakfast, blessing, and a pontifical Mass, while the Ladies Auxiliary sponsored the afternoon reception.[130] Archbishop Martinelli, the apostolic delegate, celebrated the Mass; Cardinal Gibbons blessed the first building. Bishops from Brooklyn, New York, Richmond, and Wheeling attended the ceremonies, as did representatives of other women's religious communities. The U.S. commissioner of education, members of the American diplomatic corps, senators and congressmen, and presidents of secular colleges were also present. Monsignor Thomas Conaty, rector of Catholic University, delivered the principal address, in which he predicted that Trinity's students would become both "the pride of our Church" and the "honor of our country."[131]

Conaty's pairing of phrases, as well as the combined presence of dignitaries of church and state, points to an interesting question: Was Trinity College intended to facilitate Catholic girls' assimilation to American culture, or was it designed to insulate them from its evils? At times the sisters maintained that they were trying to "keep up to the times"; at others they insisted they were trying to "counteract the tendencies of the times."[132] These statements were not so much contradictory as they were emblematic of the dual impulse to present Trinity as both a Catholic and an American endeavor. Deciding where to tilt the emphasis at various intervals was perhaps the most delicate of all balancing acts required of Sister Julia throughout the founding process.

There is ample evidence to suggest that Trinity's founding is largely a

Trinity College, 1900. Courtesy of Trinity College Archives.

story of Catholics' efforts to "keep up to the times." It was, after all, Catholic women's appeals for access to institutions of higher education that provided an important impetus to Trinity's founding. This desire testified to the development of a sizable Catholic middle class and the increasing likelihood that daughters of that class would begin to seek professional employment, a development that signaled the growing influence of Progressivism on U.S. Catholics. The Ladies Auxiliary Board, as we have seen, was decidedly American in its orientation, and the discord that Trinity occasioned between the American Sisters of Notre Dame and their Belgian counterparts further suggests that its founding is largely a story of Americanization.

In addition to showing the sisters' growing autonomy from Namur, Trinity's founding also evinced, in an unexpected way, a move away from the influence of Rome. As mentioned previously, when the machinations of Schroeder and Satolli raised the possibility of a papal prohibition, Sister Julia was well aware of the implications that a public rebuke from Rome would have on perceptions of American Catholics. In her appeal to Cardinal Ferrata in September 1897, she emphasized that "we cannot but be alive to the fact that this has now become a national affair, fixing the eyes of the whole country upon us."[133] She was worried that a forceful condemnation from Rome would fuel non-Catholics' suspicion that the Vatican was overly involved in U.S. Catholic affairs. In the long run, however, Schroeder and Satolli's attempt to assert Vatican influence actually produced an opposite effect.

Recall the wording of Rampolla's letter to Martinelli on the resolution of the Trinity question: "His Holiness . . . thinks that there should be nothing more said . . . of an Institution for females." Once that question was settled, Sister Mary Euphrasia hoped for an official statement from the Vatican that was a bit less tepid. She wanted to ask the apostolic delegate for a formal blessing of the project. Frederick Rooker refused to allow her to submit the request. The ever astute aide to Archbishop Martinelli insisted that Rome, having "stuck its finger in the pie" in the wake of Schroeder and Satolli's accusations, would not admit publicly that it had been in error. But neither would the Vatican interfere again. Once Trinity opened, Rooker predicted that Trinity could "get any amount of blessings and approbations direct from His Holiness himself." Until then, Rome would be silent on the matter. As the official representative of the Vatican, Martinelli would be unable to publicly endorse Trinity. Though he supported the sisters, he would have to refuse Sister Mary Euphrasia's request. Because of the damage that would do, Rooker pointed out, it was wiser not to put the apostolic delegate in that position. As it happened, Rooker was correct in predicting that Rome would wait until Trinity opened to send its formal blessing.[134]

Close ties between Trinity and its secular counterparts also suggest that Trinity signaled the Americanization of the Sisters of Notre Dame and their students. From the beginning, it was clear that Sister Julia intended to model Trinity on the Seven Sisters. An early report circulated about the college emphasized that Trinity would be "of the same grade as Vassar, thus giving young women an opportunity for the highest collegiate instruction."[135] As Sister Julia promised in Trinity's prospectus, it would be the "object and life of the Sisters of Notre Dame de Namur to provide the safeguards to faith and morals while they offer to women courses of study which will be equal if not superior to those of our best non-Catholic colleges."[136]

To meet this goal, Sister Julia and other members of the Notre Dame community tried to learn as much as possible about life at the secular women's colleges. Soon after the first discussion about Trinity, they began to study catalogs of Wellesley and Bryn Mawr to familiarize themselves with their curricula. Later, they actually traveled to Bryn Mawr, Mount Holyoke, Radcliffe, Smith, and Wellesley.[137] During these visits, the nuns met with deans and presidents, attended classes, visited Catholic students, and acquainted themselves with campus life. These visits forged mutual admiration between secular administrators and the Sisters of Notre Dame that would endure even after Trinity opened. M. Carey Thomas, the president of Bryn Mawr, was one of the secular educators who attended the dedication ceremony in November 1900 to demonstrate support for her "sister college."[138]

Cooperative efforts between Trinity's founders and their secular counterparts resulted in a curriculum that was virtually identical to that of Vassar and Bryn Mawr. Trinity offered three four-year courses of study: classical, scientific, and literary. Additional courses in religion explain why Trinity's students needed 132 semester hours to receive a baccalaureate while most of their secular counterparts required 120 credit hours to graduate.[139]

Given the affinity between the sisters and the leaders of secular colleges, the similarity in curricula between Trinity and those institutions, the discord that Trinity's founding occasioned with Namur and Rome, and the unmistakably American stance adopted by the Ladies Auxiliary, it is not surprising that the college was often heralded as a triumph of the forces of Catholic assimilation. A contemporary observer remarked that, because the Catholic girl was "as truly an American girl as any other, of an equally democratic and independent spirit . . . [,] it was not to be expected that there should be any difference in [her] thirst for knowledge."[140] Archbishop Thomas Beaven of Springfield, Massachusetts, commented that Trinity's founding gave the Sisters of Notre Dame a "distinctly American line" by proving that they were as "in love with country as they were with God."[141] Indeed, it seemed that Trinity's founding offered the sisters, their students, and, by association, all American Catholics an opportunity to declare themselves "American."

Interpreting this event only as an example of Catholic accommodation to American culture, however, obscures the many ways in which the sisters believed that their new initiative actually made them *less* American. Loyalty to the church and loyalty to the United States were not, of course, mutually exclusive, and neither were they viewed as such by the sisters. By founding a college, the Sisters of Notre Dame believed they were doing "the best and highest work that our vocation and our country call for."[142] Still, the rhetoric of differentiation that shaped Trinity's founding is instructive. Much like that which surrounded discussions of the New Woman, this language of differentiation allowed Sister Julia to mimic secular educators while convincing herself and others that she was doing precisely the opposite.

Soon after their first discussion about the college, Garrigan expressed his hope that Trinity would do for Catholic women "what Vassar and Wellesley and Bryn Mawr are doing for American women."[143] Garrigan's distinction guided Sister Julia's work. For all the good will that existed between the Sisters of Notre Dame and the administrators of non-Catholic colleges, the sisters never lost sight of the difference between themselves and their secular counterparts. Even as Sister Julia visited M. Carey Thomas and modeled Trinity's curriculum on Vassar's, she insisted that Trinity was essentially different from secular women's colleges. Catholicism, she maintained, was Trinity's "raison d'etre."[144]

Trinity's Catholicity did distinguish it from its secular counterparts in a number of obvious ways. The recruitment of teachers demonstrates that, despite Sister Julia's insistence on Americanness, she was committed to maintaining a substantial amount of continuity with Trinity's European Catholic counterparts. Although she had insisted that she would use only teachers who would be familiar with the new American methods, Sister Julia ensured that faculty would also be well versed in Catholic techniques. In the fall of 1899, she sent two sisters to Namur to prepare them to teach at the college level. The next summer, she gathered the ten sisters who would become Trinity's first faculty at the Notre Dame summer school in Waltham, Massachusetts.[145] As expected, Trinity borrowed professors from Catholic University to teach several courses. Garrigan taught religion and served as chaplain. Thomas Shahan taught church history, and Edward Pace lectured in philosophy.[146]

Trinity's curriculum, as previously mentioned, was modeled closely on that of secular women's colleges, with religion as an additional requirement. Church history was also taught. An early catalog emphasized the accepted wisdom that the history of Christianity was the "story of the true emancipation and elevation of womankind," noting that "it is eminently proper that the history of the Catholic Church, the divinely appointed custodian and interpreter of the will and the spirit of Jesus Christ, should be thoroughly taught in any school of higher studies for Christian women."[147] Campus life varied only slightly from life on non-Catholic campuses. Mass was celebrated every morning, and, although attendance was not required, the majority of the students went to Mass daily. Retreats occurred regularly,

Trinity students in the library, 1904. Courtesy of Trinity College Archives.

and sodalities existed along with organizations such as the Glee Club and the Athletic Association.[148]

All members of Trinity's first class were either Catholic or preparing to become Catholic. It also included several Catholic transfer students from Wellesley and Barnard, which was interpreted as proof that Catholic women had attended secular institutions only because of the lack of a Catholic alternative. The student body was also ethnically distinct. Along with most of the other early Catholic women's colleges, Trinity helped put a uniquely Irish American stamp on Catholic women's higher education. Sister Julia was one of a host of Irish-born founders of Catholic women's colleges: John Ireland's biological sister, Mother Seraphine (Ellen) Ireland of the Sisters of St. Joseph of Carondolet, Missouri, born in Kilkenny in 1842, founded the College of St. Catherine in St. Paul in 1905; Mother Irene (Lucy) Gill of the Ursulines, born in Galway in 1860, opened the College of St. Angela in New Rochelle, New York, in 1904; Mother Marie Joseph (Johanna) Butler of the Religious of the Sacred Heart of Mary, born in Kilkenny in 1860, founded Marymount College in Tarrytown, New York, in 1918.[149]

Many Irish American benevolent organizations were associated with the college. Occasional fund-raisers, such as the Reverend M. F. Foley's illustrated lecture "Rambles in Ireland," celebrated Trinity's Irish heritage. The Ladies Auxiliary of the Ancient Order of Hibernians donated a scholarship in 1905, and it maintained close ties to Trinity.[150] Perhaps the most vivid testament to Trinity's Irishness comes from its first class roster, which included names such as Dooley, Gavin, McEnelly, Linehan, O'Connell, and Kennedy.[151] Helen Loretto O'Mahoney, also a member of the first class, was a relative of Katharine O'Keeffe O'Mahoney's, the Irish American nationalist who would subsequently produce the abbreviated account of Trinity's founding years.[152] Significantly, however, Sister Julia did not wish to broadcast the college's ethnic ties: in response to a suggestion that a shamrock be used as Trinity's emblem, she politely demurred, saying it would be "too expressive."[153]

What is even more striking than these actual differences in faculty, curriculum, campus life, and student body composition is the way that the sisters, their supporters, and their students presented Trinity as distinct from non-Catholic women's colleges. The most obvious manifestation of this sense of difference was the repeated emphasis on Trinity's connection to an Irish and Catholic past. As we have seen with many other Catholic women, Sister Julia saw herself as part of a long and venerable tradition, and she and her supporters often associated Trinity with the same scholarly Catholic women of the past about whom we read in the previous chapter. In Trinity's first catalog, Sister Julia expressed her hope that Trinity would "give the women of our day every facility for becoming as brilliant lights in the intellectual world as those who have shone in ecclesiastical history in bygone ages—the Hildas, the Liobas, the Marcellas, the Paulas, the Eustochiums, the Catherines, and a host of others."[154] Sister Mary Euphrasia also believed that modern Catholic women's college students were merely following in the tradition of "St. Catherine of Sienna [sic] in the fourteenth, and St. Theresa in the sixteenth century . . . each in turn the glory of the age in which she lived." She also pointed to the women scholars at Padua, reminding sisters and students that the Catholic Church had educated women at Padua three centuries before Harvard, Cornell, or Yale opened their doors to women. In a letter to Sister Julia, she wrote, "Now *the Church approves that we take up the work of Padua!*"[155]

There was also an ethnic dimension to this sense of connection to the past among the women of Trinity. Faculty and students emphasized the close ties between the college and Ireland in an effort to demonstrate that Trinity's founding continued a long Irish tradition. One appeal, for instance, enlisted the financial contributions of Irish Americans by reminding them of this relationship. "With the memory of the College of Tara at one end of the vista across the sea and Trinity, the first Catholic college for women in America at this end of the road of learning, the support of Irish American Catholics is confidently asked."[156]

The members of the Ladies Auxiliary Board also found precedent for their actions in Catholic history. Sara Carr Upton, the board's recording secretary, evoked Trinity in her study of the fourth-century Roman palace of Marsella, a place where women gathered to study. In a publicity pamphlet she wrote for the college, Eliza Allen Starr drew parallels between the Ladies Auxiliary Board and "St. Jerome's school on the Aventine in the fourth century." Starr argued that both groups demonstrated the ways in which the church encouraged the pursuit of letters by women.[157]

The twenty-two members of Trinity's first class, according to one historian, "enthusiastically embraced their role as pioneers." If that is indeed the case, it is also true that they were repeatedly reminded that they were following in the footsteps of ancient Catholic women. Lelia Hardin Bugg, a popular Catholic writer who was a member of Trinity's inaugural class, acknowledged that the college began "a new course in the cause of higher education of Christian women." Bugg cautioned her readers, however, that Trinity College was "but reviving an old privilege conferred by the Church on women centuries before the discoverer of America was born, the privilege of being learned and good." To underscore this connection to their Catholic past, statues of "St. Paula, St. Katherine, Laura Bassi, wearing the cap and gown of the University of Bologna, Helena Bisopiagia, the sunny-haired Venetian, first among the philosophers of her time, and Novella d'Andrea" greeted the students when they walked on the terrace of Trinity's main building.[158] Envisioning new endeavors as a retrieval of the past allowed the women of Trinity—founders, supporters, and students—to blend tradition and innovation in ways that made sense to them as Irish American Catholics.

SISTER JULIA DIED ON November 12, 1901. Friends in the community reported that she remained heartbroken about the rift with Mother Aimee until the end, though she accepted it in the spirit of Christian suffering: "I have had so much success in my life," she confided to one sister, "that God in His Goodness has allowed me to suffer this."[159] Woven through this account of McGroarty's triumphs and travails are the same themes that characterized Catholics' reception of the New Woman. There was, first of all, the reliance on gender as a factor differentiating Catholics from other Americans, which in large part made possible the alliances between Sister Julia and non-Catholic educators such as M. Carey Thomas. At the same time, the limits that Catholic identity placed on those same alliances were readily apparent. Finally, Trinity's founding also testifies to the canny ability of some Catholic women to manipulate gender ideology to expand rather than constrict the opportunities open to them.

In 1897, speaking of Trinity, Cardinal Gibbons had anticipated "no rival College, of the same plane, coming into existence; in the distant future, in Chicago perhaps, there might arise a College similar."[160] As it happened, the cardinal could not have been further off the mark in his prediction about the number of Catholic women's colleges. After World War I, they would increase rapidly and reach seventy-nine by the eve of the Second World War.[161] Gibbons was more accurate in his assessment of the quality of these institutions, as few of them matched either Trinity's national reputation or its high standards in admissions, curriculum, and faculty.

The proliferation of Catholic women's colleges by the 1920s occurred in response to two factors: the growth and consolidation of the Catholic parochial school system, and the Progressive commitment to uniformity, professionalization, and state supervision of education. Once again, Catholic women, in this case teaching sisters, would be perched at the intersection of these two currents. Compelled to provide staff for a growing number of parochial institutions and simultaneously charged with improving their efficiency, teaching sisters would seek to become professionals without sacrificing the spiritual standards that were ultimately more important to them.

CHAPTER THREE   The Wageless Work of Paradise

CATHOLIC SISTERS, PROFESSIONALIZATION,

AND THE SCHOOL QUESTION

In 1905, the Archdiocese of Philadelphia sponsored an essay contest on Christian doctrine, a subject that had recently become the cornerstone of the curriculum in the city's Catholic schools. Mary Donohue, a student at Cathedral Girls' High School Centre, received a prize for her composition, "The Home Art." Donohue's teachers, the Sisters of St. Joseph (ssj), must have been particularly pleased. The congregation took a proprietary interest in Christian doctrine: one of their own, Sister Assisium McEvoy, was the author of the official archdiocesan textbook on the subject.[1] No doubt the nuns were also flattered by the essay's content. Donohue described the home as woman's true vocation, "unless she is called to one that is higher and holier . . . that of a lifework in God's own household—a vocation to religion." A sister, she wrote, "appreciates the honor of her work, even [that] which the new woman, who is *no* woman, or which the women of the world scorn . . . the wageless work of paradise."[2]

Donohue's essay touched upon common Catholic themes: the idealization of the home, which was not unique to Catholicism but was especially embraced by the members of a rising middle class; the description of religious life as a "higher and holier" vocation, which was emblematic of the two-tiered spirituality that characterized Catholicism until the Second Vatican Council; and, finally, the familiar juxtaposition of a daughter of the Old Faith and the New Woman, in this case in terms of work performed and remuneration received.

As vowed members of religious communities, Catholic sisters did not receive individual salaries for the services they provided.[3] But while the nuns who taught in parochial schools may not be understood as workers in the conventional sense, it would be difficult to find a group of women whose labor was more closely linked to the Progressive Era conversation about Catholic citizenship in the United States. Unlike the Americanist controversy, which involved high clerical politics and was debated in intellectual realms, the "school question"—at this point, actually a group of interrelated questions about how Catholics should educate their children— affected the Catholic experience at the national and local levels, especially in dioceses and parishes. And whereas the sisters at Trinity were implicated unwittingly and tangentially in the Americanist crisis, women religious throughout the country became deliberately and intimately invested in the school question. Indeed, it was the nuns' willingness to undertake "the wageless work of paradise" that enabled American Catholics to resolve it.[4]

Yet entire histories of American Catholicism, and even of Catholic education, have been written with only passing reference to sisters. Even when historians do acknowledge nuns' contribution, they have tended to oversimplify their relationship to the church. Jay Dolan's characterization of sisters as "Catholic serfs," for example, is apt in the sense that it conveys the extent to which their labor subsidized the school system. Unlike serfs, however, women religious were often committed to and empowered by the work they performed.[5]

Consider, for example, Sister Assisium McEvoy (1843–1939), the Sister of St. Joseph who published the aforementioned textbook on Christian doctrine. As a leader within one of the largest teaching communities in an archdiocese with a steadfast commitment to Catholic education, she offers a particularly revealing example of a woman religious who both was affected by the school question and figured prominently in its resolution. The key to the story is Sister Assisium's interaction with the Reverend Philip McDevitt (1858–1935), the Philadelphia priest who, as we saw in chapter 1, had tried so hard to debunk the apocryphal accounts of Mâcon. McDevitt also served as the superintendent of Catholic schools in the Archdiocese of Philadelphia between 1899 and 1916. Unlike McEvoy, McDevitt is a familiar figure in the history of Catholic education as an administrator whose innovative "Philadelphia Plan" served as a model for other American dioceses.[6] McDevitt and McEvoy were colleagues, correspondents, and friends who worked together for more than two decades to sustain and develop

Sister Assisium McEvoy, ssj. Courtesy of the Sisters of St. Joseph of Philadelphia, Chestnut Hill, Pennsylvania.

Catholic education in Philadelphia. Studying Sister Assisium and McDevitt side by side underscores how central Catholic sisters were to the project of staffing, improving, and defining Catholic schools during the first two decades of the twentieth century.

Philadelphia's large Catholic population, as well as its consistently strong episcopal support for parochial education, distinguishes it both from regions where Catholics were less dominant and from other urban dioceses where bishops showed less enthusiasm for building Catholic schools. But Philadelphia's distinctiveness enhances rather than detracts from its usefulness as a vantage point from which to observe the complexity surrounding the school question. From the creation of the Catholic school system in the mid-nineteenth century until its consolidation in the early twentieth, Philadelphia's parochial schools not only provided an inspiration for other Catholic educators but also served as a barometer of trends that would shape Catholic education until the mid-twentieth century. The problems and preoccupations of Philip McDevitt, superintendent of Catholic schools in "the historic cradle of Catholic education," serve as an ideal gateway to explore the national conversation about Catholic schools and their place and purpose in American life during the Progressive Era.[7]

As for Sister Assisium McEvoy, she was by no means unique. In Philadelphia and elsewhere, there were many teaching sisters who were equally intellectual, influential, and engaged. But, much like the city in which she worked, McEvoy is intended to be illuminating rather than representative. She offers an excellent springboard to explore how gender and American Catholic identity intersected within and shaped the cluster of concerns that constituted the school question in the early twentieth century. McEvoy's life and work dovetailed particularly well with the development of the school question; in fact, her personal involvement with the Catholic school system dated from her childhood in Philadelphia, where, in a very real sense, she had been present at its creation.

THE EVOLUTION OF THE SCHOOL QUESTION
IN THE NINETEENTH CENTURY

In 1848, Kate McEvoy, as Sister Assisium was then known, arrived in Philadelphia with her family—including her Irish-born father, Michael; her mother, Lucy; and her half sister, Maria—as emigrants from Leeds, England, where Kate had been born five years earlier. Michael McEvoy, employed as a clothing salesman, rented a home in the city's Cedar Ward, a neighborhood filled with Irish brick makers and factory men. The McEvoy residence fell within the parish boundaries of St. Patrick's, a church in which domestic servants and laborers worshiped along with members of the Catholic elite.[8]

The McEvoys arrived at an auspicious moment for the city's Catholics. Four years earlier, Philadelphia had erupted in violence over the use of the King James version of the Bible in the city's publicly funded schools. When Bishop Francis Kenrick requested that Catholic children be permitted to read the Douay translation instead, he was accused of trying to remove the Bible itself from public schools. After riots broke out at several "Save the Bible" rallies in the summer of 1844, two weeks of upheaval ensued. Thirty Catholic homes and two Catholic churches were destroyed.[9]

Philadelphia's Bible riots had followed closely on the heels of a more prolonged school controversy in New York City over government funding for religious schools. Archbishop John Hughes had petitioned for a share of the public school fund to rescue the city's struggling parochial schools. The hostile response to his bid convinced Hughes that Catholic children could never receive an unbiased education in common schools that used both the King James Bible and textbooks that routinely disparaged the Church of Rome.[10]

The school question was a relatively straightforward one for most of the nineteenth century: Should Catholic children attend public schools? Until the 1840s, most bishops could have been persuaded to say yes, provided that those institutions were truly nonsectarian. But the "school wars" in New York and Philadelphia convinced them otherwise. Hughes threw his considerable weight in support of a parallel system, coining his famous dictum: "Build the school house first, the Church after." Hughes argued that without public funding for parochial schools, Catholics who chose to send their children to them were obligated to pay a "double tax," since they would have to support the Catholic school system as well as the public. Kenrick, aware of the heavy burden a parallel system would place on an already impoverished population, was initially reluctant to agree with Hughes, but eventually he accepted the need for such a system and became a firm supporter. Kenrick and Hughes were among the most influential members of the American hierarchy, and by the time all bishops convened at the Plenary Council in Baltimore in 1852, church-sponsored schools had been defined as the "most urgent wants" of the church in America.[11]

Even after the violence of 1844 subsided, episodes of anti-Catholic bias in public schools continued to lend credence to the argument that Catholic students had no alternative but to attend their own schools. Young Kate McEvoy came face to face with anti-Catholic prejudice in her public school when she and several other Catholic children were expelled one Monday morning in May 1849. They had missed school on the previous Friday afternoon to attend practice for St. Patrick's May procession. The school principal informed Kate and her fellow truants that in order to reapply they would have to appear before the school directors. The injustice visited upon McEvoy and her friends, interpreted as evidence of anti-Catholic bigotry, prompted parishioners at St. Patrick's to initiate a fund-raising campaign for a school. Until it opened three years later, Kate McEvoy attended classes at a neighboring parish, St. Joseph's. The Sisters of St. Joseph taught students at both schools; thus McEvoy began her association with the congregation to which she would dedicate more than eighty years of her life.[12]

Miss Catherine McEvoy. This photo is identified as the pre-entrance photo of Sister Assisium. Courtesy of the Sisters of St. Joseph of Philadelphia, Chestnut Hill, Pennsylvania.

The Sisters of St. Joseph had been founded in France in 1650, with American roots established in Carondolet, Missouri, in 1836. Bishop Kenrick, who was acquainted with their work through his biological and episcopal brother, the bishop of St. Louis, asked the superior at Carondolet to send sisters to Philadelphia to staff an orphan asylum for boys. Four women arrived for this purpose in 1847. The community received its first native novice a year later. Maria McEvoy entered in 1858; Kate, along with four of her classmates at St. Patrick's, followed in 1859. The McEvoy sisters were among the many Philadelphia girls who contributed to the Americanization—or, more precisely, the Irish Americanization—of the French congregation.[13]

Kenrick's successor, Bishop John Neumann, continued his predecessor's efforts to establish parochial schools. Neumann visited the Sisters of St. Joseph during McEvoy's postulant year and emphasized his strong commitment to educational ministry. McEvoy recalled Neumann telling the postulants that "he would need for the Parish Schools all the Srs. he could get,—and the Sisters must be prepared."[14]

McEvoy entered the Sisters of St. Joseph at a time of upheaval. Repeated power struggles between the motherhouse and the local bishops forced the Sisters of St. Joseph—now scattered throughout the country—to make a choice: report to a female general superior in St. Louis or to a male bishop in their own diocese who would have complete control over their community. In 1860, the Sisters of St. Joseph of Philadelphia chose the latter option and were officially separated from the motherhouse at Carondolet. Hence they became subject to diocesan control.[15] Other communities, in Philadelphia and throughout the nation, would also be partitioned as a result of tension between the chancery and superiors of the teaching communities over the control of parish schools.

After teaching in parish schools throughout the archdiocese, Sister Assisium McEvoy returned to the SSJ convent in Chestnut Hill in 1868, where she worked as secretary to Mother St. John Fournier (1814–75). By this time, the ethnic and religious divisiveness of the 1840s and 1850s had diminished, and though anti-Catholicism would continue to shape Catholic education, it ceased to provide a primary rationale for separate denominational schools. If church leaders had created the school system in reaction to hostility toward Catholic children in public schools, they sustained their commitment to it for more complex reasons.

Foremost among these was the increasing secularization of American public schools. By the early 1880s, it was evident that Catholics' objection to public schools rested less on their antipathy toward Catholics and more on their apathy with regard to religion. In 1883 the editors of Philadelphia's *Catholic Standard* ranted against "godless" public schools, declaring that "Catholics should avoid the terrible danger of entrusting our children's salvation to teachers . . . who have no religion of any kind." Catholic criticism of public schools would increase in direct proportion to their secularization.[16]

Ethnicity provided a second explanation for Catholics' continuing efforts to build separate schools. German immigrants in the 1840s had been the first to demand that Catholic children be educated in their parents' native language. Insisting that "language saves faith," German Americans remained emphatic supporters of parish education, and Polish and other immigrant Catholics would follow their lead in building ethnic parish schools.[17]

Catholics, of course, were not the only American religious group who objected to the secularization of the public school system. Neither were they the only denomination for whom ethnicity provided a rationale for separate schools. But no other group had the resources or the population to build such a large school system. The church's institutional commitment to a separate school system was solidified by 1884, when, at the Third Plenary Council in Baltimore, American bishops decreed that every Catholic parish in the nation should have a school attached within two years. They also mandated that Catholic parents were obliged to send their children to a parish school unless they were attending a private Catholic academy.[18]

The speed at which these directives were carried out in individual dioceses depended largely on the level of episcopal support they received. In Philadelphia, Patrick Ryan was appointed archbishop in 1884, and in the tradition of his predecessors, he became a strong advocate for Catholic education.[19] At the diocesan synod of 1886, Ryan made clear that the decrees of Baltimore would be implemented, and he threatened to remove pastors who did not comply with them. Though this was no idle threat, it was the teaching sisters in the diocese, rather than parish priests, who would be most dramatically affected by Ryan's eagerness to establish parochial schools.[20] The number of Catholic schools in the archdiocese nearly doubled in Ryan's first fifteen years as archbishop, from 58 in 1884 to 103 in 1903.[21]

In the early 1890s, Catholic debate on the school question was revived briefly when it became entangled with the politics of Americanism. The three-year "school controversy" pitted conservative bishops like Michael Corrigan of New York and Bernard McQuaid of Rochester against John Ireland, who not only spoke favorably of public schools but also instituted a compromise system in his diocese.[22] But by 1901, even Ireland was convinced that "[there are] times when in the imparting of secular knowledge there is peril for faith and morals, unless secular knowledge be made to flow through the same channel as the religious. . . . Never, perhaps, as much as today, and in America, was teaching an imperative duty of the Church."[23] For the next sixty years, Catholic leaders and laity remained wholeheartedly committed to expanding and sustaining a separate school system.[24] Though the goals set in Baltimore would never be reached, the Catholic parochial school system in the United States developed into "the largest private educational enterprise known to history."[25]

Ireland had ended his 1901 brief for schools under church auspices with this plea: "To the rescue, holy Sisterhoods!"[26] His appeal underscored an obvious, if underemphasized, third explanation why Catholic hierarchy and clergy were able to muster such strong support for separate schools: the exponential growth of women's religious communities, in both size and number, provided a viable population of teachers willing to staff them. In 1840, when there were fewer than 200 Catholic schools in the United States, there were approximately 900 sisters in the country, disbursed among 15 orders. Sixty years later, with the commitment complete, the American population of nuns had multiplied to 46,583 sisters among 170 congregations. Of these, the vast majority were teaching.[27]

Over the nineteenth century, then, the increased secularization of public schools, immigration, and the exponential growth of women's religious communities created the conditions for a Catholic response to the school question in its most simple iteration: Catholic children belonged in church-sponsored schools. But while church leaders had spoken definitively to the fundamental question, Progressive Era developments raised complicated offshoots. Compulsory school laws, standardization of curriculum, more stringent health regulations, and greater expectations about teacher credentials prompted Catholic educators to consider a number of questions: How could the Catholic system be sustained and expanded? How would Catholic schools measure up as their public counterparts improved? As the state and federal government extended its reach into the realm of education, where would Catholic schools fit in?

Church leaders would respond to these and other questions by beginning to convert a loosely organized network of schools into a more centralized system. Philadelphia provided an early model of centralization on the diocesan level: Ryan created a school board in 1886, appointed a superintendent in 1889, and opened a central or diocesan high school for boys in 1890. In 1899, with the appointment of McDevitt as the third superintendent of Catholic schools, the consolidation of Philadelphia's Catholic schools began in earnest.

The founding of the Catholic Educational Association (CEA) in 1904 marked the beginning of national centralization. Speaking at the CEA's second annual meeting in 1905, the Reverend Edmund F. Gibbons urged all U.S. bishops to appoint school superintendents, both to foster "progress" in parochial schools and to represent diocesan interests in them. Gibbons, who supervised Catholic schools in Buffalo, New York, insisted that central-

Bishop Philip Richard McDevitt. Courtesy of the Archives of the University of Notre Dame, GFCL 20-58.

ization was particularly important considering the "peculiar nature" of the Catholic teaching force in his own diocese and most other American dioceses. "As a rule," he noted, teaching responsibilities were divided among several congregations, "each with its own ideas of teaching, its own rules and customs." As a result, the average teaching sister was unlikely to "ever see the inside of a school of another religious community or exchange a thought with a Sister of a different habit on subjects in which both are so intimately interested." Identifying this state of affairs as the primary barrier to educational progress, Gibbons looked to diocesan supervision as the remedy.[28]

Commenting on Gibbons's paper, McDevitt explained how he had already increased the level of diocesan scrutiny in Philadelphia by making annual visits to classrooms, compiling detailed annual reports, and presiding over the Board of Community Inspectors. This last organization had its origins in the late 1880s, when many teaching congregations had created an office of "inspector of schools" in response to what one superior described as "the want of some general and uniform superintendence."[29] McDevitt's predecessor, the Reverend John H. Shanahan, had called these congregational supervisors to periodic meetings since 1896, but it was McDevitt who not only instituted more formal meetings of the school inspectors but also increased their accountability to him.[30] This move prompted James Burns, c s c, the first historian of Catholic education, to observe that a distinguishing characteristic of McDevitt's Philadelphia Plan, and a key to its success, was that "all communities, those whose rules have the approval of Rome as well as those which are diocesan, are brought within the system of centralized control through the community inspectorship."[31] Other Catholic superintendents, citing the success of the Philadelphia model, established similar boards of inspectors.[32]

Burns described here a process by which McDevitt tightened a loophole in the church's hierarchical organization. In the late nineteenth and early twentieth centuries, many religious communities sought to have their rules approved by Rome. Once a community received canonical status, it was primarily accountable to a cardinal protector in the Vatican, rather than the local ordinary.[33] The process was invariably long and frustrating, and it did not help that most bishops were disinclined to assist communities in securing the means to circumvent their own authority. The Philadelphia ssjs began to seek canonical status in 1875, and six years later the superior, anticipating Sister Julia McGroarty's comment during the Trinity affair, wished she was a priest so she could go to Rome and plead the community's case in person.[34] The Sisters of St. Joseph eventually received provisional canonical status in 1896, but, as Burns intimated, it did little to insulate them from the effects of diocesan consolidation.

McDevitt was appointed the first chair of the Superintendents' Section of the Catholic Educational Association in 1908.[35] Within two years 30 percent of American dioceses would be served by superintendents, all of whom were priests.[36] In this respect, Catholic education in the Progressive Era replicated a defining feature of its public counterpart: the separation of male administration and female teaching staff.[37] The church's ideology of gender and hierarchical structure certainly supported such a male ascendancy. Nuns commonly identified themselves as the "spiritual children" of male superiors; one teaching sister was commended for being "as simple, upright as a little child."[38] The sisters' deference to clerical administrators became more pronounced as priests ascended the hierarchical ladder.

When McDevitt was made a monsignor in 1910, one Sister of the Immaculate Heart lamented that she would feel "further removed from you when I address you as 'monsignor' than when I could call you 'Father.'"[39] This allusive distance would increase when McDevitt was appointed bishop of Harrisburg, Pennsylvania, in 1916.[40]

McDevitt was undoubtedly a man of his time when it came to gender expectations; he was, for example, "startled" by one sister's suggestion that a woman preside at a CEA meeting.[41] At the same time, however, he did not hesitate to chastise a member of the Philadelphia Board of Education for showing insufficient consideration "to a lady who is the venerated head of a community of a thousand sisters in charge of schools where there are perhaps twenty-five thousand pupils."[42] His rebuke points to an important reality: between 1900 and 1920, the impulse to consolidate power in a Catholic superintendent's office was tempered by the considerable diffusion of authority among superiors of religious congregations. Though the Board of Community Inspectors, as well as many other aspects of the Philadelphia Plan, was indeed intended to circumscribe this authority of religious leaders, McDevitt remained well aware that the implementation of his objectives depended upon their full cooperation. Advising the newly appointed superintendent of parish schools in Manchester, New Hampshire, McDevitt assured him, "Your best work will be done through the motherhouses of the teaching communities. . . . An all important asset in the work is the confidence of the communities that arises from the knowledge that you are entirely in sympathy with them."[43]

Only by considering McDevitt's most critical needs as superintendent is it possible to appreciate not only how heavily he depended on women religious to accomplish his objectives but also how prominently women and gender influenced Catholic responses to the multifaceted school question between 1900 and 1920. McDevitt's most urgent and most obvious need was staffing the parochial schools, which increased in size and number each year. McDevitt and other Catholic educators followed a similar trajectory: once they settled on women religious as the most convenient and the least expensive solution to this problem, they realized that continuing to attract a sufficient number of young Catholic women to religious life would be a key factor in ensuring the permanency of the parochial system. The preoccupation with recruitment, both in Philadelphia and nationally, reveals that concerns about a vocation shortage became a defining feature of American Catholicism much earlier in the twentieth century than previously assumed.

In addition to more teachers, McDevitt required more "efficient" ones. As standards were raised for public school teachers in the Progressive Era, Catholic educators responded in kind. Gibbons believed that "the principal aim of diocesan supervision should be the perfecting of our teachers. . . . Upon them more than any other agency depends the efficiency of our schools."[44] Burns agreed that "the efficiency of the school is directly proportionate to the character and equipment of the teacher."[45] Identifying poorly trained teachers as the main cause of inefficiency in parochial schools, McDevitt expected the leaders of religious communities to improve sisters' education and professional preparation.[46] For their part, superiors were eager to do their "very best to make the schools as efficient as possible."[47]

McDevitt's third need, though less urgent and less explicitly stated, proved no less critical to his larger objective of sustaining and developing Catholic education in Philadelphia. Throughout his term as superintendent, he was repeatedly called upon to define the Catholic school system relative to the government-sponsored one. McDevitt's work in Philadelphia, shaped as it was by the search for efficiency, uniformity, and centralization, is undoubtedly part of the story of American Progressivism. Indeed, as McDevitt was consolidating diocesan authority in his office, Progressive school reformers in Philadelphia were creating a centralized public system in the "Revolution of 1905."[48] But McDevitt and other Catholics parted ways with John Dewey and other Progressive educational reformers in dramatic fashion when it came to articulating the purpose of education. Catholic hierarchy and clergy were appalled by the Progressive assumption that the primary goal of schooling was to prepare children for citizenship in a democracy.[49] As one historian noted, the Catholic objection to Progressivism can be summarized: "To Dewey's insistence that the 'child is for democracy,' Catholics answered, 'The Child is for God.' "[50] Nuns' predominant presence in classrooms helped Catholics underscore this fundamental difference between public and parochial schools.

Like most Catholic educators, McDevitt was suspicious of the Progressives' effort to increase government involvement in educational matters, correctly perceiving in this development a threat to nonpublic education. Catholic educators' perception of being under assault by a growing state system is evident in the militant language used by the Reverend Ralph Hayes, superintendent of Pittsburgh's Catholic schools: "If through lack of teachers, poorly prepared postulants and nuns are sent into the schools, we are committing an egregious tactical blunder of placing a weapon in the hands of the enemy."[51] Hayes's comment also suggested that the challenges of staffing, improving, and defining parochial schools were closely interrelated.

Teaching sisters in the diocese shaped and were shaped by McDevitt's response to these challenges. During his first year as superintendent, twelve communities of women religious and one community of men religious supplied teachers for archdiocesan schools.[52] In addition to the SSJS, the Sisters, Servants of the Immaculate Heart of Mary (IHM) and the Philadelphia Franciscans (OSF) were by far the largest purveyors.[53] By 1900, the SSJS, IHMS, and OSFS collectively provided 70 percent of religious teachers in the archdiocese. These three congregations would also, at McDevitt's behest, begin to offer Philadelphia's Catholic girls a high school education under diocesan auspices after 1900.

McDevitt would work closely with leaders of teaching communities in the archdiocese. Among them was the former Kate McEvoy. As mistress of novices (1887–1911) and director of sisters' studies (1911–23), she was McDevitt's most frequent point of contact in the SSJS. Katharine Drexel, the Philadelphia heiress and future saint who founded the Sisters of the Blessed Sacrament, once recalled Sister Assisium's uncanny ability to speak with "disarming frankness" to her male superiors. This candor is also evident in McEvoy's letters to McDevitt.[54] The two began working together early in McDevitt's tenure as superintendent, and throughout his term McDevitt regularly solicited her opinions and assistance on matters ranging from curriculum development to recommended reading.[55] Their correspondence, which stretched over three decades, records regular exchanges of annual feast-day greetings, Christmas gifts, occasional visits, and innumerable mutual prayers. Their friendship lasted until McDevitt's death in 1935, and McEvoy fully expected that it would endure even after that. In 1921, writing of their friendship with fondness, Sister Assisium reflected that "some ties [are] formed on earth that neither time nor eternity can break."[56]

McDevitt and McEvoy shared fundamental assumptions about Catholic schools and the role of teaching sisters in them. But Sister Assisium, like her counterparts in other communities, approached the school question from a different base of power, and with different priorities, than the superintendent did. Working in classrooms required women religious to navigate among competing loyalties—to their personal quest for religious perfection, the vows they had professed to their religious communities, their commitment to the service of the church, and, increasingly, their obligations to the state. By exploring nuns' interwoven identities as aspiring saints, efficient teachers, loyal daughters of the church, and responsible American citizens, it is possible to more fully understand the parameters of the school question and what it signified about American Catholic identity in the early twentieth century.

STAFFING THE SCHOOLS

Philip McDevitt well understood that the existence of the Catholic school system depended upon the underpaid labor provided by vowed religious. In one sermon, he described religious life as "an endowment of a vast sum, an endowment which bears the principal and heaviest burden of Catholic education. If this subsidy ceased, if the men and women of our religious communities abandoned their vocation and returned to the world, our whole educational and charitable work . . . would crumble."[57]

In retrospect McDevitt's words appear oddly prescient. In the late 1960s, a precipitous decline in the number of religious would indeed prompt many Catholic schools to close their doors. At the time, however, McDevitt was cautiously optimistic that a concerted effort to attract young Catholics to religious life could forestall such calamities. Like other church leaders, he expected that women religious themselves would play a central role in the recruitment process. It was primarily teaching sisters, McDevitt observed, who would "zealously and conscientiously turn the eyes of our youthful boys and girls away from the passing things of earth to the imperishable things of eternity."[58]

Nuns accepted this charge with eagerness. After all, many of them attributed their own decision to enter religious life to the model of beloved teachers. Sister Assisium McEvoy recalled that her vocation had been inspired by the humble example of a Sister of St. Joseph at her parish school. Though her mother had tried to persuade her to enter another community, McEvoy had chosen to enter the ssJs because of what she had witnessed as a child. In her own counsel to future sister-teachers, Sister Assisium exhorted them to be conscious of their behavior. "Remember," she admonished, "in the classroom the children are watching you, and you may repel or you may attract."[59]

But if McEvoy and McDevitt both believed that the exemplary life of religious would secure future vocations, they were also keenly aware that the ongoing multiplication of schools placed a heavy burden on communities. The perpetual need for more religious teachers was a topic McDevitt and McEvoy discussed with escalating levels of concern as the twentieth century progressed. "From every school there comes a cry for help," Sister Assisium lamented, "and there are no sisters to send."[60] Like other Catholic educators, McDevitt and McEvoy worried that a chronic shortage of vocations would ultimately compromise the parochial school system. These fears generated persistent calls for more aggressive recruitment to religious life in the early twentieth century. The heavily gendered nature of these appeals indicates church leaders' initial reluctance to entrust women with such an important work as educating children in the faith. But as church leaders recognized that women religious provided the only viable source of labor, they not only assigned nuns the task but also beseeched them to ensure the permanency of the system by convincing more of their students to follow in their footsteps.[61]

In Philadelphia, anxiety over a shortage of vocations had predated McDevitt's appointment as superintendent by at least a decade. As noted previously, the number of parish schools in the archdiocese had doubled between 1884 and 1903. Ryan had invited several new congregations of teaching sisters to Philadelphia, particularly to serve in schools attached to immigrant parishes. The Felician Sisters, for example, arrived from Detroit in 1890 to take charge of a Polish parish, and the Sisters of the Holy Family of Nazareth arrived two years later for the same purpose.[62]

Though the recruitment of new teaching congregations would continue, it was the established communities that accommodated most of the diocesan expansion. The SSJs, the IHMs, and the Philadelphia OSFs each staffed twice as many schools in 1903 as they had in 1884; their responsibilities, in other words, increased in direct proportion to the expansion of the school system. Over the same time period, the membership of the SSJs and the IHMs also approximately doubled, while the OSF membership increased fourfold.[63]

Mother Mary de Chantal Hayes, superior of the IHMs, had first noticed a marked increase in the number of applicants to her community in the late

1880s. She was initially distressed by this development, realizing that the motherhouse could not accommodate them.[64] But when she expressed her concern about this surfeit of candidates to Archbishop Ryan, he reassured her that "if those whom you receive into the novitiate are suitable subjects, you need not fear, as you will need them all . . . for pressing demands and vacancies."[65]

Less than three years later, Mother de Chantal's uneasiness over the prospect of having too many candidates had been replaced by a regret that she did not have enough teachers to accept additional missions outside Philadelphia. In 1891, the bishop of Portland, Oregon, asked Mother de Chantal to send him sisters to staff his fledgling schools. When she reported this request to Ryan, the archbishop advised her against complying with it: "It is a great mistake," he wrote, "for a religious congregation to spread itself unless it has more than members enough for home work. I feel that this is not the case with you."[66] It was likely that Ryan had other, unstated motives for dissuading Mother de Chantal. Sending sisters to Portland would certainly have decreased his own pool of available teachers. But even beyond that consideration, placing community members within the boundaries of a distant diocese would have undercut his episcopal authority. Several years later, when a priest from Coeur d'Alene, Idaho, asked Mother de Chantal to send sisters to conduct missionary work among Native Americans, Ryan denied her permission.[67]

As a community firmly rooted in Philadelphia and committed almost exclusively to teaching, the IHMs were more beholden to the archbishop than were other congregations. Between 1900 and 1920, its teaching responsibilities more than doubled. The Philadelphia Franciscans, on the other hand, illustrate how geographic dissemination and diversified ministry combined to limit obligations to individual bishops. Operating orphanages and schools in sixteen dioceses, the sisters accepted only a handful of additional schools in Philadelphia between 1900 and 1920.[68]

The experience of the Philadelphia Sisters of St. Joseph was more akin to that of the IHMs than it was to that of the Franciscans. By the beginning of the twentieth century, there were signs that the SSJs were also contending with a shortage of teachers. In 1902, Mother Clement Lannen, superior general of the congregation, turned down the request of John Shanahan, by then bishop of Harrisburg, to take charge of parochial schools in the city of Lancaster. Citing a "lack of subjects," Lannen reported that she had already

Study hall at Mount St. Joseph Academy, circa 1890. Courtesy of the Sisters of St. Joseph of Philadelphia, Chestnut Hill, Pennsylvania.

refused three schools that year for the same reason. In 1905, Lannen removed Sisters of St. Joseph from missions in Conewego, Irishtown, and Mount Rock, all within the diocese of Harrisburg, explaining, "We have had much to suffer from scarcity of Sisters to do our own work."[69] Disgruntled, Shanahan later complained that congregations were withdrawing teachers from the rural schools to concentrate in large cities. He ascribed their defection to ulterior motives: "They say that this policy is inspired by the greater glory of God—maybe, but it is quite evident that it pays better to concentrate their efforts in the great centers of Catholic population."[70]

But as the situation in Philadelphia showed, the "great centers of Catholic population" were not faring much better in terms of meeting the increased demand for teachers. McDevitt annually cited overcrowded conditions in all the parish schools of the archdiocese, and priests regularly complained to him about a shortage of sisters to carry on the educational work.[71] Not only had new schools been built, but enrollment in existing ones had risen. Between 1895 and 1905, the number of parish schools

Educational exhibit, World's Columbian Exposition, Chicago, Illinois, 1893. Sister Assisium and others in her congregation helped prepare the exhibit. Note the identification of Mount St. Joseph Academy in the upper righthand corner. Courtesy of the Archives of the University of Notre Dame, GCEX 5-7.

increased by 23 percent, while the total number of students enrolled in those schools increased by 54 percent.[72] Aware that the demand for teachers showed no sign of abating, McDevitt realized that the only solution to the problem involved increasing the available supply. Each year the superintendent defined recruiting men and women to religious life as a priority for the diocese. Noting that the future of Catholic education "depended upon the religious orders for a supply of teachers," McDevitt lamented that "the harvest is great, but the laborers are few."[73]

McDevitt was neither the first nor the last Catholic educator to use this gospel passage in reference to what was increasingly perceived as a critical shortage of new vocations. The harvest was one of souls; the laborers were religious men and women willing to serve as teachers in the Catholic school system. Quoting the passage before the Catholic Educational Association in 1908, the Reverend Bernard O'Reilly estimated that congregations of re-

Four Sisters of St. Joseph with students at the Archbishop Ryan Academy for the Deaf, 1817 Vine Street, Philadelphia, December 8, 1912. Courtesy of the Sisters of St. Joseph of Philadelphia, Chestnut Hill, Pennsylvania.

ligious teachers had refused between 75 and 95 percent of all requests to open additional schools over the previous five years.[74] In 1911, Joseph Schrembs, auxiliary bishop of Grand Rapids, Michigan, complained that an insufficient number of religious had precipitated a "crisis" in Catholic education. To avert a complete catastrophe, he urged all Catholics: "Pray ye, therefore, the Lord of the harvest that He sends laborers into His vineyard."[75] After he was appointed bishop of Cleveland, Schrembs requested Vatican permission to recite this prayer in public novenas for more vocations to the priesthood and religious life.[76] Teaching sisters also used the phrase. In 1917, one of them assured McDevitt, "I have always prayed that vocations might be multiplied and petition more fervently now, that God will send laborers for his vineyard. The fields are ripe for the harvest."[77]

The apparent dearth of vocations raised a thorny theological question: Because the call to religious life came from God, was it possible that God was not sending enough vocations? To even intimate this, as one priest noted, came "dangerously near the border-line of impiety."[78] Bishop Herman Alerding of Fort Wayne, Indiana, addressed the question squarely: "Is it a fact, as some seem to think, that there is a lack of vocations to the Brotherhood and Sisterhood? . . . I cannot believe it. The vocations exist, they must exist."[79] O'Reilly agreed, concluding that while vocations themselves were bountiful, "the germ of vocation is more easily stifled today than it was years ago."[80] Similarly, Bishop Schrembs dismissed the possibility that "God has withdrawn His spirit from us, or that He no longer inspires earnest souls with the desire for His service."[81] Many other Catholic bishops and educational leaders concurred: the vocation shortage was owed "not to the absence of divine providence, but to the lack of man's [and woman's] cooperation."[82]

The lack of cooperation was not necessarily on the part of the people who themselves were called to religious life. Rather, it was parents, pastors, and teachers who were failing to identify and nurture vocations. Vocations could not be created, of course, but they could be "stimulated," "awakened," or "interpreted."[83] One teaching sister suggested that they be "discovered" and "directed."[84] In Philadelphia, McDevitt urged that vocations be "encouraged," while another bishop asked that they be "fostered."[85] However they described it, church leaders insisted that recruitment must be undertaken more consciously and more assertively. At its second annual meeting in 1905, the Catholic Educational Association had resolved that "the fast developing system of Catholic education makes imperative the fostering of the religious vocation among our men and women."[86] The subject would be discussed at every subsequent meeting of the CEA. Calling for a "general stirring up and agitation of the matter," James Burns urged Catholics to be more deliberate in recruiting men and women to religious life, estimating that the novitiates of the teaching orders "ought to contain twice as many candidates as they have at present" if the demand was to be met.[87]

It was clear, however, that certain vocations were prized above others. Most Catholic leaders had no qualms about expressing their preference for male vocations over female ones. During his tenure as Philadelphia's Catholic superintendent, Shanahan had lamented that "men constitute only a small portion of the teaching force employed in our schools."[88] Leaders on a national level expressed similar misgivings about placing so important a work in the hands of women. As Bishop John Lancaster Spalding noted, "The teachers in our schools are nearly all religious women, just as the

The Wageless Work of Paradise   121

teachers in public schools are mostly women. What the effect of this teaching by women is likely to be on our national character, I shall not here inquire."[89] By 1908 the need for teaching brothers was defined as the "most pressing want of the Church in America."[90]

The feminization of teaching, as Spalding noted, affected public schools as well as Catholic ones.[91] The overriding concern in both venues involved the perceived impact of feminine influence on the "manliness" of young boys.[92] At the CEA meeting of 1913, the Reverend Bede Horsa, OSB, quoted educator G. Stanley Hall at length on the deleterious effects of the feminization of teaching and described the preponderance of women teachers as the "patent and material defect" of the parochial school system in the United States.[93] Given how readily Horsa expressed his manifest disdain for female teachers, the fact that one of the commentators complimented him for using a "great deal of tact" is illustrative of the consensus on the subject. McDevitt had kinder words for the sisters, observing that nothing would be gained by "minimizing the strength of women teachers and emphasizing their weakness." Nonetheless, McDevitt, like most Catholic educators, accepted that boys of "a certain age" should be taught by men, though the precise age was subject to debate.[94]

Most clerical commentators assumed that women religious would welcome relief from the burden of teaching older boys. Throughout the nineteenth century, of course, many congregations of religious women did not teach boys over seven as prescribed by their rules. But even though some communities modified their rules, as Sister Julia McGroarty had done throughout her term as provincial superior of the Sisters of Notre Dame, many sisters believed that older boys must be taught by "men who can enter into their sports, and influence or help shape their ideals and mode of action." One superior, citing the "unusual strain of coping with growing boys at the expense of shattered nerves," urged sisters to foster vocations to the teaching brotherhoods both for the sake of their own self-preservation and to build up a "virile Catholicity."[95] In Philadelphia, Franciscan superior Mother Aloysia Hofer judged boys over the age of fourteen to be "entirely unsuitable for female government."[96]

Although pleas for male vocations would continue, the gap between teaching sisters and brothers continued to widen in favor of the former. In 1907, one Christian brother estimated a proportion of twenty-five sisters to one teaching brother on the national level.[97] In Philadelphia, sisters outnumbered brothers by a ratio of seventeen to one in 1904, twenty-one to one three years later, and by 1919 there were thirty-six teaching sisters for every teaching brother in the archdiocese.[98] This imbalance did not go unexamined, and the most commonly cited explanation for the shortage of vocations to brotherhoods was Catholic boys' aspirations for ordination to the priesthood. Whereas girls who entered the convent would reach "the limit of their ambition," boys with a vocation could always choose to become priests rather than brothers.[99] In an effort to encourage more boys to consider the latter option, some recommended that Catholics distribute more literature that emphasized the uniqueness and advantages of the life of a brother. Among the latter was the avoidance of the "heavy responsibility" attached to the priesthood.[100]

Though lay male teachers would have presented a satisfying substitute for teaching brothers, most church leaders recognized that the salary paid by parochial schools would be insufficient to raise families.[101] In 1912, James Burns conceded that "the few remaining male teachers in both public and parochial schools will be replaced in time by teachers of the other sex." For good measure, he noted that "in neither case was this movement foreseen or desired."[102] Another Catholic author, admitting that teaching had "well-nigh become the monopoly of women," explained that "few consider this an ideal condition; it is, at best, a compromise, a *modus vivendi*."[103] Thus Catholic leaders grudgingly accepted nuns' dominant presence in classrooms as the price for the continued expansion of schools.[104]

As the group who had the most extended contact with Catholic children, sister-teachers were enlisted as the foot soldiers in the crusade to secure more vocations to religious life. Acknowledging their close proximity to children, Sister Assisium touted nuns' comparative advantage over priests. Priests, she noted, "cannot reach the children, and it is in the children that the seed is sown—it is watered afterward by the priest."[105] At least one bishop, Thomas Byrne of Nashville, agreed that "in some respects the office of teaching has an advantage over the priesthood." Because religious teachers were "constantly with the souls" of their pupils, they were uniquely situated to foster vocations to their respective orders.[106]

Ideally, a sufficient number of students would be attracted to religious life solely by their teachers' example. As Schrembs explained, "The dearth of candidates for the religious orders is a *spiritual want* . . . we must have recourse to *spiritual remedies*." Next to prayer, the best spiritual remedy was the piety of religious teachers. "What a power there is in the saintly life of a true religious, and how many are they who experienced the first attraction to the religious state through the influence of a saintly teacher."[107] Though Schrembs refrained from discussing the "disastrous influence" of a bad example on incipient vocations, preferring "to leave the inference to his readers," others were less diplomatic. O'Reilly warned that "children are quick to discover the defects of their superiors . . . if religious do not live up to their calling, they may become a stumbling block."[108] Chiding sisters who permitted "a slight tinge of worldliness to mingle with her piety," another priest intimated that a vocation shortage signified a loss of the community's collective religious spirit.[109] One author even implied that attending a Catholic school actually *decreased* a child's chances of entering religious life, noting that "the New England States—with an almost entire absence of parochial schools—have given the Church more vocations to the priesthood than the States in which the parochial school system has been best established." Explicitly comparing Boston with Philadelphia in this regard, the author hinted that teachers in Catholic schools were responsible for the disparity.[110]

While some religious insisted that their own exemplary conduct should attract a sufficient number of children to religious life, others disagreed.[111] Noting that "vocations do not always present themselves spontaneously," one teaching brother observed: "The power of suggestion, in the way of good, had produced surprising results."[112] Here again, this recommendation treaded upon dangerous theological ground: Suppose one were to encourage a "false" vocation? McDevitt attempted to assuage this concern in Philadelphia after it surfaced in 1908. Acknowledging that some had questioned the "wisdom, even the theological soundness" of appeals for vocations, he emphasized that "religious communities have no intention to swell their ranks with persons who are without a religious vocation." McDevitt explained that religious "merely wanted to awaken their consciousness of it, or remove irrational fears attached to it."[113]

Fears of nurturing a "false vocation" became entangled with a little-remembered controversy over the doctrine of priesthood. In 1909 a French cleric named Joseph Lahitton challenged the widely held assumption that one's vocation derived from interior inspiration. Instead, he argued that a vocation could only be *conferred upon* the candidate by the bishop. This claim elicited so much controversy in France that Pope Pius X created a

Commission of Cardinals to study the question. In 1912, this commission vindicated Lahitton, declaring that a vocation "does not consist, at least necessarily and ordinarily in a certain inclination of the subject," but in the call of the bishop. Because this ruling assigned the task of judging a candidate's suitability for religious life to the bishop or religious superior, it was interpreted as a sign that others, including teachers, could "more easily, without imprudence, directly and repeatedly urge one who is fit to enter the priesthood."[114]

Though both Lahitton's argument and the pronouncement of the Holy See referred specifically to the vocation to the priesthood, several religious in the United States applied it to religious communities. In a speech delivered to a group of Catholic teaching sisters, the Reverend John Delaunay, csc, declared that the resolution of the Lahitton controversy had "highly practical bearing" for their work in classrooms. He offered it as "proof that should remove their dread of making a mistake" in guiding particular students in the direction of the religious life. The teacher would not be "giving" the child a vocation; nor would she be discovering a vocation that the child previously had. Instead, she would be "merely judging that her charge exhibits certain signs which will . . . compel the bishop or religious superior to call the candidate either to the Altar or religious profession."[115] One superior of a women's religious community, referring to "the recent ruling of the Holy See which makes the call of the Superior of the Seminary the sure outward sign of vocation," emphasized that the decision should "consequently lighten the responsibility of those instrumental in encouraging a boy or girl to enter the novitiate."[116]

Meanwhile, thousands of vocations were supposed to be lost because of teachers' lack of attentiveness. One Catholic superintendent speculated that "God had a religious vocation for hundreds of American Catholic girls who remain in the world, and the failure of response is partially due to the neglect and sometimes apathy of those whom God asks to cooperate with Him in the guidance and training of His children."[117] Sisters were often suspected of even greater apathy with regard to their male students. One teaching brother in Philadelphia grumbled that the only applications to their community came from among the boys of his own community's schools.[118]

Teaching sisters were exhorted to use "conscious propaganda" throughout the school day in order to attract students to religious life.[119] Sisters were to be particularly attentive to the manner in which they presented the privileges of life in the world: "Can it be said," one priest asked, "that the attractions of the ballroom, the theatre, the picture show, wield so powerful an influence over American maidens, that the sanctuary and the cloister, which in days gone by could draw princesses from their palaces and queens from their thrones, have lost for them their secret yet potent charms?"[120] Another priest worried that sisters might inadvertently give "undue prominence to the 'almighty dollar'" by emphasizing business courses to the exclusion of catechetical ones, thus dealing a "death blow" to many vocations.[121]

Teaching sisters were also advised not to confine their "watchful eye" to the classroom alone. Careful observance of children during the Mass might reveal an incipient vocation. Sacramental preparation was also declared a "good time to work upon the souls of the young and point out to them the advantages of religious life." The period of preparation for First Holy Communion was judged particularly opportune, but the months preceding Confirmation were also seen as a favorable time to plant the seed.[122] Sisters were also encouraged to increase personal contact. In Massachusetts, church leaders encouraged them to "ask at least four or five girls, especially high school or normal school pupils, to visit them during the year at the convent and urge them to join the community."[123]

What did sisters stand to gain from more energetic recruitment? For one thing, they could compensate for what they might perceive as their personal spiritual deficiencies. For the benefit of a group of teaching sisters, Delaunay conjured an image of an otherwise unworthy dying nun finding consolation in the number of vocations she had inspired: "O my God, Thou Knowest that I have not been a fervent religious. I have too often neglected the service of my rule. . . . But see, O Lord, how many children I have gained for Thee. See all those priests saying Mass for their teacher; all those religious praying for me."[124] Occasionally, sisters could use the increased numbers as leverage. In 1914, Mother Bonaventure Stimson of the Philadelphia SSJs petitioned Archbishop Edmond Prendergast (who had succeeded Ryan in 1912) for financial assistance to enlarge the novitiate: "If we do not build," she warned, "we shall soon have to refuse postulants." Another congregation in Philadelphia, the Sisters of Our Lady of Charity of the Good Shepherd, also asked Prendergast to purchase property for them to enlarge the novitiate.[125]

Nuns' most obvious inducement for securing more vocations was undoubtedly the perpetuation of their community. Most communities attracted the largest number of candidates from among their own pupils.[126] In one of the ssjs' parish schools, fifty-six graduates entered women's religious communities over a thirty-five-year period. Thirty-seven girls had chosen the Sisters of St. Joseph, while the other nineteen had entered other congregations. Reflecting on these nineteen, Sister Assisium McEvoy conceded that "the garment of the Spouse is woven of many colors."[127] Not all nuns were as circumspect. One superior chided sisters who did not "scruple to throw cold water on the ardent admiration a girl might give expression to for an institute other than their own. . . . What matters it in what portion of the vineyard she selects, so long as she works in the vineyard?"[128] In practical terms, of course, it mattered a great deal to communities who were expected to furnish an endless supply of laborers for the harvest.

The battle for vocations provides important context for understanding the development of diocesan-sponsored secondary education for Catholic girls. While central high schools did not promise sisters the tuition benefits of their private academies, they compensated by providing a potentially rich source of new vocations. According to one superior, cities that had a diocesan high school were the envy of other congregations: "The teaching orders there are re-enforced year after year with numbers of candidates graduated from these schools—candidates solidly grounded in religion. . . . It is during the high school age that the strongest and most enduring ties are formed."[129]

When Catholic Girls' High School opened in 1912, Philadelphia became the first archdiocese to offer Catholic girls a free high school education under diocesan auspices.[130] The precursors to the high school had actually been established twelve years before, when McDevitt had authorized four congregations to open "Senior Centres" attached to selected parish schools. These centers would be open to female graduates of parish schools who wished to continue their education in a two-year course of study.[131] The Sisters of Saint Joseph opened a center at Cathedral Parish (the school attended by the prizewinning essayist Mary Donohue). The IHMS opened one at St. Teresa's, and the Sisters of the Holy Child Jesus began another at Assumption Parish. In 1903, the Franciscans established a center at St. Elizabeth's Parish.[132]

Vocational needs were used to justify, at least in part, an unprecedented and controversial arrangement at Catholic Girls' High School. While Mc-Devitt had promised that each center "would be in absolute control of the community teaching it," he had different plans for the high school.[133] Admitting privately that it was "an interesting experiment," McDevitt proposed that sisters from different communities share teaching responsibilities at Catholic Girls' High School.[134] McDevitt invited the congregations who ran senior centers to be part of a "union faculty." The SSJS and the IHMS readily agreed, while the Franciscans did so after a brief period of deliberation.[135] The Sisters of the Holy Child Jesus refused, explaining that the shortage of teachers was so acute that "all except the infirm are doing a full days' teaching."[136]

The institution of the union faculty ensured that authority in the school would be vested with McDevitt rather than with any one community superior. In an unmistakable physical sign of his overall control, he moved his office to Catholic Girls' High School and became known as its acting principal. McDevitt defended the decision by appealing to a sense of fairness. To select any one order, he argued, would be perceived as showing favoritism. But to make the prospect more attractive to the nuns themselves, he observed that with the union faculty "the opportunity of getting vocations would be enjoyed by several communities instead of one."[137] This carrot, in other words, softened the impact of what was actually a considerable transfer of power from community motherhouses to the chancery.

As in the parish schools, recruitment at the high school level was tied to devotional life. Following the lead of Pope Pius X, Catholic educators encouraged frequent communion, pointing to a correlation between the number of frequent communicants and the number of vocations at particular schools.[138] The Philadelphia Franciscans developed a "Eucharistic Army" to encourage devotion to the Blessed Sacrament. One Franciscan sister urged another member of the community to "pray for recruits to the army," reporting that "the first seven high school pupils who became generals in the army entered our novitiate and are now professed sisters."[139]

Other communities saw similarly encouraging results. One IHM sister identified "the harvest of vocations [as] one of the many blessings bestowed by God upon the Catholic Girls' High Schools of Philadelphia."[140] Of the 114 novices in the SSJS with a high school degree in 1916, 75 had graduated from Catholic Girls' High School.[141] As for McDevitt, he often referred to the high number of vocations from the centers and the high school and was known for showing particular pride in his graduates who had chosen "the better part."[142]

IN AN EFFORT TO ENCOURAGE former students to consider a vocation, teaching communities in Philadelphia sponsored annual retreats for the graduates of their academies and the senior centers as early as 1907. These would continue for alumnae of the Catholic Girls' High School.[143] To solve the wrinkle introduced by the union faculty, sisters proposed that two tiers of alumnae associations be established: a "Special Alumnae" chapter under the direction of each community and open to the graduates of that community's parish schools, as well as a "General Alumnae" group for the high school in general, with a rotating directorship to "minimize rivalry" among congregations.[144] McDevitt's successor, the Reverend John Flood, advised other congregations to institute similar programs for alumnae of their high schools in order to foster more vocations.[145] Members of working-girls sodalities were also thought to provide a "very fertile field for vocations," especially when they were "properly managed by the sympathetic and tactful Sister."[146] In Sister Assisium's view, these candidates were particularly welcome because they brought with them the experience of having "earned money."[147]

When measured strictly in terms of numbers, these efforts to attract new vocations were certainly successful. The Philadelphia SSJS doubled in size between 1903 and 1925, and the IHMS nearly tripled.[148] By 1920, there were more than 90,000 women religious in the United States, up from 46,583 in 1900.[149] In terms of actually resolving the crisis, however, recruitment campaigns fell far short of the goal. By 1920, calls for vocations assumed an almost fevered pitch. At the CEA meeting that year, the Reverend Ralph Hayes identified "a need of systematic, concerted action in this matter of fostering vocations." Noting that this need had come to the fore "with increasing urgency," Hayes took pains to specify that he was not initiating a "drive" for vocations. To label it as such, he maintained, "would indicate a total lack of appreciation of what a religious vocation really means."[150]

Hayes's distinction notwithstanding, the pleas for additional vocations often had the appearance of a "drive." One teaching sister had no compunction about labeling it as such: " 'Pray ye the Lord of the harvest that He send laborers into His harvest.' In this age of campaigns and federations . . . ought we not bestir ourselves for a common vital cause and form an alliance?"[151] In the diocese of Brooklyn, the superintendent of Catholic schools tried to popularize the slogan "One Vocation from Every Priest and Teacher."[152] In Philadelphia, John Flood, noting a "constantly enlarging field," suggested that "it should be the ambition of every parish . . . to repay the obligation in part by sending every year into their ranks a just quota of suitable subjects."[153] American bishops also made vocations a part of their 1919 pastoral letter on education, urging all teachers to "remember that after the home, the school is the garden in which vocations are fostered."[154]

The demand for teachers continued to climb. Even worse times lay ahead, as the number of parish schools increased in 1920 and high school education became more widespread. Meanwhile, however, Sister Assisium and other teaching sisters were preoccupied with answering a related question: What was the *purpose* of vocation? As Mother de Chantal, IHM, was fond of saying, "The number means nothing without the spirit."[155] In other words, discussions about vocations were not simply about their quantity. They were also about quality, both of teaching and of religious life.

IMPROVING THE SCHOOLS

McDevitt's entreaties for more teachers were matched in intensity only by his pleas for better ones. In his view, if overcrowded conditions posed the gravest threat to the Catholic school system, inadequately trained teachers presented a close second.[156] Unlike many other church leaders, McDevitt grasped the connection between the two problems: the "urgent demand for teachers," he realized, might force religious communities to send untrained sisters into classrooms. Observing that "the teachers make the school," Mc-Devitt predicted that Catholic education "will rise and fall in public estimation on the evidence borne for or against it in the lives of the pupils it sends forth."[157] Unless religious communities assigned a high priority to the proper training of teachers, he warned, the entire enterprise would collapse.[158]

Recognizing that the motherhouses of each community bore "the heaviest burden" of teacher training, McDevitt depended largely upon congregational leaders to create a more efficient cadre of archdiocesan teachers. They responded eagerly. Sister Assisium McEvoy was undoubtedly one of the women McDevitt had in mind when he commended "the authorities of the teaching orders" for their willingness "to cooperate in everything that makes for the betterment of the parish schools."[159] McEvoy once promised McDevitt that she would welcome any development that "open[ed] a wider and longer vista in educational projects," and she never gave him reason to doubt the sincerity of that pledge.[160]

But no matter how indefatigable McEvoy was in her efforts to raise the SSJS' standards for professional preparation, the model of "professionalization" is of limited usefulness in understanding her commitment to excellence. For McEvoy, a vowed member of a religious community, protecting the integrity of the religious vocation took precedence over all other considerations. "Religious must be engaged in the work of their *profession*," she told future sister-teachers. "What is their profession? Not music, nor botany, nor any one study but the *science* of the *spiritual life*."[161] As for "efficiency," she wryly observed to McDevitt, that was a quality that would be measured "only in eternity."[162]

The key to understanding Sister Assisium's approach to improving teacher training lies in a sermon that she often paraphrased in her conferences with future sister-teachers. "You cannot be admirable Marthas unless you are first ardent Marys. . . . The fecundity of your works depends on your interior life."[163] In the gospel passage to which the sermon refers, two sisters compete for Jesus's approval. Martha prepared and served the meal, while Mary devoted her full attention to Jesus. When Martha demanded that Jesus rebuke her sister for ignoring the tasks, Jesus chastised her instead: "Martha, Martha, you are anxious and worried about many things. There is need of only one thing. Mary has chosen the better part, and it will not be taken from her."[164]

The passage had specific meaning in the context of Catholic religious life. Like Mary, women who became nuns were understood to have chosen "the better part."[165] For sisters in apostolic communities, however, emulating Martha was also an essential component of their vocation. Though the institutional church did not recognize apostolic congregations as true religious until 1900, nuns had been engaged in active ministry for centuries.[166] As Sister Assisium observed, her own congregation had been founded in 1650 with the purpose of supplementing the "cloistral central duties of Mary" with service to the destitute, the ignorant, and the suffering.[167]

While achieving a balance between the interiority of religious life and the intrusions of the world was hardly a new challenge for women in apostolic communities, the unrelenting shortage of teachers in the early twentieth century amplified the metaphorical tension between Martha and Mary.

Moreover, the consolidation of the Catholic school system, combined with rising expectations about teacher credentials in the public schools, directed unprecedented attention of church leaders at the diocesan and national level to the "Martha" component of women's religious vocation.

Until the late nineteenth century, the call to religious life itself was largely interpreted as sufficient foundation for whatever apostolic work sisters would undertake.[168] It was also common practice to pair inexperienced teachers with veterans in order to facilitate on-the-job training. Signs of professionalization began to appear in the mid-1880s. At the Third Plenary Council in Baltimore, the American Catholic hierarchy recommended that bishops "confer with the superiors of congregations dedicated to the office of teaching in the schools, in order that Normal schools be established where they do not exist." By this point, many communities had already begun to supplement the apprenticeship system with formal instruction at summer schools, though the sessions were often erratic. In the Philadelphia SSJs, Sister Assisium characterized the education of novices as "irregular" throughout the 1880s, and the IHMs' summer school at Villa Maria was suspended during its second year because of construction on the motherhouse.[169]

In the Philadelphia OSFs, the appointment of Sister Eberharda Jones as director of the Glen Riddle Normal School in 1892 marked a turning point in the education of the community's novices. Born Charlotte Jones to a brick maker of English birth, Sister Eberharda was a graduate of the Philadelphia Normal School who had spent three years teaching in the city's public schools before she entered the OSFs.[170] Both the degree and the prior experience made her the exception rather than the rule among the novices, a fact that Jones accepted with equanimity: "God does not always grant vocations to the religious state to those who have had the most and best educational advantage," she observed. "Therefore we take the young aspirant as God sends her to us."[171] Throughout her thirty-five years as director of the community's normal school, Sister Eberharda dedicated herself to improving teacher preparation, recognizing that the "efficiency [of the parish schools] must be upheld if we are to save the children of this generation to the Church."[172] It was through that work that Jones met McDevitt, and she, too, became one of the superintendent's collaborators in the quest to improve the quality of teaching throughout Philadelphia.[173]

Another sign of professionalization among teaching sisters was the

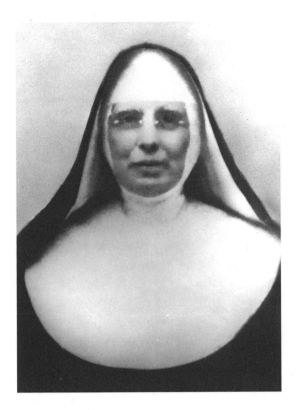

Sister Eberharda Jones, OSF. Courtesy of the Archives of the Sisters of St. Francis of Philadelphia, Aston, Pennsylvania.

aforementioned appointment of congregational supervisors of schools. One of the first women to serve in this capacity was Mother Camilla Maloney. The daughter of an Irish immigrant laborer in Susquehanna, Pennsylvania, Elizabeth Maloney was born in 1852 and entered the IHM novitiate in 1870. After teaching in Philadelphia parish schools and serving as the community's mistress of novices, Maloney was appointed inspectress of schools in 1892. When community inspectors began meeting regularly at the superintendent's office, Mother Camilla also became an ally of McDevitt, who depended on her "invaluable experience" and "mature wisdom." She remained in this position until 1904, when she was elected superior of the community after the death of Mother de Chantal.[174]

By the early twentieth century, church leaders became increasingly defensive about religious teachers' lack of credentials.[175] In his 1903 annual report, McDevitt criticized the tendency of some Catholics to allow state schools to set the standard of excellence: "We candidly say we shall not be satisfied with

Mother M. Camilla Maloney, IHM, 1906. Courtesy of the Archives of the Sisters, Servants of the Immaculate Heart of Mary, Immaculata, Pennsylvania.

our schools simply when they compare favorably with those of the State . . . the efficiency of the latter is far from being well proven."[176] In fact, that same year Pennsylvania's superintendent of schools suggested that public school teachers should emulate Catholic sisters, who spent "the greater part of their vacations in some form of preparation for the year's work."[177]

Still, as states began to impose uniform standards for teacher preparation, McDevitt and other Catholic educators became increasingly convinced that more formal pre-service training would improve the "efficiency" of teaching in the archdiocese. Unlike their secular counterparts, Catholic supporters of improvements in teacher training had to confront an apparent paradox: professional preparation was often at cross-purposes with the goals and mission of religious communities. As James Burns explained, "As a religious order, with its rules, constitutions, and traditions, the ideal of the community is to avoid change; as a teaching organization, its ideal must be that of continual progress, through better equipment, better methods of instruction, and the more thorough preparation of teachers."[178]

In the ideal, there was no tension between sisters' religious and professional identities. In distinguishing between the primary and secondary ends of vocation, canon law placed one's own sanctification over the sanctification of others.[179] Church leaders often reinforced this message. In one profession ceremony, Archbishop Ryan reminded the new sisters that "a Religious imbued with love . . . for her Divine Spouse will do more for the welfare of God's children, even with fewer intellectual gifts, than one who has made a brilliant study of the sciences, without acquiring a deep religious spirit."[180] Another priest preached to the Sisters of St. Joseph in their chapel at Chestnut Hill: "Why did you become a religious? To teach children? No, no, you came to be a religious for the sake of Jesus Christ, for His Glory—the rest is secondary."[181]

Clear prescriptions often obscured complicated reality. Skirmishes routinely broke out between bishops and superiors over the sanctity of the novitiate (the period devoted to religious formation). The increasing demand for teachers often prompted diocesan officials to recommend accelerating religious formation to place sisters in classrooms sooner. Both Shanahan and McDevitt, for example, proposed that novices in their second year do their practice teaching in parish schools.[182] Early on in her term as superior, Mother Camilla extracted a promise from Ryan that the IHMs' canonical year would remain intact, and "no argument, however strong, could induce her to abandon her resolve."[183] Mother Clement, SSJ, also insisted that she would not use novices in school or anywhere else outside the novitiate.[184] Her successor, Mother Bonaventure Stimson, would later use the requirement of the "keeping of the novices for the canonical term" to explain to Ryan's successor why the order could not accept too many more candidates.[185]

Yet congregational superiors often had little choice, and the strong demand for sister-teachers often left communities overextended. In her history of the Philadelphia Franciscans, Sister Mary Adele Gorman tactfully discusses the "rapid—often too rapid—expansion of the congregation in its first fifty years," explaining that "the too-generous Mother Agnes had responded to appeals that tore at her heart, apparently putting the good of the congregation in jeopardy in order to answer what she considered to be a stronger call to minister among the people of God."[186]

No matter how imperfectly applied, directives that privileged religious over professional preparation compelled advocates for teacher training to defend their proposals against charges that increased pedagogical instruction would erode the religious spirit. At one CEA meeting, a priest exhorted superiors to keep their priorities ordered: "The cloister first, and then the classroom. Let religion lead and pedagogics follow and both will greatly profit by the transaction." Without the proper interior disposition, he maintained, neither talents nor accomplishments would matter.[187] Another cleric urged teaching nuns to be faithful to "that intensely Catholic spirit, without which neither the order nor the individual has any reason for existence."[188]

A 1908 article in the Philadelphia-based *Ecclesiastical Review* forced McDevitt to confront pleas "for greater devotion to the spiritual side of the Teaching Sister's life" and warnings about "the danger of giving too much attention to her training in class-room work." But while he recognized the fear that "the religious spirit of our teachers might suffer diminution under insistent demands of modern civilization," the superintendent refused to back down from his commitment to higher standards, noting, "If the preparation of a Religious for her duties in the parish school be a bar to the religious life, or incompatible with it; if the insistence that Religious be trained for pedagogical work, either at the Motherhouse or elsewhere, is to be looked upon as an unreasonable hardship—then there must be a total change in our educational policy." McDevitt expressed complete confidence in the ability of the sisters to carry on their work. He was convinced that "the Religious Order that could not preserve its religious spirit under the requirements of proper preparation for the classroom, would abandon at once the work of teaching and devote itself to the personal sanctification of its subjects."[189]

It was probably not a coincidence that, at the time McDevitt wrote this, one community in Philadelphia was scaling back its commitments because "the work supercedes striving for perfection." Two years earlier, Mother Aloysia Hofer had succeeded Mother Agnes Bucher as superior of the Franciscans. A former mistress of novices, Hofer had long been concerned about the consequences of the community's rapid expansion on its collective religious spirit. Because she believed the community was already stretched too thin, Hofer decided to accept no new missions during her first term, which lasted from 1906 to 1912.[190] Sister Marilla Stoddard, Mother Aloysia's assistant, explained to her spiritual adviser: "We may be wrong in our judgment, but it seems to us that the Community has under-

Classroom in school staffed by the Philadelphia Franciscans in Spokane, Washington, 1900.
Courtesy of the Archives of the Sisters of St. Francis of Philadelphia, Aston, Pennsylvania.

taken more than it can accomplish. It is, to use a very common expression, being like a 'Jack-of-all-trades and a master of none.' We begin a little of everything and bring nothing to completion."[191] After a period of "stabilization," the community resumed accepting missions, both in Philadelphia and in fifteen other dioceses throughout the country.

The sisters' own discussions of vocation corresponded closely to official pronouncements in that they invariably distinguished between primary and secondary ends. As Sister Assisium told the novices, "If you are not saints, you are only good women clothed in the religious habit. What is the end of our vocation? First, my own sanctification; second, to help sanctify other souls."[192] She reminded sisters that they would be "religious first and religious teachers second . . . if you are putting your secular work first you are not living up to your vocation."[193] Speaking of the religious life, Mother de Chantal of the IHMs insisted that "no one has ever left home and all dear to her without the desire of becoming a saint" and that "next only to our personal sanctification comes the welfare of our pupils."[194] Sister Eberharda echoed: "We must be great saints. The people in the world must be saints;

we must be great saints. . . . We are in the convent first for our own sanctification, then only for the sanctification of others."[195]

Unlike many clerics, however, the women religious charged with improving teacher preparation tended to present Martha and Mary as collaborators rather than competitors. In other words, they argued that achieving a higher level of competency in the classroom would help to secure the teacher's sanctification as well as that of her students. In her "Canticle of the Classroom," Sister Assisium wrote about how the quotidian tasks of the teacher could provide a path to the beatific:

> Lord of the books and blackboards
> > Since I have not time to be
> A Saint by doing lovely or heroic
> > things for thee
> By kneeling long before Thy throne,
> > There free to pray and think
> Make me a saint by praising thee
> > In Hectographic ink![196]

Sister Assisium speculated that the urgent need for Catholic schools would have prompted at least one canonized saint to revise her understanding of where one could encounter the divine: "St. Teresa says 'God walks among the pots and the pipkins.' Had she lived in the twentieth century, she would have added, 'And among the books and blackboards.' "[197]

These themes recurred in other teaching sisters' reflections on vocation. Mother Camilla reminded her sisters that teaching was a "sacred privilege" and that preparation for it was to be their most important occupation.[198] Sister Eberharda Jones tied the scholarly to the spiritual in her description of the novitiate as "the normal school of the religious life."[199] Martha and Mary also joined forces in the work of nursing Franciscans. As Mother Aloysia observed, "The sister engaged in nursing the sick should endeavor to become more and more perfect in the work of her calling. Indeed, it is her *sacred duty*, for she is not merely a hired lay nurse but a *religious nurse*, one who has assumed weightier obligations and who is laboring for a reward that is eternal."[200]

Ideally, Mary's example could offer a sister consolation and encouragement when the duties of Martha overwhelmed her. One new teacher, daunted by the amount of work to accomplish, took solace in her youthful vigor: "I have such health," she told Sister Assisium, "that I know God expects me to turn it all into love and love into energy."[201] In an effort to calm a nervous new teacher, Sister Eberharda assured her that as long as "your zeal and energy are directed toward being a good Religious . . . God will bless your efforts in the education of his little ones."[202] Mother Camilla, counseling a sister who had experienced difficulties at her parish school, reminded her, "Nothing injures health like sadness, melancholy, bitterness. Live in holy joy. . . . God who has chosen you for the good of many will give you the spirit, strength, courage and the love for many."[203]

The same sense of "chosenness" appears in Sister Eberharda's reflections on religious life. As "God's co-laborers," each sister had "a special place in God's plan, a special work to do for Him."[204] In the ssjs, Sister Assisium advised novices that "there is a work for me to do here that no one else shall do."[205] She always emphasized that a sister's work, whether in the classroom, hospital, or kitchen, derived from her primary commitment to her religious community. "Labor," she counseled the novices, "is the vocation of St. Joseph's daughters." She had stern words for sisters who were not prepared to work hard or well, identifying laziness and mediocrity as the two most serious threats to community's religious spirit.[206] Although work was important, devotion to the community came first.

The similarities across congregations notwithstanding, it is important to note that these women identified themselves not as generic "sisters" but as "daughters of St. Joseph," "children of the Immaculate Heart," or "daughters of St. Francis." Sister Assisium declared, "The Rule is our gospel: there is, as we well know, a gospel according to St. Matthew, St. Mark, St. Luke and St. John and there is a gospel according to the Sister of St. Joseph—our holy rule—and we will be judged by it."[207] She admitted that while "religious vows in substance, are the same in every community," "every community does not observe them in the same way."[208] Writing about her congregation in a letter to McDevitt, Sister Assisium boasted that proud "intellectual almsgiving as well as spiritual is our *forte*."[209]

Congregations' sense of their own uniqueness shaped their relationship to one another and to the diocese, with significant implications for the development of teacher training. Before the twentieth century, members of different communities had little reason or opportunity for sustained contact. Though the superiors of the ihms, osfs, and ssjs knew and even admired one another, they kept a polite distance.[210] Sister Eberharda once observed that communities were so disconnected from each other in the early twentieth century that "one was often led to think they were all not laboring in the same cause."[211]

Along with other diocesan superintendents, McDevitt was very critical of the "narrow parochialism" that segregated communities from one another.[212] He viewed the Board of Community Inspectors, as well as the Girls' High School centers, as ways to bring the communities into closer collaboration. When the centers opened in 1900, Mother Clement, ssj, insisted that "there must be no rivalry" with members of other congregations. "It is hard enough to find religious criticized and deprecated by those outside of us," she noted; "we should all support each other."[213] Mother de Chantal also commended the ihms who taught at St. Teresa's Centre for not criticizing members of other communities or the students who had been educated by them.[214]

The "union faculty" at Catholic Girls' High school, of course, required an unprecedented amount of cooperation among communities. Many sisters approached the prospect of working in such close proximity with trepidation.[215] McDevitt hoped bringing the teachers of various communities together at one institution would "modify the self-satisfied attitude that all that is best in pedagogical knowledge and religious spirit is in 'our community.'" At the same time, he expected to capitalize on congregational rivalry, hoping it would stimulate excellence.[216] McDevitt himself reported no significant problems with the union faculty, and several sources suggest that he deserves much of the credit for its success. One sister recalled, "No one community was more important in his eyes than another. We were all sisters, all teachers, all equally important."[217]

Another of McDevitt's proposals, establishing a central diocesan normal school, was also intended both to improve teacher training and to encourage more intercommunity collaboration. John Lancaster Spalding had recommended creating such institutions in 1890, and the proposal was revived by McDevitt and James Burns in 1904. McDevitt explained that "where a religious community depends solely on its own members for training its teachers it is quite possible for faulty as well as excellent methods of instruction to be transmitted."[218] Each community's sense of its own unique response to the call of "Martha," however, made it unlikely that communities would relinquish control over the education of their novices to the diocese. McDevitt later conceded that responsibility for training devolved exclusively upon congregations: the motherhouses, the local superior, and the community inspector.[219] This last office was the only one with direct accountability to him.

Although McDevitt occasionally visited novitiates to supervise and administer examinations, it was not until sisters were actually teaching that he was in a position to assess their pedagogical acumen.[220] Annually, he made personal visits to every parish school and sent individual teachers detailed evaluations.[221] His office also sponsored occasional lectures and published quarterly "Educational Briefs" designed to enrich sisters' intellectual life. (Margaret Buchanan Sullivan's "Chiefly among Women," in fact, had been one of these.) McDevitt also encouraged communities to join the Catholic Educational Association, which was established in 1904.[222]

If the institutional church provided minimal structural support for the education of its teaching sisters, it also offered little material assistance. Superiors felt the pinch acutely. Mother Bonaventure Stimson of the SSJS noted that the community had tripled its expenditures on training and education between 1907 and 1912 alone.[223] The Philadelphia model points to a facet of the school question that was true in other dioceses throughout the country: supportive of sisters' education in the abstract, most bishops were reluctant to allocate funds for it. Even McDevitt, a self-defined champion of sisters' education, routinely subordinated it to other priorities. In 1911, for example, the head of the summer school at the University of Pennsylvania proposed that McDevitt solicit money from lay Catholics to fund scholarships for sisters to attend classes. Admitting that improving sisters' education was a noble goal, McDevitt insisted that all fund-raising efforts in the archdiocese be channeled to the Catholic Girls' High School.[224]

Communities could, in theory, have pooled their resources to minimize their expenses, but again the commitment to the practical efforts of Martha made this unlikely. In case after case, "each community tried to distinguish itself from others, jealously guarding its own traditions, textbooks and grading systems and resisting efforts to develop uniform policies. . . . Each maintained that its distinctive teaching methods were intrinsically superior."[225] This mind-set, combined with the lack of diocesan support, explains why most teaching communities engaged in parallel rather than cooperative ventures.

Ensuring that all sister-teachers had a high school degree was the first step in improving standards. In Philadelphia, the SSJS, IHMS, and OSFS had their novitiate normal schools "affiliated" with Catholic University around 1915, a process that gave "a definite, standardized course of study" to sisters who had one or two years of high school before they entered.[226] Levels of education at entrance, meanwhile, were steadily improving. Among the women who entered the SSJS between 1909 and 1916, 78 percent had an eighth-grade education or less. Of the women who entered the community between 1916 and 1922, only 47 percent did not have a high school education.[227]

Communities often focused on "educating the educators," usually the directors of normal schools. James Burns explained how "a few thoroughly educated men or women, with the high ideals and noble enthusiasm that spring from the pursuit of the scientific study of education, will be able, through the training of young teachers in the normal school, to improve the quality of teaching in hundreds of parish schools."[228] Burns was speaking specifically of sister-students who attended the Catholic Sisters College in Washington, D.C. Opened in 1911 and spearheaded by Thomas Shields, a sociologist at Catholic University, the Sisters College represented the most ambitious attempt to develop a national plan for Catholic teacher training. Beginning in 1912, the Philadelphia SSJS, IHMS, and OSFS all sent a few members each year to the college. Sister Eberharda Jones was a student there between 1914 and 1916.

Many discussions about the Sisters College focused on the way the institution helped students mediate the demands of Martha and Mary. Pope Pius praised the college for allowing nuns to pursue their education "without in any way slackening the observance of their religious rules."[229] Sister Assisium, responding to fears that "taking degrees may incite Sisters' pride and self-sufficiency," defended the decision to send Sisters of St. Joseph to the college: "But if one wants to keep our place in the educational work, one must keep pace with modern requirements."[230] She did allow that "in every good there is a danger. I suppose an inspectress must see that the written work does not displace unduly the recitation of the spiritual life."[231]

It was not feasible, practically or financially, to send more than a few sisters to Washington, D.C., so the Philadelphia teaching communities looked to local colleges to provide members with postgraduate education. In the IHMS, Mother Camilla arranged extension courses through the University of Pennsylvania and through Westchester University, a state teachers college only a few miles away from Immaculata.[232] Significantly, Mother

Camilla differed sharply from her counterparts in the SSJS or the OSFS with regard to her opinion of state schools.

Invited to reflect on the question "Should Our Religious Attend State Normal Schools," Sister Assisium responded with an impassioned negative. "Why," she demanded, "should our religious be asked to drink at poisoned wells, or imbibe knowledge from sources agnostic or pantheistic, nay, even antagonistic to faith?"[233] Sister Eberharda agreed, observing that "the State Normal school and non-Catholic college or university are not the proper professional training schools for our religious. . . . Our teachers must imbibe their training from a Catholic viewpoint." Like Sister Assisium, she referred to godlessness of the public schools as a "poison," describing it as "so insidious that even the keenest intellect often fails to detect it in our readers, histories and scientific texts . . . if we do not guard our religious against this outside influence, our schools will become Catholic only in name."[234] Several members of both the SSJS and the OSFS studied at Villanova College, a local college founded by the Augustinian order.

The nuns' strong opposition to state normal schools must be understood in the context of Catholic educators' abiding suspicion of increased government involvement in educational matters. The editor of *America* railed against "Prussianized" schools, and the dean of studies at the College of St. Thomas in Minnesota conceded that while "the 'Big Brother' idea is all right in its place, in the matter of State supervision over certain phases of the educational process, as at present constituted, it is apt to be overdone."[235] In Philadelphia, McDevitt grew increasingly concerned about "a tendency on the part of the State . . . to modify the civil authority's passive or indifferent attitude toward private schools."[236]

The prospect of state certification of private-school teachers, in particular, provoked widespread uneasiness. While Sister Eberharda recognized that "the State may insist on a standard of excellence," she was worried about granting "public authority" control over Catholic teachers, curriculum, or textbooks.[237] In an anxious letter to McDevitt in 1919, who was then the bishop of Harrisburg, Sister Eberharda asked him to confirm rumors "that the Government intends to take control of the Parochial Schools and that the Teachers will have to take State Examinations." McDevitt offered little reassurance: he observed that "it is not at all likely that the civil authorities, National or State, will continue indefinitely the present policy of leaving our educational system go on in its own independent fashion." To this end, he advised Sister Eberharda and other religious leaders to prepare teachers for state examinations, as he predicted that individual states would gradually enact laws to compel all the teachers in parish schools to pass a state examination. He told her to "hope for the best, but prepare for the worst."[238]

The "worst" would happen in 1924, when the state of Pennsylvania mandated that all teachers be certified by January 1, 1927.[239] Mother Camilla Maloney of the IHMs had anticipated this development by two decades and felt that, on the whole, it would bring positive changes to Catholic education.[240] Mary Molloy of the College of St. Teresa in Winona, Minnesota, was one of the few who shared Maloney's sanguine view, observing that "the State is exercising no more scrutiny over the teaching profession than it exercises over law or medicine." Furthermore, Molloy argued, certification was in their best interests. Unless religious teachers had "equal rank with the rest of their professional sisters . . . our carefully nurtured, most dearly treasured possession, the parish school, will be taken from our keeping."[241]

While Malloy and Maloney may sound sensible in retrospect, the prospect of state certification did represent the worst-case scenario to most Catholic educators before 1920. To understand why, it is necessary to consider how Catholic educators perceived their schools in relation to state-sponsored ones. Considering the amount of time and energy Catholics poured into differentiating their schools, allowing "the enemy" to set the standard was indeed unthinkable.

DEFINING THE SCHOOLS

Defining Philadelphia's parochial schools in relation to state-sponsored ones often involved emphasizing the similarities between them, especially in terms of the effectiveness of each in cultivating loyal citizens. McDevitt and his public counterpart, Superintendent Martin Brumbaugh, frequently tussled over Catholics' right to educate their children in denominational schools. The most heated dispute erupted in 1910, when Brumbaugh stated publicly that attendance at state schools should be made a condition for citizenship.[242] Always careful to emphasize that he was protesting not as a Catholic but as an American citizen, McDevitt responded to these and other challenges with a three-pronged defense of Catholic education: first, he argued that Catholic schools performed a great service to the state, both by saving the government a great deal of money and by relieving it of responsibility for educating a large percentage of school-age children; second, he pointed out that Catholic taxpayers willingly bore an unfair double burden in supporting two parallel school systems; and third, he insisted that Catholic schools were at least as "American" as their state-supported counterparts, and perhaps even more so because they produced morally responsible citizens.[243]

Though McDevitt was a thoughtful and eloquent spokesman for the cause, there was nothing particularly unique about his reasoning. In a sense, he was only repeating the arguments that John Hughes had made fifty years earlier and rehearsing the ones that supporters of school choice would advance later in the twentieth century. McDevitt's preoccupation with differentiation, however, reveals a much more distinctive and less examined aspect of Catholic school definition in the Progressive Era. For Catholics in Philadelphia, as for Americans in general, the state loomed larger in the first two decades of the twentieth century than it ever had before. During his first few years as superintendent of Catholic schools, McDevitt could justly claim that "the parish system has scarcely any relations with the civil authorities."[244] That would not hold true for long. Increasingly, McDevitt aspired to meet standards set by the state, sought more benefits from the state, and watched schools become more subject to state control. Like other Catholics, he was deeply suspicious of the Progressive impulse to increase the reach of state and federal governments. In reaction to the state's efforts "to extend its jurisdiction in matters educational," McDevitt devoted more time and attention to highlighting the differences between Catholic and state-sponsored schools.[245] McEvoy and other teaching sisters not only participated in this process of differentiation but also proved integral to it both practically and symbolically.

The ssj convent at Chestnut Hill was one of many places where McDevitt spoke of Catholic teachers' obligation to form not only "citizens for the state" but also the future "citizens of God's kingdom."[246] In a paper written for the cea meeting, McEvoy echoed this theme by observing that while "the unreflecting" might focus on the similarities between parochial and public schools, more discerning observers grasped the essential differences between them. "The State school," she noted, "ignores the formation of the soul, and it keeps in view, it teaches only for the things of time; in the Catholic school, the culture of the soul is the primary object, for we teach in time to prepare for eternity."[247] "Teaching in time to prepare for eternity" pointed once again to the ongoing spiritual challenge to accommodate the intrusions of this world while keeping one's eye on the next. But the phrase also captured the crucial distinction that Catholic educators used to distinguish parochial and public education during the Progressive Era.[248]

Others used teleological arguments to explain why the two systems were fundamentally different, despite their deceptively similar appearance. The Reverend Thomas Shields, the Catholic educator most sympathetic to Progressive reformers, acknowledged the necessity of educating for citizenship. But because Catholics recognized each boy and girl as not only "a future citizen" but also as "a child of Heaven," they could not accept state citizenship as the ultimate aim of education.[249] Students at the Catholic Sisters College described Catholic and public schools as "two systems with divergent aims." Athough the two systems "may run parallel to each other in some lines of work," the state system "is found to stop at the point where the other considers that the more important part of its work begins."[250] John Tracy, comparing the public and Catholic school systems to "two great ships," observed: "Twin sisters they appear to be. . . . The only difference between the two palatial vessels is that one is without compass or rudder."[251] While public school students sailed along aimlessly, in other words, Catholic schools offered children a clear destination.

Different ends required different means. In Philadelphia, McDevitt pointed to "religion in education" as the most critical navigational tool that would keep Catholic school students on course.[252] In holding up religious education as the primary distinguishing factor, McDevitt was certainly not inventing anything new. As we have seen, the removal of religion from public schools had long been used to justify separate denominational ones. In the first two decades of the twentieth century, however, religious education took on additional significance for Catholic educators, in view of both Progressive educational reform and the ongoing secularization of public schools. James Burns noted that the public schools had "changed considerably in character since the days of Bishop Hughes." Although they had lost their "Protestant tone," a development that Hughes would presumably have cheered, they had gradually eliminated any form of "positive Christian teaching" to an extent that neither Hughes nor any other American could have anticipated. Appalled by this, Burns, along with other Catholic educators, insisted that "religion must be taught *in the schools*."[253]

It was against this backdrop that McDevitt, soon after becoming superintendent, set out to make religious education the "predominating factor, the informing element of our educational system." In addition to inaugurating the aforementioned essay contest, McDevitt also organized an archdiocesan catechetical exhibit.[254] The main thrust of his efforts, however, was directed at reforming the teaching of catechism and church history. McDevitt was motivated in part by his dissatisfaction with how Christian doctrine was taught, a sentiment he shared with other Catholic educators.[255] In his annual report for 1903, McDevitt urged Philadelphia teachers "to make the study more pleasant and attractive" so that students could take a more "lively interest."[256]

McDevitt's quest to vivify the teaching of Christian doctrine led him to Chestnut Hill, where Sister Assisium McEvoy prepared ssj novices to teach the subject based on a teaching manual that she had developed for community use in 1899. Introducing the manual to the community, Mother Clement had observed that "the battleground of the Church now lies in the school room and each Sister should take valiantly her part in spreading there the kingdom of Christ to the souls God sends her."[257] In her own words, Sister Assisium characterized the curriculum as her effort to reconcile Progressive transformations in education with immutable Catholic doctrine: "The Course of Religious Instruction," she wrote, "is the outcome of the attempt to bring the 'New Education' to bear on the sacred and unchangeable truths, and to lead children not only to know, but to love and practice them."[258] Duly impressed with Sister Assisium's methods, McDevitt encouraged the Sisters of St. Joseph to publish the curriculum so that it could be made available to other archdiocesan teachers. *The Course of Christian Doctrine: A Handbook for Teachers* was released by Dolphin Press in 1904. In order to "secure close uniformity" among schools, McDevitt required that all archdiocesan schools adopt the textbook, and it remained the official syllabus in Philadelphia until 1928.[259]

The *Handbook*'s publication made Sister Assisium as famous as it was possible for most women religious to become early in the twentieth century. Admirers from Philadelphia and beyond sent her exuberant praise. Shanahan of Harrisburg described the book as "the most valuable contribution to our pedagogical literature that has ever been made in America." Teaching sisters from many different congregations used it throughout the United States and in Australia. A lay settlement worker at Brownson House in Los Angeles reported that it worked well in a kindergarten curriculum.[260]

Sister Assisium offered instruction in the teaching methods to the IHMs, the Sisters of the Blessed Sacrament, and other Philadelphia-based communities. She also traveled to other dioceses at the invitation of Catholic school superintendents or religious communities for the same purpose.[261] One teaching sister, praising McEvoy, remarked that she knew of no other religious who had done more for the church; she ascribed "the universality" of McEvoy's work to a uniquely Philadelphian spirit: "Did you get that spirit from the city or did the city get it from you?" she asked. "I wonder."[262] McEvoy presented her work at the CEA meeting in 1914, and her instructions on how to present Christ's death contain what was, according to one scholar, the earliest plea to avoid anti-Semitism in the history of American catechetics.[263]

McEvoy also applied her "new methods" to the teaching of the Mass, and this, too, resulted in several publications, some of which elicited criticism. "Like all other progressive methods that savor of innovation," one of her friends noted, "it has its enemies."[264] The most prominent critic was an unnamed Sister of Charity writing in *America*, who chided McEvoy's textbooks for their "graphic representations of eternal truths."[265] McDevitt dismissed this critique as nonsense, and another Catholic school superintendent speculated that the anonymous author had attended a non-Catholic university.[266] Sister Assisium later attributed both the popularity of her methods and the deflection of any major criticism of them to McDevitt's advocacy.[267]

Less than thirty miles away from Sister Assisium's classroom at Chestnut Hill, Sister Eberharda Jones also spent much of the first quarter of the twentieth century applying Progressive theories of pedagogy to the Catholic school curriculum. Like McDevitt, Sister Eberharda believed that Christian doctrine should not only be taught as an isolated subject but "must be brought into and permeate every branch of discussion if we are to give our parish schools their distinctive characteristic."[268] Insisting that "religion should be correlated with other branches of the curriculum and should be the dominant note in all training and discipline," Jones developed a curriculum that highlighted "the principles of our Holy Religion" in her chosen field of mathematics.[269] In 1923, she completed a doctoral thesis in the subject, becoming the first person to receive a Ph.D. from Villanova University.[270]

As Margaret Mary Reher has noted, it is possible to overstate the influence of Progressive methods on catechetical instruction in Catholic schools. But though it may be true that "rote memorization" would continue to "carry the day," the efforts to reshape the teaching of Christian doctrine imply that Progressive influence may have been more widespread than previously assumed.[271] Moreover, the work of Sisters Assisium and Eberharda suggests that, while scholars of Catholic and Progressive education have assumed that women religious were "hardly involved" in curriculum development, it might be more accurate to say that their contributions were hardly recognized.[272]

In the case of McEvoy's *Handbook*, the author was identified only as "S.S.J." The use of initials was fairly standard practice, as nuns rarely used their names in publications. In this case the author's anonymity was even further protected by the omission of "Philadelphia" as a community identifier. It had been left out on the recommendation of the Reverend Herman Heuser, the editor of Dolphin Press. Though Mother Clement and Sister Assisium both objected to this proposal initially, they acquiesced in the face of Heuser's persistence.[273] He subsequently commended the sisters for their "excellent religious disposition of unselfishness" in their acceptance of the omissions. Typically, he held out the promise of a heavenly reward as compensation for the lack of an earthly one, reminding the sisters that "we work for eternity and are very sure of our Divine Master's not forgetting whom the credit of faithful work and use of talents is due."[274] Sister Eberharda received similar admonitions, from both Heuser and other priests, in the wake of her various accomplishments. When she earned her Ph.D., her thesis director dismissed any praise as "not acceptable to the spirit of humble saint Francis that is so exactly yours."[275] Another priest ascribed her desire to publish her book to the "religious motive of community devotion" rather than the "spirit of self-glory."[276]

This spirit of humility and detachment figured prominently in the ubiquitous paeans to teaching nuns that appeared in Catholic sermons and devotional literature in the early twentieth century. This phenomenon was undoubtedly connected to the desire to stimulate more interest in religious life among young Catholics. It was also a symptom of Catholics' defensiveness about their comparative lack of professional preparation, as many Catholic educators opined that the "intangibles" inherent in religious life amply compensated for any deficiencies in formal training.[277] But the widespread obeisance paid to teaching nuns also served another purpose: by their very presence, Catholic sisters attested to essential differences between parochial and public schools. In other words, if sisters were practically integral to the rhetoric of differentiation through the subjects they taught, they were symbolically so because of what they represented.

Next to religious education, McDevitt pointed to the "unqualified and unselfish consecration of our teachers to a calling they consider divine" as the second most important factor distinguishing Catholic schools from their secular counterparts. He insisted that Catholics' dependence on teaching nuns did not "arise from economic necessity alone; it is of deliberate choice," and he observed that while "some of our teachers have not a special professional training . . . there are elements of power in the work of religious of which the secular teacher has little acquaintance."[278] McDevitt and other Catholic educators latched on to three particular distinguishing characteristics: the relative longevity of a teaching sister's "career," her removal from the world, and her lack of financial remuneration. According to McDevitt, sisters' lifelong vows lent "a permanency to our teaching body, which is confessedly wanting in that of the Public Schools."[279] James Burns agreed that whereas the "Catholic teacher takes up teaching as a life profession, and is, as a rule, a teacher for life," public school teachers who served only a few years "can scarcely be said to be a body of professional teachers at all."[280] Even one of the most vociferous opponents of female teachers conceded that the teaching nun who "devotes her life to the mastery of the difficult art of teaching" was at least preferable to secular teachers, who, by viewing the teaching profession as temporary, represented an even "nearer and more prolific source of evil."[281]

Nuns' supposed seclusion gave them another comparative edge over public school teachers. According to Burns, sisters' lives "centered on the school," and their "conversations, recreations, and prayers" focused on their students. The Reverend John Mullany paid homage to the men and women who renounced "all other duties and responsibilities in life that they may devote themselves . . . to the noble work of educating Catholic youth."[282] Thomas Shields noted that, unlike the secular teachers, who carried the social and economic burdens of the world into the classroom, the religious teacher was "withdrawn from the world and lifted above its strife and turmoil," thus better poised to elevate society through the school.[283] Sister Eberharda observed that "even non-Catholic school superintendents admit that herein lies the strength of the body of religious teachers—they have no distractions, no intercourse with the world. They live in community, and there is ample opportunity for an exchange of ideas on educational subjects, and each can learn from the experience of the other."[284] Entering the classroom from "the quiet seclusion of their convent homes," sisters turned to teaching with a singleness of purpose that set them apart from their preoccupied counterparts.[285]

Sisters' lifelong commitment and singular devotion to teaching, while worthy of praise, paled in comparison with their most admirable qualification: their refusal to accept "no other compensation than that which is barely sufficient to clothe and shelter them."[286] Praising sisters' "sacrifices, self-denial, the rigid economy, and the whole-souled consecration to a high calling," McDevitt held up the teaching sister as a refreshing contrast to her mercenary public school counterpart.[287] Burns noted that unlike public school teachers, for whom work was "a matter of bread and butter," teaching sisters were "not bothered about salaries."[288] Another priest pointed out that "teachers in the non-Catholic institutions . . . have made no vow of poverty. They work for a salary. They wish to keep their positions, or even to obtain promotion." Sisters' aspirations for their own religious perfection, in contrast, offered a much loftier incentive for attaining pedagogical excellence.[289]

Thomas Shields even seized upon nuns' renunciation of temporal wealth to make his case that Catholic schools formed the basis for "true Americanization." While the state was "obliged to use self-interest as the main motive in attracting her teachers and keeping them in her service," the religious vow of poverty freed religious teachers from such crass motives, enabling them to devote their lives and services "unreservedly to the children who may come under [their] care, without thought of personal gain or benefit in return." In teaching sisters, Catholic school students witnessed a powerful example of "disinterested citizenship."[290] The truth of this statement is obviously difficult to assess, but as Mary Donohue's essay makes clear, nuns' willingness to perform "wageless work" was not lost on their students.

It is striking how many Catholics gloried in nuns' lack of material compensation; the word "pittance" was used more than once to describe their salaries.[291] For James Burns, it was obviously a matter of pride that "the

Sister Marita Anne McGonigle, IHM, third-grade classroom, St. Agnes School, West Chester, Pennsylvania, 1940. Courtesy of the Archives of the Sisters, Servants of the Immaculate Heart of Mary, Immaculata, Pennsylvania.

salaries of Sisters teaching in the parochial schools rarely rise above two hundred fifty dollars per annum . . . more commonly it is from one-hundred fifty to two hundred dollars per annum," whereas teaching brothers earned twice as much.[292] As noble as it might have been, nuns' underpaid labor created manifold problems for teaching communities. Often sisters did not even receive "the pittance requisite to maintain them"; moreover, low wages impeded efforts to improve sisters' education. Even Shields, for all his celebration of nuns' superior motivation, believed that sisters' salaries should be raised enough to support the attendance of several community members at the Sisters College.[293] Nuns' supposed lack of need for money also compromised, to say the least, their ability to negotiate for higher wages. In 1912, Mother Bonaventure Stimson of the SSJS asked pastors to increase each teaching sister's stipend by $50 per year, bringing the total to $250. One pastor refused on the grounds that the people of his parish would be indirectly taxed to support the motherhouse.[294]

Philadelphia teaching sisters received some financial relief in 1920, when a newly elevated Dennis Cardinal Dougherty raised their salary to $300 per year.[295] Though in this instance teaching sisters were the beneficiaries of Dougherty's unilateralism, this would be less true in the grand scheme of things. Renowned for his autocratic style of leadership, Dougherty would sharply circumscribe nuns' activities and influence during his more than three decades as head of Philadelphia's archdiocese. Although there is some evidence that a few superiors bristled at Dougherty's autocratic proclivities in the early 1920s, it seems they were far more concerned about the prospect of ceding authority over teacher training to the state than about ceding it to the archdiocese.[296] Within a decade, however, sisters would surrender much of their autonomy to both entities.

EVEN THOUGH THEY NO LONGER worked in the same diocese, Sister Assisium and McDevitt continued to correspond frequently throughout the 1920s. As she became "the dean of octogenarians" at Chestnut Hill, McEvoy began to anticipate her death as "the most complete detachment from the baubles of time."[297] This escape would elude her until 1939, but her infirmities increased in number and severity each year, and her letters to McDevitt invariably contained requests for blessings and prayers. The bishop, too, was experiencing the ravages of aging. After one illness he recuperated at the ssj vacation home in Cape May Point, New Jersey.[298]

The two old friends continued to discuss the overcrowding of Catholic schools, which worsened as Dougherty, fancying himself "God's Bricklayer," embarked on a frenzied building crusade.[299] A second central diocesan girls' high school, which opened in Philadelphia in 1927, became, according to Sister Assisium, "another drain on the number of teachers available," and she was disturbed that the constant demand left the Sisters of St. Joseph "forced beyond our capacity."[300] Of even greater concern was the scramble to meet state requirements. In 1922, reporting that the "Normal" classes were in full swing, she wondered to McDevitt "what the outcome will be for ultimate progress."[301] In her letters to McDevitt, Sister Assisium reported that she was thankful to be "old enough to be out of these rushes." While "the coming generation would be better prepared for them," she predicted that "if the spirit of religious retirement goes, it would rob communities of many graces."[302] She noted that "the increase of intensive work of the schools, the certification of teachers, the reaching out for degrees is not promotive of peace of mind or health of body. . . . Yet what can be done?"[303]

Though McEvoy had lamented McDevitt's departure for Harrisburg, she had reason to be grateful for it in the 1920s. His contacts in the state capital proved helpful in her now routine dealings with Pennsylvania's Department of Public Instruction. In particular, McDevitt assisted the Sisters of St. Joseph in securing a charter for Chesnut Hill College in 1924.[304] By this time, the IHMs had already opened Immaculata College (1920), and the Sisters of the Holy Child had established Rosemont College (1921). The close proximity of these Catholic women's colleges was representative of a national pattern of proliferation. One prophetic observer, citing "the overlapping, duplication, and undignified scramble for students," recommended that "the multiplication of colleges, and especially of colleges for women, should be halted" and replaced by the creation of collaborative, regional universities.[305] Considering the commitment to educating its own for the "Martha" component of the vocation, as well as the need for each community to finance college degrees for all their teachers, there was little chance that communities would have responded positively to that suggestion. Had they done so, however, it is likely that more Catholic women's colleges would have survived the upheaval of the late 1960s and 1970s.

Implicit in Sister Assisium's critique of "the credit craze" was an understandable degree of defensiveness. One of her contemporaries, Sister Stanislaus Quigley, recalling the excellent education she had received as a child, lamented that the nineteenth century was "spoken of by the present day intelligentsia as 'the Dark Ages,' the time in which 'the poor Sisters did not know how to teach.' I wonder!!! I wonder, indeed."[306] Resenting the implication that the Sisters of St. Joseph had not always been committed to teaching excellence, Sister Assisium felt a sense of vindication in 1928, when the Pennsylvania State Board of Education ratified a charter that had governed the community since 1870.[307]

Vindication for Catholic schools in general came in 1925, when the U.S. Supreme Court's decision in *Pierce v. Society of Sisters* secured the right of nonpublic schools to exist. This decision made the need to define Catholic schools less urgent even as the need to staff and improve them intensified. The idealization of the teaching nun continued and hastened the gradual process of the subordination of the individual to the congregation that was part of the Americanization of religious life in the early twentieth century.[308]

The lives of Sister Assisium McEvoy and the thousands of other sisters who performed "the wageless work of paradise" in Catholic classrooms reinforce the themes that shaped the discussions of the New Woman and the debates over the founding of Trinity College. By "teaching in time to prepare for eternity," sisters joined other Catholics in affirming their qualifications for U.S. citizenship while at the same time limning the boundaries that divided them from non-Catholic citizens. Sister Assisium could certainly not be labeled a New Woman, and she would hardly have recognized herself as such. Yet her work, shaped as it was by the mandate for more efficiency, professionalism, centralization, and state oversight, is as much a part of the history of Progressivism as is that of any other woman in the United States at the time.

Two high schools are named for Philip McDevitt, one in Philadelphia and one in Harrisburg. There is, of course, no Sister Assisium McEvoy High School; nor are there many diocesan institutions in Philadelphia named for nuns. Considering the power differential between McDevitt and McEvoy and recognizing the former's failure to support teaching sisters in tangible ways, contemporary feminists would be justly appalled to hear Sister Assisium describe McDevitt as her "friend." But in the world she inhabited, McDevitt was indeed her friend, far more so than a non-Catholic wage-earning professional or a union organizer. At the same time, it is possible to detect in this story the seeds of gender discontent that would sprout in the Sister Formation movement a few decades later and eventually lead some Catholic nuns to stand at the vanguard of the social movements of the 1960s. Meanwhile, however, the inability of women religious to unite across congregations is immensely telling. If at this juncture Catholic women were unable to see one another as allies against a male-dominated hierarchy, it was even less likely that they would be interested in collaborating with non-Catholic women in a crusade to challenge gender subordination. The limits that religious identity placed on Catholic women's perceptions of the possibilities of sisterhood are the subject of the next chapter.

CHAPTER FOUR

The Morbid Consciousness
of Womanhood CATHOLICISM, ANTISUFFRAGE,

AND THE LIMITS OF SISTERHOOD

Katherine E. Conway, a journalist and author based in Boston, frequently
commented on the constellation of issues that constituted "the woman
question" in late nineteenth- and early twentieth-century America. Like
most other Catholics, Conway had little patience for the New Woman's
wholesale renunciation of ties to tradition, family, and community, and she
criticized her for "clamor[ing] for new spheres of influence, or the reform
of the universe."[1] Most significant, however, Conway despised the New
Woman for introducing a scourge into American society, a disease to which
she believed she and other Catholic women were immune: "the modern
malaria of the morbid consciousness of womanhood."[2]

This is a curious turn of phrase, and it is especially puzzling to learn that
Conway first used it in 1893. Historians of U.S. women have interpreted the
1890s as a period in which many middle-class women were actively *cultivating* a consciousness of womanhood by attending women's colleges, working
in social settlements, joining women's clubs, and expanding their participation in reform movements and church organizations.[3] Because all of these
are understood as positive developments for American women, both in and
of themselves and as preconditions for the emerging feminist movement,
"morbid" seems a puzzling choice of adjective to define feminine consciousness.

Yet the modifier would have resonated with many of Conway's contemporaries. Margaret Buchanan Sullivan, as we have seen, spent the 1890s as
she had spent the previous two decades, using her position as "the best man

Katherine
Conway,
1886.

on the paper" as a way to deepen Catholics' understanding of their own history and to dispel myths about that tradition held by non-Catholic Americans. In establishing a women's college, Sister Julia McGroarty might have been more open to developing a feminine consciousness had she not been painfully aware that alliances with women outside her religious tradition, cast in a certain light, would place her primary objectives in jeopardy. Sister Assisium, who like Sister Julia inhabited a community of women, had a definition of sisterhood that did not extend very far beyond her bond with other members of the Sisters of St. Joseph. All three of these women's lives were marked by an overwhelming sense that being part of a Roman Catholic tradition distinguished them from other American women, a belief that shaped their respective responses to New Womanhood, women's higher education, social reform, and professionalization. Although it is true that all of them occasionally bristled at the limitations of their sex, it is also true that they felt far more marginalized as Catholics in American society than as women in the church. Consequently they established barriers that, while not exactly impermeable, limited their ability to identify with other women.

The same would be true of Katherine Conway. In her case, the limits of sisterhood manifested themselves most clearly in her protests against woman suffrage. Her views on the subject provide an ideal starting point to examine the factors behind Catholic women's collective lack of enthusiasm for suffrage, factors that are far more complex than many interpreters have appreciated. Though Americans of both sexes protested the enfranchisement of women on a wide variety of grounds, U.S. Catholics have been presented as exceptionally united in their opposition to women's political and legal equality. Historians have usually ascribed Catholics' lack of support to a prevailing ideology of gender that sharply circumscribed the public activities of Catholic women.[4] Other often cited explanations include widespread clerical opposition to the cause and, for Irish American Catholics, the persistence of Irish patterns of gender segregation that dissuaded women from political participation.[5]

Historian James J. Kenneally has written extensively about Catholic women and suffrage. In 1984, he observed that Catholic women's collective absence from the suffrage movement made it difficult to situate them within the history of American feminism. Suggesting that support for suffrage might not be the best barometer by which to gauge Catholic women's commitment to their own emancipation, Kenneally proposed that historians essentially circumvent the suffrage question and ask instead whether "Catholic women, to the same extent as Protestants, contribute[d] to the development of a more significant and meaningful life for their sisters."[6] Over the past two decades, historians of Catholic women have answered this second question with a resounding affirmative, producing an impressive body of scholarship on the legions of women religious who provided hundreds of thousands of Americans with education, social services, and medical care and on the many laywomen who organized labor unions, pioneered in charitable work, and spearheaded social reform.

While it is clear that this new research has enriched the history of U.S. Catholicism, far less certain is the extent to which it has permeated the narrative of American women's history. The problem Kenneally alluded to in 1984 persists: Catholic women hold little appeal for women's historians, who privilege as subjects women who either espouse or prefigure modern feminism, of which support for woman suffrage is simply the earliest of litmus tests. If skirting the question of Catholic women and antisuffrage has not solved the problem, perhaps it is time for historians to reexamine the question in greater depth. What exactly was it about woman suffrage that so alienated the majority of American Catholics?

In seeking to answer this question, we discover Catholic antisuffragists in the same historiographical position that antisuffragists in general occupied until fairly recently. Scholars had viewed them as retrograde, primarily because what little information we had about them was provided by their opponents. As historian Gerda Lerner pointed out, suffragists consistently underestimated both the scope and the significance of their opposition. Over the past decade, scholars such as Thomas Jablonsky, Jane Jerome Camhi, and Susan Marshall have shown that remonstrants (the term used for antisuffragists in the 1890s) were neither pawns of men nor dupes of special interest groups. Antisuffragist organizations were characterized by defined leadership structures, and they used well-implemented strategies that eventually came to resemble the very organizations they so vociferously scorned.[7]

None of the studies just mentioned, however, has focused explicitly on Roman Catholics. As a group they did not figure prominently in the campaign against suffrage for many of the same reasons they did not participate vigorously in the pro-suffrage movement: members of both constituencies were disproportionately drawn from the elite. As had been the case with regard to antisuffragists in general before the publication of these illuminating studies, information about Catholics and the suffrage debate has often been supplied by suffragists, many of whom assumed that "priest-ridden" Catholics obeyed official church prohibitions against supporting suffrage. At a minimum, a deeper explanation of Catholic antisuffragism complicates that assumption. Beyond that, it challenges the reliance on traditional rhetoric as a factor used to explain Catholic women's behavior. Katherine Conway, for example, rarely missed an opportunity to parrot the Catholic ideology of True Womanhood. Even Kenneally, who is ultimately sympathetic to Conway and other Catholic antisuffragists, interprets their use of rhetoric as evidence of their "inconsistency" on women's issues or the "constraints that faith imposed" on them. Other scholars are much harsher in their evaluation of Conway and other women who accepted traditional female roles. In her perceptive study of Catholics in Boston, for example,

Paula Kane argues that Conway "exhibited a disappointing reluctance to see what doors had been closed on her own life by not regarding women as a class doubly bound by gender and religion." In her study of Irish immigrant daughters, Hasia R. Diner classifies Conway as part of an Irish American group of women who "emphatically went on record against the ideas of the 'new women,'" interpreting Conway's antisuffrage views as a "puzzling problem and a historic irony."[8]

A comparison between Conway and leaders in the broader antisuffrage movement reveals interesting similarities and even more illuminating differences. Among the latter is this: whereas most antisuffragists launched their protests as classic American insiders, anxious to defend their wealth, status, and privilege, Conway approached the question very much as an outsider. She was convinced that because Catholics' experience in the United States had been indelibly marked by "the poison of utterly unfounded prejudices, misunderstanding, misrepresentation, and downright slander and calumny," their loyalty to the church would automatically supersede all other allegiances. All Catholics, she assumed, were "intent, first of all, on the glory of the Church in whose membership [they] are one."[9] This assumption blinded her in obvious ways. She believed, for example, that Catholics would overlook substantial ethnic and class differences to group themselves under the banner of religion. Yet in other respects Conway was clear eyed. She understood that many of her "sister women of diverse faiths" viewed her, "a daughter of the Old Faith," as inherently suspect. Thus she was attuned to the need to defend her religious interests from assaults against them.[10]

In the end the distinctive factor about Conway was not her opposition to suffrage but the way she perceived it as intertwined with the need to define an American Catholic identity. Though she and other Catholics would repeatedly insist that suffrage was "not a Catholic question," discussions about it, like those about the New Woman, higher education, social reform, and professionalization, were inextricably linked to larger Catholic questions in the Progressive Era: How should members of a minority religious tradition relate to Protestants? How might Catholic influence be increased? How could Catholics defend their church from perceived threats against it? These questions are important in understanding where to place Catholic women in the history of American feminism, a social movement that emerged in the second decade of the twentieth century. In many respects

Conway and other Catholic women were the historical foremothers of modern antifeminism, a subject that has recently received more attention with the rise of the New Right.[11] Yet they also testify to how much has changed over time, both for American women and for Catholics in the United States.

The reasons behind Conway's opposition to suffrage are not as straightforward as they appear to be. As is the case with Sullivan, McEvoy, and McGroarty, it is impossible to understand Conway's response to transformations in gender roles without appreciating how she perceived herself as a Catholic in American society. For Conway, even more than for the other three, answering that question begins with an exploration of Irish American ethnicity.

IRELAND, IRISH AMERICANS, AND CATHOLICISM
AT THE TURN OF THE CENTURY

Not long after young Kate McEvoy (later Sister Assisium) was expelled from her Philadelphia public school, another Katherine, also the second daughter of the family, was born to Irish immigrants in Rochester, New York. Her parents, James and Sarah O'Boyle Conway, had several advantages over their compatriots in Philadelphia and other eastern cities. James, a native of western Ireland, had arrived in Rochester shortly after the completion of the Erie Canal (1825). He soon prospered as a contractor overseeing the building of bridges and railroads throughout the region. As one of many new arrivals in western New York, James Conway avoided the harsh treatment that thwarted the Irish in Philadelphia and other more established urban centers. Years later, his daughter remembered Rochester as a place where "the native and foreign-born started with an equal chance." Katherine would spend most of her life, however, in Boston, a city in which she felt herself and other Irish Catholics to be the victims of "racial and religious prejudice."[12]

Had Katherine Conway ever met Sister Assisium, it is virtually assured they would have gotten along famously. They both believed wholeheartedly in the necessity of education under church auspices, and both distrusted state involvement in it.[13] Conway was also cut from the same cloth as Margaret Buchanan Sullivan, who became one of her closest friends. Conway's life paralleled Sullivan's in many respects. They were both educated by the Society of the Sacred Heart; both began their professional employment in a classroom; and both became writers who looked upon their work as a spiritual vocation. From her early days as a reporter in Rochester, Conway envisioned herself as an employee of the church's "publicity branch," and in the early 1890s she became an enthusiastic participant in the Apostolate of the Press, the loosely organized movement spearheaded by the Paulist fathers that sought to harness Catholic writing in service of the Old Faith.[14]

Conway also allied herself solidly with the forces of a Catholic past. Her biographical sketch reads like a list of "firsts": she became the first woman journalist in her native Rochester; the first woman editor of the *Pilot* (Boston); and one of the first lay professors at Saint Mary's College in Notre Dame, Indiana.[15] Yet Conway never championed herself as a "first" in anything; nor was she likely to acknowledge the pioneering efforts of her contemporaries. Like many other educated Catholic women, Conway admired and sought to emulate Catherine of Alexandria and Catherine of Siena. She once described Saint Mary's College as the modern counterpart of "a Benedictine convent of the first years of the sixteenth century, springing up again in America and brought right to date." It was also Conway who proclaimed Sister Julia McGroarty to be acting in a manner that was "perfectly logical, religiously and socially," in founding a Catholic women's college. By anchoring Saint Mary's and Trinity firmly to a Catholic past, Conway was able to become a faculty member at the former institution and a fervent supporter of the latter. An ally of Sister Julia's, she contributed to fund-raising efforts for Trinity, served on its Associate Board in Boston, and publicized the college through newspaper articles and essays.[16]

Katherine's mother, Sarah O'Boyle Conway, was reportedly descended from a highly educated family in Ireland, and she was evidently determined that her American-born children receive the best education available to them. For Katherine and her sisters, as for other daughters of upwardly mobile Irish American families, that meant attending a local convent school run by the Society of the Sacred Heart. Conway completed her course of study at St. Mary's Academy in Buffalo, also run by the Sacred Heart. With the encouragement of one of her teachers, whom she remembered as "a singularly gifted woman," she published her first poem at the age of fifteen.[17] As we have seen, the proscriptions against coeducation, combined with the dearth of Catholic women's colleges, prevented many

Catholic women from pursuing an education beyond the high school level before 1900. In some cases, however, Catholic women of Conway's generation found alternative means for advanced study, through either additional work at the academy level or private tutoring. Conway's opportunity came as a result of her family's friendship with Rochester's bishop, Bernard McQuaid. He was a champion of higher education for women—or at least those women who were "destined for the teaching or other learned professions." Upon her graduation from St. Mary's in Buffalo, Conway began a private course of study in church history, literature, and theology under McQuaid's tutelage. She compared her mentor to Saint Jerome, "who thought it no way beneath his dignity, but a good investment of his time, to instruct studious women." Conway maintained a close relationship with McQuaid until his death in 1909.[18]

Clearly, not all Irish American women followed the same path. But while the extent of Conway's education may have been extraordinary, the difference is, in some sense, only a matter of degree. Irish Americans in general valued education for their daughters as well as their sons. Historian Janet Nolan has explained how this emphasis on female education led many Irish immigrant daughters to become teachers, and indeed Conway's first regular employment was at the normal school of Nazareth Convent in Rochester, where she taught rhetoric and literature.[19]

Conway's real aspiration, however, was to become a writer. She would produce several volumes of poetry, as well as two novels, over the course of her lifetime, but her primary work would be in the field of journalism. While teaching at the normal school, she edited the *West End Journal*, a Catholic monthly published for the benefit of Catholic orphanages. In the early 1870s, just as Margaret Sullivan was securing her own position at the *Chicago Evening Post*, Conway became the first woman to write for the *Rochester Daily Union and Advertiser*. She also worked as a correspondent for several New York City newspapers. Conway's decision to pursue journalism as a career was determined largely by financial considerations, as James Conway had experienced a reversal of fortune in the early 1870s. Again in the manner of many Irish immigrant daughters, Conway used her earnings to supplement the family income.[20]

In 1883 Conway's writing attracted the attention of John Boyle O'Reilly, the editor of the *Pilot*, the most widely circulated Catholic newspaper in the country at that time. Impressed by Conway's talent, O'Reilly offered her an editorial position. The prospect of addressing a larger audience appealed to her; she accepted the invitation and moved to Boston. Here again, Irish gender traditions shaped her decision. Whereas living apart from family, and in particular from a male protector, would have been virtually inconceivable for a woman from an Italian or Polish background, Irish immigrant daughters were permitted a relatively wide berth. Katherine's elder sister, Mary Conway, traveled even farther from the family circle. In 1877, she went to Buenos Aires to open a school that she ran until her death in 1903.[21]

Far from severing her ties with her immediate family, Katherine's move to New England actually increased their dependence on her. Her parents soon followed her to Boston, and she became their sole means of financial support until they died within a few months of each other in 1892. Conway also supported her mentally ill sister, a burden of care that presented "a constant source of anxiety" and "robbed her of all peace."[22] That sister died in 1898. Once Mary died in faraway Buenos Aires five years later, Conway was left with James, the youngest and the only brother in the family, as her last surviving sibling. After spending a number of "rootless years," James had also settled in Boston, where Katherine helped him obtain a municipal job.[23] For the rest of her life she had a close relationship with him. Her diary records frequent visits to James's home, and it is evident that she formed a particularly close connection with one of his four children, her niece Helena. Conway's devotion to her brother and sisters was representative of many Irish American families, in which sibling connections often "constituted the most positive and least problematic relationships in Irish society."[24]

Conway's move to Boston sharpened her sense of ethnic and religious awareness in two ways. As noted previously, she perceived much more antipathy directed against Irish Catholics in Boston than she ever had in Rochester. New England, she believed, was the most inhospitable place in the country for Irish Catholics.[25] Another reason why Conway's move to Boston heightened her sense of ethnic identity was that with it she began a seven-year apprenticeship with John Boyle O'Reilly, a prominent Irish American. Born in Ireland in 1844, O'Reilly had been exiled to an Australian prison as punishment for his involvement in the Fenian uprising of 1866. In 1869 he escaped from captivity and traveled to the United States. He began to write for the Pilot a year later and assumed its editorship in 1878. O'Reilly's use of the paper to publish information about Ireland and Irish Americans prompted its nickname, "the Irishmen's Bible."[26]

O'Reilly was notoriously skeptical of women's abilities. Yet Conway's writing talent so impressed him that he eventually assigned her responsibility for the Catholic, editorial, and features sections of the newspaper. The admiration was mutual. Conway described O'Reilly as "a generous and considerate employer, a man to be thoroughly respected as well as liked by all those who are associated with him." O'Reilly's death in 1890 left her bereft, and throughout her life she would attribute most of her literary success to his guidance.[27]

Conway's connection with O'Reilly provided her access into Irish America's "first literary coterie." Other members included her colleague at the *Pilot*, James Jeffery Roche; Louise Imogen Guiney; and Mary Elizabeth Blake, the Irish American woman who had used Catherine of Siena to argue for a more expanded public role for modern Catholic women. According to literary historian Charles Fanning, O'Reilly's cohort represented the first encroachment on the Yankee Protestant literary establishment in New England.[28] John "Honey Fitz" Fitzgerald, mayor of Boston and good friend of Conway's, claimed that these writers "tore away the curtains of New England prejudice and won a definite position for Catholics (especially those of Irish blood) in the stronghold of the Puritans."[29]

It is Conway's fiction that demonstrates perhaps most clearly how closely her own fate was linked to that of other members of her ethnic group. Fanning has classified Conway as a successor to the "famine generation" of Irish writers, a group who had produced sentimental and moralistic novels that sent readers an unambiguous message: success and happiness in the United States depended upon hard work, family unity, and, most important, "keeping the faith." These writers had repeatedly contrasted the miserable fates of characters who "lost the faith" with the good fortune of those who remained loyal to Catholicism.[30] In contrast, Conway and other Irish American writers at the turn of the century left this simplistic sentimentality behind as they began to probe deeper into life in the Irish ethnic community. As Fanning noted, however, they had not yet adopted the intense self-scrutiny that would characterize a more mature generation of Irish America. Instead they are best known as a bridge between the didactic fiction of the early nineteenth century and the harsh realism of a novel such as James Farrell's *Studs Lonigan*, which would be published in the 1930s. Fanning has described Conway and other Irish American writers of this period as "caught and confused between *Heidi* and *Maggie: A Girl of the Streets*."[31]

This confusion surfaces throughout *Lalor's Maples*, an autobiographical novel in which Conway confronted many of the dilemmas that faced the newly middle-class Irish throughout the second half of the nineteenth century. The novel is set in Baychester, a thinly disguised version of Rochester, in 1860. The protagonist is Mildred Lalor, the second daughter of a prosperous Irish American contractor who had arrived penniless sixteen years before. The novel opens with the family's move to The Maples, a house that John Lalor built in a section of Baychester that had previously been the exclusive domain of "Yankees." The plot revolves around the impending loss of The Maples as a result of a series of financial setbacks, caused in part my Mrs. Lalor's extravagance and her desire for material goods. Palmer Ellis, a Protestant who holds the mortgage on their house, falls in love with Mildred and proposes marriage to her. Mildred's heart belongs to Raymond Fitzgerald, but her mother begs her to marry Ellis in order to rescue the family dwelling. After spending a month in prayer and in consultation with the bishop of Baychester, Mildred accepts Ellis's proposal in order to save her family's social status. When Ellis refuses to consent to a Catholic ceremony, however, she breaks the engagement and leaves Baychester for Boston. The vengeful Ellis forecloses, and the Lalors leave The Maples.[32]

Conway was among the first Irish American writers to introduce the archetype of the dominant mother and the central symbol of the house, both of which would become central features of Irish American literature. The novel also captures the anxiety about the costs of assimilation that had inspired much of Irish Catholics' wariness about the New Woman. But while Conway raised probing questions about the structure of the Irish American family and the dangers of being seduced by middle-class temptations, these questions ultimately proved too difficult for her to sustain. The novel's denouement bears more resemblance to that of *Heidi* than it does to that of *Maggie*: the villain repents after Mr. Lalor saves his life, and Ellis reveals that his first name is not Palmer but Patrick. His attempt to conceal his Irish Catholicism had led to his evil ways. As for the Lalors, they return happily to The Maples, and Mildred marries her true love.[33]

Though Conway's personal and professional life dovetailed neatly with patterns prevalent throughout Irish America, she rarely acknowledged how profoundly her ethnic background had shaped her life. She attributed her own sense of detachment from Ireland to the influence of her father. In contrast to his wife, who "idealized the land of her birth," James was truly "an American born in exile" whose love for his adopted country far exceeded his affection for his native one. Like her father, Conway professed an innate preference for "the present tense" and therefore claimed to be astonished when, on a trip to Europe in 1898, she responded powerfully to her first glimpse of Ireland. Until that moment, she contended, she had disavowed any connection to a country that so clearly belonged to the past. But when the Irish coast appeared on the horizon, she received a new appreciation for "the heritage of blood": "Then up leaped that quicksilver current, fluttering my heart, and throbbing in my temples, and filling my vision with the misty shapes of inherited memories." These surprising emotions evidently prompted her to take a more sympathetic view of the past tense, as she magnanimously forgave the young lads who "brought on yesterday's papers."[34]

Conway's blithe dismissal of Ireland as a "land of yesterday" implies that she believed that the country had no impact on her life other than a romantic attachment. The reality was much more complicated, for, as we have seen, Irish traditions played a decisive role in the person she became. Though she may have indeed inherited it from her insouciant father, Conway's sense of detachment, like the tensions that characterized her fiction, also reflected the ambivalence of a transitional generation. By 1900, two-thirds of Irish Americans had been born in the United States, and as their collective ties to Ireland grew more tenuous, many Irish Americans began to accentuate their Catholicism at the expense of their Irishness. As Timothy Meagher, Ellen Skerrett, and other scholars of the Irish experience in the United States have noted, ethnic identity increasingly found expression as religious identity in Irish American communities at the turn of the century.[35]

Certainly this phenomenon is evident among many of the women whose lives we have already explored. Even Margaret Buchanan Sullivan, who was without question among the most ardent of Irish American nationalists in the 1880s, had reduced her writing about the Irish and Ireland significantly in the 1890s as she focused more on Catholicism. And though they were both members of religious communities densely populated with Irish American women, neither Sister Julia McGroarty nor Sister Assisium McEvoy evinced any notable desire to ally themselves with other members of their ethnic group. In contrast to the obvious ways in which their lives were organized around religion, their references to their ethnic background were few and far between. Sister Julia may well have been speaking metaphorically when, upon seeing the Irish coast for the first time in her adult life, she described it as "a cloud on the horizon, misty and indistinct." For her part, Sister Assisium spoke of her Irish heritage only rarely, and when she did, she usually associated it with her Catholicism. At one point she noted, "There are few who love Ireland more than I for all she has suffered and done for the Faith."[36]

This muting of ethnic identity under the umbrella of religious identity is even more pronounced with respect to Conway, who believed that by the end of the nineteenth century "Irish" and "Catholic" had become, "for all practical purposes, convertible terms."[37] In marked contrast to her blithe dismissal of Ireland, Conway readily acknowledged her faith as her perennial guiding principle. Reflecting on why she always acted with "implicit Catholicity," she asked: "Wherefore if a Catholic really believes what he professes religiously, that his faith is precious above all worldly assets, and that it should guide him alike in all his acts and omissions, should he hesitate to reveal himself in any effort or under any circumstances as fully and completely a Catholic?"[38] This conviction had an obvious impact on her writing, as she believed it was very difficult to "draw the line between author and churchman" and that all Catholic writers were compelled to promote the interests of the church.[39] Speaking at the 1892 convention of the Apostolate of the Press, Conway outlined three goals of the Apostolate: strengthening the faith in practicing Catholics, rekindling it in lapsed ones, and convincing Protestants of the "Catholic truth." As was true for many other Catholic writers of the period, these goals became the defining purpose of her professional life.[40]

Conway's assumption that all Catholics would join her in acting with "implicit Catholicity" testified both to her sense of ethnic superiority over more recent Catholic immigrants and to her unwillingness to accept their demographic impact on the U.S. church. After all, she could not have been more wrong in her assessment that "Irish" and "Catholic" had become essentially interchangeable by the end of the nineteenth century. On the contrary, the Catholic Church was growing more ethnically diverse each year, as thousands of Catholics from eastern and southern Europe arrived on American shores. By 1915, members of twenty-eight different ethnic groups constituted the Catholic Church in the United States. In addition to arousing the suspicions of non-Catholic Americans, the presence of these newcomers created uneasiness among their more acclimated Irish co-religionists, who felt that their hard-won status was threatened by association with these more recent arrivals. As Skerrett noted in her studies of the Irish in Chicago, the increasing tendency to identify as Catholics prompted many Irish not only to "downplay their ethnic identity" but also to attempt "to force other Catholic immigrants to do the same."[41]

Conway's impulse to conflate Irishness and Catholicity, along with the myopia of privilege that made it possible, was hardly uncommon in a place like late nineteenth-century Boston, for it was there that the episcopate, the clergy, and religious communities were characterized by a preponderance of Irish Americans. Even other members of the laity assumed Irish hegemony over other Catholic ethnic groups. Marian Dogherty, for instance, was another Boston Irish American whose career as a teacher in the city's public schools roughly coincided with Conway's years at the *Pilot*. In her memoirs, Dogherty recalled the day that Jennie Soreno, one of her most promising students and the children of two Italian immigrants, had refused to identify herself as Italian in response to the query of a visiting statistician. The girl's unwillingness to label herself an Italian mystified Dogherty as well as the principal of the school until a visit from her father clarified the situation:

> PRINCIPAL: "But, Mr. Soreno, if both you and your wife are native Italians, does that not make Jenny of Italian blood? She is not English or Scotch or Jewish; don't you see that?"
> MR. SORENO (in accented English): "No, no, signora, 'scusa me teacher, scusa me. Jennie not Italian—never! She born in Boston. She Irish Roman Catholic!"[42]

Though the time that elapsed between this incident and Dogherty's recounting of it may well have distorted her recollection, the presumption that an Italian immigrant child would have identified herself as an Irish Roman Catholic is suggestive of the kind of wishful thinking that underlay Conway's belief that all Catholics would, like her, overlook differences of class, race, and ethnicity and allow religion to determine all their "acts and omissions."

If Conway's tendency to understate the strength of ethnic and class bonds and to overstate the power of religious ones is important for understanding how she perceived herself in relation to other Catholics, it is even more significant in illuminating her relationship with non-Catholics. From her childhood in New York through her old age in New England, Conway persistently divided the world into the people who shared her faith and those who did not. Whenever she lectured, she recorded in her diary how many of "her own"—Catholics—had been present in the audience. It was not that this strict dividing line could not be crossed; in fact, she often relished the opportunity to associate with non-Catholics so that she could "rub in" things that were not "known to [them] as they should be."[43] But the divide was always there, and it would become a decisive factor in shaping Conway's relationship with non-Catholic women and her resistance to woman suffrage and, later, to what she and others perceived as suffrage's "ugly attendant," feminism.[44]

CATHOLICS AND THE CASE AGAINST SUFFRAGE

Katherine Conway launched her formal protests against suffrage in the mid-1890s, when she contributed to a series of roundtable discussions entitled "The Woman Question among Catholics" in the *Catholic World* and *Donahoe's Magazine*.[45] These and other articles that appeared in Catholic periodicals followed a nearly two-decade hiatus in substantial discussions devoted specifically to woman suffrage. The reasons for this gap have little to do with events in Catholic circles and instead reflect the rise, fall, and reemergence of suffrage as a powerful force on the American scene. Though the suffrage movement had been set in motion at the Seneca Falls Convention in 1848, it had weakened twenty years later when its leaders had disagreed bitterly over whether woman suffrage should take a back seat to the post–Civil War effort to enfranchise African American men. This dispute split the movement in half, and it was only after the two competing branches reunited in 1890 that woman suffrage began to gather the momentum and grassroots support that would culminate in the passage of the Nineteenth Amendment thirty years later.[46]

Though it was widely assumed that the Catholic Church as an institution was categorically opposed to women suffrage, most discussions of it—both pro and con—began with the proviso that Catholics were free to express their own opinion, as the church had adopted no official position. In 1913, the *Ave Maria* quoted one archbishop's reminder that "no matter how strongly opposed any Catholic may be to the grant of the franchise of women, he should bear in mind that until the Church has pronounced upon the question, any other Catholic is quite free to hold and express a contrary view."[47] Even Cardinal Gibbons, whose opposition was well known to both Catholics and non-Catholics, always stipulated that he was only offering his opinion on the question, as the church "has neither approved nor disapproved" of woman suffrage.[48]

Writing in the *Catholic World* in 1915, Helen Haines used the metaphor of "longitude" and "latitude" to explain to the secular press the complexity of the suffrage question among Catholics. While longitude denoted "the line of thought and action which converge toward the two poles of faith and morals," latitude defined "great zones—fervid, temperate or austere— which have produced so infinite a variety of flora and fauna." The diversity, which "arose from individual freedom which the perverse critic affects not to grasp," made it impossible to identify one Catholic position on the war that was then raging in Europe. It also made it difficult to discern a unified Catholic position on "another great question—the political enfranchise- ment of women."[49] Though Haines's article appeared relatively late in the game, when suffrage had already been passed in several states and when the movement had garnered much more mainstream support, her argument had been sound all along: never at any point did the American bishops or the Vatican release an official statement on woman suffrage, and there had always been and would continue to be Catholics on both sides of the debate.

Haines herself supported suffrage, and not surprisingly she reminded her readers that her position constituted no significant break with the past. She pointed out that Margaret Brent, a Catholic from sixteenth-century Virginia, had been one of the earliest American crusaders for women's vote. Haines also cited a number of contemporary Catholic women who agreed with her. Among them was Jane Campbell, who enthusiastically combined her service to the American Catholic Historical Association with leadership of the Philadelphia Suffrage League. As we have already seen, Campbell justified her support for suffrage by pointing to the considerable public influence that certain Catholic women had exercised in the Middle Ages. Sara McPike, a Catholic supporter of suffrage, also suggested an association with Catholic women of the past when she founded a pro-suffrage group in New York City named after Saint Catherine of Siena.[50]

Haines could have pointed to a number of other pro-suffrage Catholic women. Many of them were Irish American, including Marguerite Moore, the Irish American nationalist who, as we saw in the first chapter, had gone to such lengths to distinguish the savior of Foxford, Ireland, from the New Woman. Moore spoke in support of suffrage as early as 1894.[51] Margaret Haley, an Irish immigrant daughter born in Joliet, Illinois, in 1861, became a public school teacher in Chicago and subsequently a leader of the Chicago Teachers' Federation. Like many other Irish American teachers, Haley supported suffrage because she believed that enfranchising women would lead to the allocation of more money to schools.[52] Other Irish American women explained their support of suffrage by comparing their battle for enfranchisement with the Irish struggle for home rule. At the very least, the prosuffrage views of these and other Irish American women challenge the argument that the "cultural baggage" of gender segregation dissuaded Irish women from political participation in the United States.[53]

Like the Catholic women who supported suffrage, the handful of priests who spoke in favor of it were also quick to point out that they spoke as individuals rather than as mouthpieces for the church. Anticipating Helen Haines's complaint, the Reverend Elliott Ross of Chicago objected to being asked to present the Catholic view of suffrage: "For the Catholic view of this question, to put it in an Irish way, is that there is no Catholic view. You might just as well speak of the Catholic view of the tariff, or the weather, or the corn crop. There is no Catholic view of suffrage, because it is not a Catholic question." Ross was one of several clerics whose testimonies in favor of suffrage appeared in pamphlet form in 1914.[54] In many cases, these priests hailed from states that had already granted women partial suffrage, a fact that some clerical opponents suggested should be used to undermine their credibility. Nevertheless, they offered their testimony as proof that women were capable of using the vote wisely and judiciously, thereby challenging the argument that enfranchisement would contaminate the family and society in general.[55]

Not all clerical supporters came from places where women had already secured the right to vote. Among the most prominent of these was Katherine Conway's mentor, Bishop Bernard McQuaid of Rochester, who spoke in favor of suffrage at a national convention in 1904, thirteen years before suffrage passed in New York.[56] The fact that Conway took the position opposite that of the American bishop she most admired suggests that clerical opposition and pressure is an inadequate explanation for her views.

Like others, she recognized that Catholics were free to express their own opinions on matters that did not relate to dogma. When it came to literature and politics, she once observed, "The Church asks us simply to put conscience into both."[57] Conway's reference to politics is also telling, as it calls into question another common explanation offered for antisuffragism: Irish women's adherence to patterns of gender segregation, which supposedly prevented them from participating in the all-male domain of politics. As reluctant as Conway was to tout the influence of ethnicity on her choices, she attributed her own unflagging support of the Democratic Party to her Irish background, maintaining that she was political "both by nature and inheritance." She often proved adept at using party politics to her advantage. She once pulled strings to obtain a city job for her brother, and long before she was able to vote, she was in the thick of Boston politics as editor of the *Republic*, a paper owned by Boston's Irish Democratic mayor John "Honey Fitz" Fitzgerald.[58]

So the question remains: If the Church did permit so much latitude on the question, and if Irish gender traditions did not necessarily preclude participation in politics, why did Katherine Conway—and the majority of Catholic women—remain unpersuaded by arguments in favor of woman suffrage? The most convenient answer, of course, is to attribute their opposition to the pervasive influence of a restrictive Catholic gender ideology. Indeed, it is true that Conway repeatedly endorsed Catholic proscriptions against women's public role, observing that "it seems settled beyond question that woman, as woman, can have no vocation to public life." In a popular guidebook for Catholic girls, she insisted that "the vocation of the overwhelming majority of women is to wifehood and motherhood; . . . the fixed aversion, or at least indifference, of most of them to public work" is a safeguard "raised by God's own hand about the sanctuary of life."[59]

Conway allowed for several exceptions to this general rule. Catholic sisters, she pointed out, were often exempted from the exclusively private life because their higher calling forced them to perform educational or charitable services in the public sphere. Of course, she noted, since the "instinct against publicity" was intensified in them, nuns were actually the exception that proved the rule that Catholic women were preternaturally adverse to public life. In other cases, "some women by virtue, not of their womanhood, but of their strong individualities, marked ability, and the demands of unusual environment, may have a special call to public duty."[60]

Conway's contemporaries criticized her for allegedly including herself in this category. Mary Dowd, a schoolteacher from New Hampshire, was almost certainly referring to Conway when she wrote, "One brainy, strong-minded woman stands out in the broadest, most glaring light of publicity, that of the press, and advises other women to court seclusion, gingerly admitting, however, that there are a few exceptional women who may choose public lives. But she leaves the impression that such examples are so very few that the reader would never dare to consider herself one."[61]

Conway did consider herself exceptional, but for a different reason than Dowd implied. She believed the secret to her own success, like that of most extraordinary women, "lay largely in the necessity of providing for the dependent parent or household, which forced them to do their best work, for the sake of larger money returns."[62] Since Conway was the sole supporter of her parents and sister, her finances were always precarious. Even after her dependents had died, Conway remained perennially anxious about money, a situation that resulted in part from the refusal of some of her male superiors to pay her a salary commensurate with her responsibilities. Given her lifelong status as a self-supporting woman, it is no wonder that she was very sympathetic to any crusade that helped to secure rights for women who earned their own living. She agreed with Mary Blanche O'Sullivan, another Boston Catholic writer, that the energies of "women's rights advocates" would be better spent pursuing a much nobler cause, "the emancipation of working women."[63] Conway's perennially fragile economic position underscores an important point: though her education, ethnic background, and social status may have placed her in a relatively privileged position within the American Catholic community, she was hardly a member of a wealthy elite, a distinction that is important to consider in analyzing her relationship to the broader suffrage movement.

Conway joined the Massachusetts Association Opposed to the Extension of Further Suffrage to Women (MAOEFSW), a state organization founded in 1895 that subsequently became a model for similar groups in other states. She was also a member of another antisuffrage organization in New York, the state that she would consider her "home" long after she left it permanently in 1883. But she never became a leader in either group. As Thomas Jablonsky has explained, the ethnic and class composition of both the Catholic and the Jewish population ensured that their members would be virtually absent from the top offices of antisuffrage organizations. Molly

Elliot Seawell, the lone Catholic among the leadership of the MAOEFSW, may have been correct in asserting that the suffrage movement "necessarily involved privileged classes."[64] But the same could be said of antisuffrage organizations, and while Conway enjoyed a number of economic and social advantages over many other American Catholics, her lack of inherited wealth, her ongoing financial problems, and her daily work demands placed her in a different position than that of the majority of remonstrants.

There was certainly a great deal of overlap in the rhetoric used by Conway and by other antisuffragists. Like many of them, Conway claimed that a woman could exercise more political influence through her exalted social position than she could through the ballot. It was for this reason, she explained, that she had joined the New York Society for the Political Education of Women, which promoted "the acquisition of much and intimate knowledge of political affairs, believing that with this and the tact and high standards of good women they could most effectively influence city, state, or national politics."[65] Conway also echoed other remonstrants in her insistence that Catholic women would simply vote with the heads of their household. She worried, too, that voting would compromise women's special role as mothers and caregivers. Ironically, many suffragists shared this assumption of women's moral superiority and argued that women should be allowed to apply their maternal skills to society at large.[66]

Beyond the parallel use of traditionalist rhetoric, it is possible to discern other similarities between Conway and other leading antisuffragists. Susan Marshall has argued, for example, that remonstrants relied on traditionalist language to mask the true extent of their political activism.[67] Certainly this was true of Conway, who had long utilized obfuscation as strategy to challenge the prescriptions of True Womanhood. Working for the church's "publicity branch" permitted Conway to live a public role without challenging Catholic True Womanhood. While she admitted to a friend that "few Catholic women have seen as much of public life as I have," she presented a different picture of herself publicly. "I am in no sense a public woman," she told one interviewer. "I hide away at my editorial desk in the *Pilot* office with the cloak of my beloved profession wrapping its protective folds around me." This view was not uncommon; many Catholic women saw writing as a spiritual vocation rather than a public one.[68]

Despite these similarities, there were deep differences between Conway and the majority of antisuffragists. Marshall and others have shown that remonstrants predominantly used their protests to protect their positions of privilege and access to power. Conway, by contrast, opposed woman suffrage from a marginal position. This marginalization was not merely economic, although, as previously noted, she clearly she did not enjoy the "stable, cushioned surroundings" that most remonstrants did.[69] Instead, it was as a Catholic that Conway felt herself to be most distant from privilege and power in American society. How deeply she perceived the suffrage movement as a threat to her religious interests becomes clear upon a deeper examination of what lay behind her distaste for "the morbid consciousness of womanhood."

"TRUE SOLUTION OF THE WOMAN QUESTION"

On the surface, Conway's objection to feminine consciousness had nothing at all to do with religion. She had coined the phrase "morbid consciousness of womanhood" in 1893 in reference not to suffrage but to a proposed Woman's Day at the World Columbian Exposition in Chicago. In a series of letters to William Onahan, the chair of the exposition's Catholic Congress, Conway insisted that women should be included on the basis of merit, not sex, and that segregating them would lead not only to paltry attendance but also to substandard quality. Integrating women on the regular program, in contrast, would show "the observant non-Catholic public that clever women are not a nine days' wonder in the Catholic Church."[70] Conway repeated her arguments publicly in a *Pilot* editorial: "It is by no means good for the feminine intellectual health to be dwelling incessantly on any work in this world of men and women as exclusively women's work. Such habit of mind creates false and inadequate standards, and is the fertile source of narrowness and triviality." She further insisted that "all the great work of the world represents the united efforts of men and women. . . . We trust that Catholic women . . . will escape what they have heretofore escaped— the modern malaria of the morbid consciousness of womanhood."[71]

Woman's Day proceeded as scheduled in spite of Conway's protests. Conway delivered a paper on Catholic reading circles and the Catholic summer school a day earlier and held firm to her conviction that fostering sex pride would inevitably lead to inferior work and lower standards. She never reconciled herself to the prospect of separate events for women. More than a decade later, she wrote that "every compilation and periodical restricted to the representation of women writers, every 'woman's building' or 'women's exhibit' . . . every 'women's day' in a convention, religious or otherwise, is a distinct drawback to worthy and dignified work among women."[72]

Conway would subsequently apply the argument she had made against Woman's Day to the burgeoning woman suffrage movement. Allowing that the wisdom of the woman suffrage movement was itself subject to debate, Conway was distressed by what she understood to be the movement's "reflex action," the tendency to encourage women to think of themselves primarily as women. According to Conway, this "reflex action" was positive in that it "accelerated the opening of new and befitting avenues for the woman wage-earner on the industrial or intellectual lines." A far more ominous effect of the "reflex action" was that it "exaggerated feminine self-consciousness and endeavored to introduce into women's life that baseless thing, sex pride."[73] "Who," she wondered, "would protect the individual woman from the tyranny of the organized woman?"[74] Conway predicted that Catholic women would find the suffrage movement particularly unappealing in this regard, given that they evinced "no appreciable tendency . . . to organize aggressive or defensive leagues of women as women, no consciousness of the distinctly feminine—as apart from human—interests to be agitated for; in short, no morbid consciousness of womanhood."[75]

Conway's belief that the descriptor "womanly" was inherently derisive speaks volumes about her struggle to succeed in a profession dominated by men. Her editor, John Boyle O'Reilly, once praised Conway for having "the heart of a woman and the brain of a man."[76] However distasteful this compliment would be to a modern feminist, it pleased Conway immensely. She would, in fact, use the same compliment in her eulogy for her friend Margaret Sullivan, who, noted Conway, was "ranked, from the first decade of her career, among the most eminent men of her profession."[77] Conway once claimed that "if you want from [a woman] her true opinion of the womanly, especially in the intellectual order, just note how she purrs with delight, if some work of hers is described as virile. We all do it."[78]

This argument that separation was actually counterproductive to women's pursuit of equality surfaced elsewhere in the campaign against women's enfranchisement. As part of her case against suffrage, Boston novelist Margaret Deland echoed Conway in describing the Women's Building at the 1893 World's Fair "mortifying and humiliating" to women. "How much better," she mused, "if the [women's art] had been placed among their peers, and not set aside as noticeable because women did them. . . . Such insistence upon sex in work is an insult to the work, and to the sex, too."[79] But though Conway might have agreed with Deland on this point, the two women found little other common ground.[80] In fact, Conway despised Deland for reasons that are hardly mysterious: as with many antisuffragists, Deland's opinions were shaped by deep-rooted prejudices against Catholics, particularly those of Irish descent. In a 1910 essay that appeared in the *Atlantic Monthly*, Deland accused the New Woman of being so hungry for power that she was willing to extend the vote even to "her cook." According to Deland, the New Woman was "willing to multiply by two the present ignorant and unconscientious vote which many thoughtful persons, anxiously doubting democracy, believe is already threatening our national existence." In case the implication was not entirely clear, Deland spoke more specifically, observing that "we have suffered many things at the hand of Patrick; the New Woman would add Bridget also."[81] Deland was not alone in holding these sentiments, as the prospect of "the ignorant Catholic vote"—particularly the ignorant Irish Catholic vote—motivated many antisuffragists, who worried that "should the women of New York State obtain the franchise, the Pope of Rome will become the next President of the United States."[82]

Ironically, if anti-Catholicism pervaded the campaign against woman suffrage, it also shaped the crusade in favor of it. Early on, suffragists such as Elizabeth Cady Stanton argued that Catholics were unable to comprehend the American ideal of individual rights.[83] Later, as women with wealth, status, and privilege increasingly joined the cause, the case for suffrage rested on the argument that if African American, uneducated, or "foreign" men were able to vote, then white, middle-class women surely deserved the franchise. Although the racial and class biases of the suffragists are widely acknowledged by historians, scholars have paid little attention to the significance of the fact that the majority of the uneducated and foreign "undesirables" were Catholic.[84]

Many contemporary Catholic observers, in contrast, were well aware of the religious biases lurking behind the arguments in favor of extending the vote to women. We have already seen how Catholic clerics blamed the apocryphal accounts of Mâcon on vengeful woman suffragists, and even ordinary women presumed that it was suffragists who were the architects of the "have women souls?" debate. One Catholic woman from Chester, Pennsylvania, was not at all surprised to discover a group of "ardent suffragists" repeating "horrible calumny" of Mâcon at an Emergency Aid meeting in the city.[85] Catholic publications regularly called attention to the class and religious biases of prominent proponents of suffrage. In 1912, for example, the *New World*, Chicago's Catholic newspaper, accused Jane Addams of being "badly afflicted with nativism." It cited as evidence Addams's recent testimony before Congress, in which she had reportedly argued that by doubling the total vote woman suffrage would "materially decrease the proportion of the immigrant vote to the total vote," thereby diminishing the adverse effects of the former.[86]

Thomas Shields, Catholic University professor and founder of the Catholic Sisters College, also highlighted the biases that undergirded suffrage arguments. Shields himself actually supported limited suffrage for women. He argued that, because they played such an influential role in shaping citizens, all teachers of children, nuns included, should have the "power and duties of the ballot." But in 1907 he published a lengthy imagined conversation between a priest, several prominent educators, a Catholic mother, and a suffragist who was also a graduate of a non-Catholic college. In one of her frequent tirades, the suffragist rants that "man has always shown himself impatient of every attempt made by woman to gain her rights. He grants suffrage to the illiterate, to the ex-convict, to the negro, and to the hordes of immigrants from Russia and southern Europe. . . . But woman must not be given the ballot lest by its use she might gain her freedom!" Of course, the Catholic mother eventually put this disagreeable woman in her place by demonstrating that true freedom and contentment were not to be found in the ballot but under the auspices of the Catholic family and the church.[87]

For her part, Conway placed "women-suffrage leagues" in the same category as the virulent anti-Catholic American Protective Association.[88] She claimed that Catholic women, though disinterested in suffrage in general, would happily use the franchise to combat "the attacks of bigotry on the civil and religious rights of any citizens.[89] In both her speeches and published material, Conway often paired criticism of suffrage with a spirited defense of Catholicism's suitability for the United States. In *The Christian Gentlewoman and the Social Apostolate*, for instance, she followed her critique of suffrage's "reflex action" with a criticism of the people who would perceive the Catholic Church as "narrow." Any "intelligent reader of history," she contended, could only conclude that the Catholic Church was the only church "with room about her hearth for all mankind," paraphrasing James Russell Lowell's description of the United States.[90]

Conway's perception of the suffrage movement as anti-Catholic, combined with her own desire to act with "implicit Catholicity," points to the deeper reason behind her disdain for the "morbid consciousness of womanhood." While she might have been convinced that "sex pride" would have a detrimental effect on American women, she believed that a heightened feminine consciousness would present a much graver threat to American Catholics. By founding and joining separate women's groups, Conway argued, Catholics were in danger of imitating Protestant Americans. The "woman business," she insisted, was "overdone in non-Catholic circles."[91] The establishment of too many Catholic women's organizations would perpetuate the "the erroneous notion popular in certain circles that Catholicity cannot make its way except in borrowed attire." More ominous, it would also imply that the bonds of womanhood were somehow stronger than the bonds of religion, a proposition that Conway considered to be very dangerous.[92] Unless Catholic women identified themselves primarily as Catholics, she feared, the "morbid consciousness of womanhood" threatened to fracture the Catholic community by gender at a time when its cohesiveness was of paramount importance. As Catholics struggled to overcome the religious prejudices of their fellow citizens, it would be foolish to segregate themselves by sex or, for that matter, by any other category.

The Catholic community in the United States, already divided by ethnicity, class, and race, was nowhere near as unified as Conway believed it to be. Nonetheless, Conway assumed that Catholics would present a united front not only in the battle for their own acceptance in the United States but also in the war to defeat the larger forces that she and others deemed antithetical to Catholicism. Her complaints that "individualism" found its fullest expression in suffrage tapped into language that Catholic intellectuals of the period used to critique liberalism, and when she cautioned that the "state" would overreach its authority in foisting suffrage upon an unwilling population, she echoed Catholic educators' response to federal and local attempts to assert state authority over parochial schools.[93]

Other Catholics mentioned the threat of socialism and the "tyranny of the state" in their arguments against suffrage.[94] Martha Moore Avery, for example, was a former socialist whose 1903 conversion to Catholicism had resulted in part from the influence of her convent-educated daughter who had become a nun. In a series of articles, Avery made clear that it was not outdated notions of women's intellectual inferiority that prompted her to oppose suffrage but her conviction that suffragists supported abortion, birth control, and state efforts to supplant the family with the individual as the key unit organizing civil society. In addition to these evils Avery raised the specter of secularization, interpreting suffrage as one plank in a larger rebellion against religion.[95]

The suffrage movement did not, as Avery and other Catholic critics claimed, "smack of irreligion."[96] It was, however, accompanied by a critique of patriarchal religion. The most radical of these critiques was Matilda Joslyn Gage's *Woman, Church and State*, which had contained among its many "objectionable" passages an account of the "have women souls" debate at Mâcon. Equally disturbing to many Christians was Elizabeth Cady Stanton's 1895 publication of *The Woman's Bible*. Though some Catholic antisuffragists dismissed Stanton's Bible as "a painful absurdity," other Catholics perceived it as part of an attempt to destroy religion. The editors of Philadelphia's *Catholic Standard*, for example, wrote that while it was one thing for Catholics "to amuse ourselves with the 'new woman,' [and] to laugh at her caprices," the New Woman's version of the Bible was no laughing matter. Stanton and her collaborators, the editors insisted, had "turned into a mockery the truths of both 'Old' and 'New.' "[97]

Stanton and Gage collaborated on the voluminous *History of Woman Suffrage*, which, according to Avery, demonstrated that the premise of the woman suffrage movement was that "woman would not only outgrow the power of the priesthood, and religious superstition, but would invade the pulpit, interpret the Bible anew from her own standpoint, and claim an equal voice (with men) in all ecclesiastical councils."[98] Avery interpreted this premise as proof that the modern woman suffrage movement had its origins in "that rebellion inaugurated more than 300 years ago," the Reformation. Citing Jane Addams as a prominent example of a woman whose interest in women's rights had led her to turn her back on religion, Avery insisted that Addams's popularity showed that "the religion of women dominant in the secular affairs of our country" was certainly not Christianity.[99]

Of course, Avery presented the Catholic Church, not Christianity in general, as the historical and ongoing emancipator of women, a fact that distinguished her and other Catholics from Protestants who claimed that

Christianity had rescued women from the perils of heathenism. The appendix to Stanton's *Woman's Bible* contained a series of responses to the question, "Have the teachings of the Bible advanced or retarded the emancipation of women?" The replies ranged from Josephine K. Henry's clear condemnation of the Christian Church as modern civilization's most tyrannical and unjust institution with regard to women to the more measured reply of Frances Willard, the founder of the Woman's Christian Temperance Union, who pointed out that "the nations which treat women with the most consideration are all Christian nations." Among the evidence Henry used to support her claim was the fact that when Christianity was "at the zenith of its power . . . it was denied that woman has a soul." Willard, meanwhile, repeated an argument often made by Christian missionaries, reformers, and advocates of American imperialism: Christianity's elevation of women signified its cultural superiority over heathen nations.[100]

As we have seen, American Catholics often put a much finer distinction on the institution that had rescued women from heathenism: it was *Catholic* Christianity, rather than Christianity in general, that would guard women's rights as attentively in the future as it had done in the past. Avery, for example, contended that women's rights were best secured in "the Court of Rome," not through the ballot box.[101] Conway made the same distinction in her antisuffrage arguments. By turning their back on religion, she insisted, suffragists were following along the dangerous path that they had chosen during the Reformation. Indeed, daughters of the "old historic Church" continued to be granted so many privileges by the church that they would find any rights proffered by the government to be superfluous. Conway maintained that, thanks largely to the protection their church afforded them, "Catholic women did not feel that their interests are menaced from any quarter." In fact she "marveled" that Catholics even raised "the woman question," pointing out that the sanctuary and the pulpit were the only doors the church had kept closed to women.[102]

As we have seen, Conway and Avery were hardly the first to insist that Roman Catholics had emerged from the Reformation divide as the true heirs to Christianity's historical role as the emancipator of women. Nor were they the first to apply this premise to suffrage. In 1869, English convert Blanche E. Murphy had written one of the first discussions about suffrage to appear in the *Catholic World*. Whereas other Catholic antisuffragists relied on the argument that women were divinely consigned to the domestic sphere, Murphy presented her case with a different twist. The history and tradition of women in the church, she argued, testified that women's best hope for the future lay in their solidarity with other Catholics, rather than with the women's rights advocates who were overwhelmingly Protestant. Using an argument that would soon become very familiar to Roman Catholics, Murphy suggested that "women's rights' associations" had become necessary only because "women's wrongs" had been multiplied since the Reformation. "The present movement," she claimed, "is a reaction against the Protestant atmosphere of repression which has suffocated women's highest aspirations for three hundred years." Throughout her four-part survey of the history of women and the church, Murphy argued that the Roman Catholic Church had "historically marked out a noble margin for women's genius in the state and in public life."[103]

Conway and Avery were among the many Catholics who revived Murphy's argument after the reunited woman suffrage movement began to gain more strength in the 1890s. In 1893, Conway's friend Mary Elizabeth Blake claimed that the "true solution of the woman question could be found in the Church." Because it could help women respond to their newly active lives, it was the church and its "saving grace," rather than women's rights advocates, that deserved Catholic women's loyalty. Blake's life closely paralleled both Conway's and Margaret Sullivan's: Born in Ireland, Blake was educated by the Society of the Sacred Heart and attempted in much of her published work to spread the Catholic truth among nonbelievers. Unlike either Sullivan or Conway, however, Blake was a married mother of eleven, a status that gave her more credibility when she described suffragists and other women who came from "childless homes" as "a menace to the nation."[104]

Blake, Avery, and Conway all publicly lent credence to the argument that Catholic women "had nothing to gain by suffrage." They agreed that "the true and consistent action" of the Catholic Church "as the champion and protector of women's rights, is sufficient assurance of its future."[105] All of them often called upon Catholic women of the past to buttress their arguments against suffrage. Conway, for instance, cited various examples of Catholic women throughout history who gained access to power and education despite "the absence of a woman suffrage movement."[106] Among them were many of the same figures who had been touted by male clerics seeking to dispute the notion that the church was the historical oppressor of women. Speaking to group of non-Catholic women, Conway pointed to the University of Bologna, eight centuries old, as evidence that the church had never "underrated women's intellectual activity." In fact, she noted, the female graduates of Bologna far outnumbered educated women of "our favored, and perhaps too boastful times, when Columbia's one female graduate evokes national applause."[107] She believed that it was merely "fear of Papal sympathies" that had prevented non-Catholic women from acknowledging the "name and fame" of women such as Catherine of Siena, Joan of Arc, and Isabella of Castile. Like many of the writers who sought to craft the Catholic pages of American history, Conway also believed that prejudice against her religious faith had masked the contribution of women such as the Louisiana Ursulines and Elizabeth Ann Seton.[108] These daughters of the Old Faith, of course, had been successful, accomplished, and content in the halcyon days before the "woman suffragist" had arisen and complicated the relationship between the sexes.[109]

Like other Catholic men and women, Conway offered these historical figures not only as lessons from the past but also as guides for the future. Not surprisingly, the woman she pointed to most consistently as a model for Catholic women to emulate was Mary, the mother of Jesus. Certainly it is true that, like many of her contemporaries, Conway emphasized Mary's domesticity and obedience. In devotional and advice literature of the late nineteenth century, Mary was often anachronistically cast as a "housewife" who tended to the needs of husband and child. According to the *Catholic Girls Guide*, published in 1905, the Blessed Mother made her home inviting and comfortable for Saint Joseph when he came home from work. For his part, Joseph was pleased to see "his evening meal ready and everything as orderly as possible."[110] Eleanor Cecilia Donnelly also used Mary's status as a housewife to protest the extension of the vote to women. Since Mary was the "immaculate source" from whom all rights flowed, she observed that "the stream could not rise higher than the source." Catholic women, in imitation of Mary, should therefore content themselves with domestic pursuits and eschew political ones.[111] These and other examples support one contemporary feminist scholar's observation that "if the Protestant Church has succeeded in oppressing women by eliminating Mary, the Catholic Church has oppressed women by domesticating her."[112]

But while Mary could undoubtedly be used to control and contain women, she was always a more elastic symbol than these idealistic descriptions would suggest. In arguments that presaged the ones feminist theologians would make a century later, a few Catholic women in the late nineteenth century emphasized that what was distinct about Mary was not her obedience and virginity, as clerics would have women believe, but her courage and ability to act independently, as she did at the wedding feast at Cana. Mary Dowd, specifically responding to the analogy Eleanor Donnelly had made, observed that if all good Catholic women should be housewives, as the Blessed Virgin was, then all men should be artisans because Jesus was a carpenter. Dowd used this fallacy as her basis to argue in support of woman suffrage.[113] In another contribution to the discussion, Philadelphia Catholic Mary Spellissy protested the frequent characterizations of the Blessed Mother as deferential and submissive. These portraits, she argued, led Catholic women to "commit serious blunders whose consequences are far-reaching and deplorable."[114]

While Conway did not carry the argument this far, she did depend upon Mary not only to differentiate Catholic women from seekers of women's rights but also to justify expanding opportunities for Catholic women. In 1889, Conway was invited to speak at Boston's Women's Educational and Industrial Union, an organization that had been founded in 1877 by upperclass Boston women to support the working women of the city. The invitation to Conway, the first Catholic to address the organization, was no doubt intended to help build this bridge between social classes. Acutely conscious of this distinction, Conway chose to speak on the Blessed Virgin Mary, declaring that there was no other subject on which "a daughter of the Old Faith" and "her sister-women of diverse faiths" could find "more points of agreement and fewer of divergence."[115] But the remainder of the speech, which she devoted to a discussion of Catholic women's special alliance with Mary, belied the ecumenism of her opening statement. In claiming that "no woman has done more for the elevation of her sex than this Blessed Mother of whom I speak," Conway identified Mary as the inspiration for modern Catholic women's intellectual and economic advancement.

Conway's assumption that her "sister-women of diverse Faiths" envied Catholic women their ability to draw inspiration from Mary was not entirely unfounded. As Sally Cunneen has recently shown, a number of nineteenth-century Protestant reformers evinced a surprising enthusiasm for Mary as a model for women. Margaret Fuller, Anna Jamison, Frances Power Cobbe, and Harriet Beecher Stowe were among those who questioned whether Protestants had, by eliminating "Mariolatry," not also deprived themselves of a powerful advocate for advancing women's social position.[116] Several former Protestant women celebrated the ways in which their conversion to Catholicism afforded them the special services of Mary as an advocate. Emma Forbes Cary, with whom Conway served on Trinity College's associate board in Boston, suggested in a variety of venues that having Mary as a model insulated women from the harmful influence of misguided and ridiculous advocates of women's rights.[117]

In much the same way that "the cloak of her beloved profession" protected her from being labeled a public woman, Conway's association with Mary immunized her from criticism that she was too openly subverting gender prescriptions. Mary, in other words, functioned in much the same way that suffrage did. She provided Conway and other Catholic women with an easy way to affirm that the bonds of Catholicism were indeed stronger than the bonds of womanhood. This did not mean that they did not seek to advance their sex in other ways. Indeed, setting her fondness for traditional rhetoric aside, there can be little doubt that Conway challenged gender prescriptions, both by example and by encouragement. She acted as a "literary god-mother" to aspiring Catholic writers and was instrumental in opening a school of journalism at a Catholic women's college.[118] Many scholars have interpreted the gap between her rhetoric and reality as inconsistent or symbolic of a "polarity in Catholicism that required women to stay at home . . . at a time when Progressive women were demanding the chance to improve society through activism and feminist radicals fought for civic equality."[119] But it is also possible to see it as the space in which it was possible for Catholic women to renegotiate, however slowly, their position within society and the church.

EPILOGUE: CATHOLIC WOMEN AND
TWENTIETH-CENTURY ANTIFEMINISM

By 1917 it was clear that woman suffrage was imminent. The election of Carrie Chapman Catt in 1914 as president of the National American Woman Suffrage Association had signaled a new direction for the movement. Over the next few years, Catt's "Winning Plan" had increased support for a constitutional amendment even as more state organizations sought to enfranchise women through referenda. She had predicted that a victory in one southern state and one eastern state would turn the tide in favor of national success. This milestone was reached in 1917 when women received the right to vote in Arkansas and New York. The suffrage cause was also helped by women's visible participation in U.S. efforts in World War I. In 1918 the House of Representatives passed the federal suffrage amendment, and on August 26, 1920, it became part of the U.S. Constitution when Tennessee became the thirty-sixth state to ratify it.[120]

Katherine Conway reacted to the passage of the Nineteenth Amendment as a "good sport" and cast her vote in the next election. From that point on, her only suffrage-related protest concerned the injustice of the Massachusetts requirement to specify one's age on the ballot: at age seventy-two, she felt it was too insulting! Conway's response was characteristic of the majority of remonstrants, who quickly put aside their reservations about voting once suffrage became an accomplished fact. This was in many respects inevitable: in the process of protesting women's political participation, scores of women had become very politically savvy, and once in possession of the right to vote, they were just as likely as other women to exercise it.[121]

Conway did demonstrate remarkable consistency in one respect: whether Catholic women had the right to vote or not, she argued, their paramount concern should be maximizing Catholic influence. Whereas she had previously contended that the movement for woman suffrage would divide Catholics and thus diminish their power, she now prevailed upon newly enfranchised Catholic women to use the ballot to increase that power. In a particularly bold proposition, she urged Catholic women to mobilize in order to elect one of their own to the presidency, in partial reparation for the outrageous prejudice that Catholics had experienced throughout U.S. history. Conway did not live to see Al Smith nominated as the Democratic candidate in the election of 1928. Had she done so, however, it is certain she would not only have supported him but would also have been incensed at the anti-Catholic rhetoric his nomination unleashed.[122]

Catholic clerics who had been opposed to women's enfranchisement adopted a stance similar to Conway's: they assured Catholic women that, since suffrage had been "thrust upon" them, they were simply bound to vote in a manner that demonstrated continued solidarity with the church.[123] Addressing the women of New York in 1917, the editors of *America* used the occasion of the Feast of the Immaculate Conception, a special day that honored Mary, to juxtapose the Blessed Virgin with the now smugly victorious suffragist. As many had done in the past, the editors asserted that

Mary's example, coupled with the church's historical record of liberating women, not only would guide Catholic women to make reasonable choices at the polls but also would deter them from establishing alliances with the kind of women who had pushed for suffrage in the first place.[124] Several weeks later, writing in the same publication, the Reverend John Ryan provided more specifics about the particular women Catholics should avoid. Even the women who had accepted suffrage "with great reluctance," he insisted, were now morally and civically bound to use "their votes against feminism and all other forms of extreme radicalism."[125]

Ryan's description of feminism as a form of extreme radicalism was representative of most Catholics' views on the subject. Unlike the woman suffrage movement, which had been in existence for seven decades by the time Ryan's article appeared, "feminism" represented a new development in the United States. According to historian Nancy Cott, the term, usually capitalized, emerged in the American lexicon around 1910 and became commonplace by 1913. The extensive communication networks established by suffragists had helped to lay the groundwork for feminism, but feminists went far beyond suffragists in their goals and assumptions. Feminists looked beyond the ballot toward a social revolution, which included "freedom from all forms of women's active expression, elimination of all structural and psychological handicaps to women's economic independence, and end to the double standard of sexual morality, release from constraining sexual stereotypes, and opportunity to shine in every civic and professional capacity."[126]

In contrast to the diversity of opinions they held on suffrage, Catholics expressed near universal disdain for feminism. One man observed that feminism "sets itself a broader purpose than mere voting; it gazes determinedly into flattering vistas of prospective sex-equality and civic achievement."[127] The ballot, in comparison, seemed tame. With venom previously reserved for the New Woman, Catholics assailed the feminist as a byproduct of the Reformation, an affront to the social order, and a threat to Catholic unity. Many believed that "irreligion" was at the root of "feminist agitation," and Catholic women were frequently exhorted to consecrate their lives to "counteracting that insanity of sin which is too painfully manifest in modern forms of 'feminism.' "[128]

Catholic women's collective failure to identify with feminism raises a number of interesting historical questions, not least of which is why women who stood to gain the most from feminism did not prove to be more receptive to it.[129] It is not difficult, for example, to sketch a scenario in which a woman such as Katherine Conway might have followed a different path and sympathized with a social movement intended to increase women's economic independence and expand their professional opportunities. In her history of modern feminism, Cott has shown that a sense of shared gender identity—women's willingness to say "we"—was crucial to the development of feminist identity.[130] As should be obvious by now, Conway was nowhere near as immune to the "morbid consciousness of womanhood" as she believed herself to be. She treasured her friendship with a number of other Catholic women writers, among them Margaret Buchanan Sullivan and Mary Elizabeth Blake, and she encouraged other young women to follow in her footsteps by joining the church's "publicity branch." And despite her fear that Catholic women might become overorganized, Conway undoubtedly enjoyed and benefited from her participation in all-female Catholic groups, such as the John Boyle O'Reilly Reading Circle, as well as secular women's organizations, such as the New England Women's Press Association. The most significant irony attending Conway's disdain for the "morbid consciousness of womanhood," however, was that she spent what were probably the happiest years of her life in a community of women at Saint Mary's College in Notre Dame, Indiana.[131]

Conway's relationship with the Sisters of the Holy Cross at Saint Mary's had begun in 1907, when nearby University of Notre Dame had awarded her its most prestigious honor, the Laetare Medal. Conway served as Saint Mary's commencement speaker in 1911 and, at the invitation of Mother Pauline O'Neill, the college president, joined the faculty the next year. Though Conway left Boston with reluctance, the salary Mother Pauline offered her was "better than any [she] had in her life," and the prospect of teaching young Catholic women about the history of their church also appealed to her.[132]

Sister Madeleva Wolff, csc, was a student of Conway's who later became the president of Saint Mary's College (1934–61) and one of the most important figures in the history of Catholic higher education. Wolff remembered the time she spent "walking with [Conway], talking with her daily, reading proof, commenting on editorials" and described it as "a rich apprenticeship, such as few young teachers have ever known." Another former student, Sister Eleanore Brosnahan, csc, remembered Conway's living quar-

Katherine Conway, 1907, wearing the Laetare Medal. Courtesy of the Archives of the University of Notre Dame, GLAE 1-15.

ters on campus as "a gathering place for literary aspirants." Conway taught her students that "women could take their writing talent as well as their faith into the marketplace without compromising either." In particular she was instrumental in founding a school of journalism at the college, so that graduates would be better prepared to earn a living in the field.[133] Conway remained at the college for four years, when illness forced her to resign and return to Boston. Though her health had never been robust, it deteriorated significantly during the last decade of her life, and while she would continue to publish prodigiously, she was mostly confined to her home until her death in 1927.[134]

If, in retrospect, the time she spent in all-female environments might have provided Conway with a positive reason to gravitate toward the emerging feminist movement, her recognition of the limitations of her sex might have also provided her with a negative motivation to do so. Throughout her career Conway was aware that being a woman was a liability in the field of journalism. She realized, for example, that Catholic periodicals were more likely to reprint her *Pilot* articles without attribution than they were to do so with pieces written by men. But when she first complained that her work was "appropriated without a line of credit," John Boyle

O'Reilly assured her that nothing mattered, as long as "the good ideas are circulated."[135] O'Reilly's advice echoes that given to both Sister Assisium McEvoy and Sister Eberharda Jones with regard to their own publications: even outside religious life, Catholic women were often consigned to anonymity. Though the knowledge that all would be rewarded in time usually consoled her, Conway was also subject to periods of disillusionment: "Of course, I know all about the reward to come and all the rest," she confided to a friend, "but there are times when courage flags, and Heaven seems a long way off."[136]

Conway felt the limitations of sex more acutely during her last years at the *Pilot*. James Jeffrey Roche succeeded John Boyle O'Reilly as editor in 1890, and Conway never admired Roche the way she had his predecessor. While assigning her the lion's share of the work, Roche offered Conway little in terms of either recognition or remuneration. The friction between them escalated to open hostility in 1904, when Roche slanted the paper heavily in favor of the Republican presidential candidate, Theodore Roosevelt. Conway objected to the betrayal of the Democrats, "the party through which the grandfathers of most of us won their civic standing."[137] Ironically, Roosevelt's election solved her problems, at least temporarily, as Roche was rewarded with an appointment to the American consulate in Rome. Comparing Roche's departure to "shaking off a nightmare," Conway succeeded him and became the *Pilot*'s first woman editor.[138]

Unfortunately this turn of events offered Conway brief respite. In the early years of the twentieth century, Irish Americans' loyalty to the *Pilot* declined as more of them became further removed from the immigrant generation. Moreover, the *Pilot* increasingly faced competition from diocesan newspapers whose costs were underwritten by local bishops. Though Conway struggled to rescue the paper from financial ruin—even forgoing her own salary at times—it continued to lose money. The situation took a turn for the worse in 1907, when Boston's new archbishop, William Henry O'Connell, dismissed Conway from the paper's staff after what Paula Kane has described as a prolonged "contest between gender and power." Throughout all these struggles Conway was aware that her sex was a significant factor. During particularly tense times at the *Pilot*, she insisted that "a man would not stand for it."[139]

Despite her recognition of sex-based subjugation, Conway not only remained decidedly aloof to the possibilities of feminism but did everything she could to convince other Catholic women of its destructive potential. In this respect, Conway invites comparisons with a modern antifeminist, Phyllis Schlafly. Both women used their own weighty public influence to protest women's legal equality, albeit with different outcomes. While suffrage passed despite Conway's opposition to it, Schlafly is credited with single-handedly derailing the Equal Rights Amendment. Both women were intelligent and highly educated; both were prolific writers. Both also envisioned themselves as "exceptional," and both were reluctant to recognize the degree to which their own contributions were undervalued because of their gender. Finally, both Conway and Schlafly were Catholics who frequently used the language of gender essentialism to defend church teaching on women's proper place.

Noting the parallels in upbringing, social class, and experience between Schlafly and Betty Friedan, the mother of second-wave feminism, feminist scholar Sheila Tobias has asked much the same question of Schlafly that we have asked of Conway: Why did she become an antifeminist instead of a feminist? Tobias concludes that the answer lies in Schlafly's innate conservatism: "Simply because a woman is female or a housewife or has a problem that has no name does not mean she will become a feminist *unless*—and feminists took a long time to understand this—she leans toward a progressive agenda."[140] Kane has explained Conway's antifeminism in much the same manner, noting that her "emancipated life did not override her conservatism."[141]

Perhaps, however, Conway's failure to identify with feminism may be attributed not to its inability to override her "conservatism" but rather to its inability to overcome her need to act with "implicit Catholicity." Throughout her life, the bonds of Catholicism remained stronger than the bonds of womanhood, and as long as this remained true, feminism would hold little appeal. Conway and the other Catholic women who turned a blind eye to early feminism thus prefigure not only vociferous antifeminists such as Schlafly but also the members of the far more numerous "I'm not a feminist, but . . ." crowd. Through their reflexive opposition to sex hierarchy, their commitment to equal worth for both sexes, and their pursuit of gender parity in the professions, these women often tacitly endorse feminism through their actions and assumptions. Yet they remain deeply suspicious of feminism because of the movement's association with a number of "radical" causes, especially the pro-choice movement. Consequently, what was true early in the twentieth century remains true a century later: feminism has been unable to attract substantial support from women from conservative religious traditions.

But if a comparison between Conway and a modern Catholic antifeminist reveals illuminating historical parallels, it can also illustrate how much has changed over time. Consider another comparison, this time between Conway and Mary Ann Glendon, the Harvard Law School professor who was recently appointed the first woman to head a Vatican commission. As Conway had done at the beginning of the twentieth century, Glendon plays a crucial role in convincing a majority of her Catholic sisters that feminism is incompatible with their religious beliefs. She is a champion of Pope John Paul II's "new feminism," an ideology of gender that, through its language of "complementarity," evokes the traditional church teaching that women are defined relative to men and through their self-sacrificial role within the family. In 1995, Glendon observed that "a Catholic woman impatient with the pace of change might consider asking herself: 'Where in contemporary society do I feel the most respected as a woman, whatever my chosen path in life?'" Asserting that she could find no other institution that surpasses the Catholic Church in this respect, Glendon maintained that feminist critiques of the church, such as those implicit in arguments in favor of women's ordination, are both misguided and beside the point.[142] Recall that Conway had spoken very similarly a century earlier, when she "marveled" that the woman question was even raised among Catholics, given that the only places from which the church barred them were the sanctuary and the pulpit. And we have seen how strongly she believed that it was the church, not the women's rights movement, that offered the best hope for women's advancement. This conviction shaped her own as well as countless other Catholic women's perception of suffrage, higher education, social reform, and other developments judged to be crucial for the expansion of women's role in society.

Yet the line connecting Conway to either Schlafly or Glendon is hardly a straight one. When Conway noted that the church allowed women everywhere but the sanctuary and the pulpit, the same could have been said of all but a few Christian denominations. But by the time Schlafly's crusade against the Equal Rights Amendment was at full tilt, all the mainstream Protestant churches, including the tradition closest to Roman Catholicism, were ordaining women. When Conway, Margaret Sullivan, or any of their contemporaries insisted that their church had done more for them than any other institution, their statement rang more true than it would when Glendon paraphrased it a century later. There is no doubt that since the late 1960s a Catholic woman in American society has had vastly more opportunities for education, meaningful work, and leadership outside church structures than within them. But from Conway's birth in the mid-nineteenth century until the late 1960s, quite the opposite was true. The Catholic Church had provided her with a purpose, a sense of meaning, and a profession; neither Schlafly nor Glendon needed the church for any of those things. Transformations for women in American society had far outpaced changes for women in the church.

If the world had changed a great deal for women over the twentieth century, it had also changed dramatically for Catholics. By the time Schlafly and Glendon came to national prominence, Catholics in the United States had witnessed the election of one of their own to the presidency. While the significance of Kennedy's election can be overstated, it was a development that had been only a fantasy to Conway. Moreover, Schlafly and Glendon and others of their generation lived in a Catholic world that had been transformed by the Second Vatican Council. Again, while its significance can be exaggerated, there is no doubt that the council empowered the laity and opened the door for dissent in a manner that Catholics in the early twentieth century could never have predicted or even imagined. Finally, the Irish Catholic community had been transformed demographically from a largely immigrant population on the margins of U.S. society into a largely well-educated and affluent group constituted of quintessential American insiders. In other words, the seeds of gender discontent that had lain dormant throughout the Progressive Era would be watered in the 1960s by Vatican II, massive social change, and major demographic transformations. Consequently a greater number of Catholic women would respond differently to American feminism in its second incarnation than they had done in its first.

In this respect, Conway should not only be seen as the historical foremother of Phyllis Schlafly, Mary Ann Glendon, or any other "conservative" contemporary Catholic woman. We might also find her modern counterpart in journalist Anna Quindlen, who acknowledges the centrality of Catholicism in her life but often finds herself alienated from the church because of her outspoken views in support of legal abortion. Similarly,

Sister Assisium McEvoy's modern counterpart might be found in Sister Mary Scullion, a Philadelphia nun whose work with the homeless has made her a local hero. Unlike McEvoy, Scullion neither wears a habit nor lives in a convent, and she frequently collaborates with both laypeople and the state. Yet she resists the label of a "nontraditional" nun, presenting her work as a creative adaptation of tradition rather than a radical departure from it. As we have seen, McEvoy followed the call of "Martha" by providing a minority with an education under church auspices; a century later, Scullion lives out the same call by standing in solidarity with the poor.[143] A similar comparison might be drawn between Sister Julia McGroarty and Sister Helen Prejean, the contemporary nun whose work with death row inmates has been made famous through the book and film *Dead Man Walking*. In 1897, McGroarty came to Washington, D.C., to provide Catholic daughters with the means to access professional occupations; more than a century later, Prejean visits the nation's capital with a different purpose in mind. Having found her work in the classroom to be "too ethereal, too disconnected" in the wake of Vatican II and social change, she sees lobbying for the abolition of the death penalty as an essential part of her religious vocation.[144]

All such comparisons require historical caution. But these connections between Catholic women of the past and present do reinforce the premise I stated in the introduction. The privileging of pre-feminists within the historiography of American women, as well as the tendency to view the past through the lens of an unrelentingly patriarchal contemporary church, has left women like Conway, McEvoy, McGroarty, and Buchanan oddly frozen in time. There is no room to understand that, far from being insulated from social changes as daughters of the Old Faith, they became active participants in the Progressive project to mediate between old and new.

Notes

ABBREVIATIONS

ACQR   *American Catholic Quarterly Review*

ARSPS   *Annual Reports of the Superintendent of Parochial Schools of the Archdiocese of Philadelphia*. Vols. 1–25. Philadelphia: M. P. Lewis, Jr. and Co., 1895–1919.

ASJPH   Archives of the St. Joseph Provincial House, Archives of the Daughters of Charity, Emmitsburg, Maryland

ASSFP   Archives of the Sisters of St. Francis of Philadelphia, Aston, Pennsylvania

ASSJ   Archives of the Sisters of St. Joseph of Philadelphia, Chestnut Hill, Pennsylvania

BJMC   Bishop Bernard J. McQuaid Collection, Archives of the Diocese of Rochester, Rochester, New York

CEAB   *Catholic Educational Association Bulletin*

CLSC   Charles Leon Souvay Collection, University of Notre Dame Archives, Notre Dame, Indiana

DEHC   Daniel E. Hudson Collection, University of Notre Dame Archives, Notre Dame, Indiana

ELD   Ella Lorraine Dorsey

EPC   Archbishop Edmund Prendergast Collection, Philadelphia Archdiocesan Historical Records Center, Philadelphia, Pennsylvania

FSC   Brothers of the Christian Schools

FY   Founding Years, Trinity College Archives, Washington, D.C.

IHM   Sisters, Servants of the Immaculate Heart of Mary

JAMC   James A. McMaster Collection, University of Notre Dame Archives, Notre Dame, Indiana

KEC   Katherine Eleanor Conway

KECC/BC	Katherine E. Conway Collection, John J. Burns Library, Boston College Archives, Boston, Massachusetts
KECC/SMCA	Katherine E. Conway Collection, Saint Mary's College Archives, Notre Dame, Indiana
LAB	Ladies Auxiliary Board Collection, Trinity College Archives, Washington, D.C.
MMCP	Mother Mary Camilla Papers, Archives of the Sisters, Servants of the Immaculate Heart of Mary, Immaculata, Pennsylvania
MMDCP	Mother Mary de Chantal Papers, Archives of the Sisters, Servants of the Immaculate Heart of Mary, Immaculata, Pennsylvania
MMJP	Mother Mary James Papers, Archives of the Sisters, Servants of the Immaculate Heart of Mary, Immaculata, Pennsylvania
OLCGS	Sisters of Our Lady of Charity of the Good Shepherd
OSF	Order of St. Francis
PJRC	Archbishop Patrick J. Ryan Collection, Philadelphia Archdiocesan Historical Research Center, Philadelphia, Pennsylvania
PRMC/ND	Philip R. McDevitt Collection, University of Notre Dame Archives, Notre Dame, Indiana
PRMC/PA	Philip R. McDevitt Collection, Philadelphia Archdiocesan Historical Records Center, Philadelphia, Pennsylvania
RACHSP	*Records of the American Catholic Historical Society of Philadelphia*
ROPM	Religious Orders Printed Material, University of Notre Dame Archives, Notre Dame, Indiana
RSCJ	Society of the Sacred Heart
SA	Sister Assisium McEvoy, SSJ
SAMC	Sister Assisium McEvoy Collection, Archives of the Sisters of St. Joseph of Philadelphia, Chestnut Hill, Pennsylvania
SCSE	Special Collections—Sister Eberharda Jones, Archives of the Sisters of St. Francis of Philadelphia, Aston, Pennsylvania
SEC	Sisters Education, Archives of the Sisters of St. Joseph of Philadelphia, Chestnut Hill, Pennsylvania
SEJ	Sister Eberharda Jones, OSF
SEJC	Sister Eberhardha Jones Collection, Archives of the Sisters of St. Francis of Philadelphia, Aston, Pennsylvania
SHCJ	Society of the Holy Child Jesus
SJM	Sister Julia McGroarty, SND

SJMC   Sister Julia McGroarty Correspondence, Trinity College Archives, Washington, D.C.

SMCA   Saint Mary's College Archives, Notre Dame, Indiana

SME   Sister Mary Euphrasia, SND

SND   Sisters of Notre Dame de Namur

SSJ   Sisters of St. Joseph

TCA   Trinity College Archives, Washington, D.C.

UNDA   University of Notre Dame Archives, Notre Dame, Indiana

WJOC   William James Onahan Collection, University of Notre Dame Archives, Notre Dame, Indiana

INTRODUCTION

1 Ludden, introduction to Mullany, *Pioneer Church*, ii (emphasis in original).

2 Hoy, *Good Hearts*; Coburn and Smith, *Spirited Lives*; Morrow, *Persons of Color and Religious*; Moloney, *American Catholic Lay Groups*; Skok, *More than Neighbors*; Brown and McKeown, *Poor Belong to Us*.

3 Kane, Kenneally, and Kennelly, *Gender Identities*; Kennelly, *History of American Catholic Women*; Kennelly, *American Catholic Women*; Kane, *Separatism and Subculture*.

4 Kane, "Review of John T. McGreevy."

5 Braude, "Women's History *Is* American Religious History."

6 Brekus, "Introduction," 1.

7 See, for example, Evans, *Born for Liberty*, 298, 305–6, 319.

8 The standard anthology in women's history did not contain a single essay about Catholic women religious until its fourth edition, and even that essay was subsequently dropped from the fifth edition to accommodate topics such as the sexual revolution and abortion. Jane S. De Hart and Linda Kerber to Suellen Hoy, June 24, 2003, courtesy of Suellen Hoy. Among the recent studies of Catholic nuns in France are Curtis, *Educating the Faithful*, and Rogers, *From the Salon to the Schoolroom*.

9 Boylan, *Origins of Women's Activism*; Fitzgerald, *Habits of Compassion*.

10 Braude, "Review of Anne M. Boylan's *The Origins of Women's Activism*."

11 Braude, *Radical Spirits*, xvii. Patrick Allitt noted that many Catholic women, "subservient to men, deferential, self-effacing, sometimes anti-suffrage, would seem the least enticing and least likeable to historians seeking avatars of modern gender-role transformations." Allitt, "American Women Converts and Catholic Intellectual Life," 79.

12 *Official Catholic Directory of the Philadelphia Archdiocese*, 112.

13 I am indebted to Catherine A. Brekus for making this comparison and for sharing her research on Protestant female preaching. Stewart, *Marvels of Charity*, 565.

14 I have borrowed this phrase from Natalie Zemon Davis, who used it in *Women on the Margins*, 203.

15 Cott, *Grounding of Modern Feminism*, 39. See also Bordin, *Alice Freeman Palmer*, 2–3. See, for example, Nancy Woloch, "The Rise of the New Woman," chap. 12 in Woloch, *Women and the American Experience*, 269–307, and Matthews, *Rise of the New Woman*.

16 Finley Peter Dunne, "The New Woman," May 4, 1895, reprinted in Dunne, *Mr. Dooley and the Chicago Irish*, 145–47.

17 O'Reilly, *Mirror of True Womanhood*, 6–7, 55–57, 338–39. See also Karen Kennelly, "Ideals of American Catholic Womanhood," in Kennelly, *American Catholic Women*, 1–16, and Becker, "Rational Amusement and Sound Instruction," 55–90.

18 Dolan, *American Catholic Experience*, 309–11; McAvoy, *Great Crisis in American Catholic History*; Gleason, "New Americanism in Catholic Historiography," 4–5.

19 Sr. Julia to Cardinal [Mariano] Rampolla, September 8, 1897, TCA.

20 Flanagan, *America Reformed*, 46; Hoy, *Good Hearts*, esp. chaps. 4 and 5.

21 Brekus, "Introduction," 23.

22 Nugent, "Catholic Progressive?"

23 McShane, *Sufficiently Radical*, 1–2.

24 More than a decade ago Leslie Woodcock Tentler implicitly highlighted the disparity between the attention given to Catholic women and to Progressive reformers such as Addams. Noting the vast network of institutions founded by nuns, she argued that "had women under secular or Protestant auspices compiled this record of achievement, they would today be a thoroughly researched population." See Tentler, "On the Margins," 108. Suellen Hoy's recent study of Catholic sisters in Chicago stands to balance the historical record. By examining nuns' widespread assistance to the city's immigrant and African American poor, Hoy shows how Catholic women's support for that population both antedated and exceeded that provided by Addams and Hull House. Hoy, *Good Hearts*.

25 De Hart and Kerber, "Introduction," 5–12; Brekus, "Introduction," 25.

26 White, *Too Heavy a Load*, 17 (emphasis in original).

27 Braude, "Review of Anne M. Boylan's *The Origins of Women's Activism*," 183.

28 Higginbotham, *Righteous Discontent*, 1, 2, 14.

29 Anderson, "Negotiating Patriarchy and Power."

1 Sullivan, "Chiefly among Women," 324; Sullivan quotes Gladstone on 324. This article would be reprinted a number of times, with Margaret Sullivan subsequently identified as its author. The original version will be cited.

2 Sullivan later observed that Gladstone "was born with a detestation of the Catholic Church, and he died in it." [Margaret Sullivan], "Morley's Life of Gladstone," *New World* (Chicago), October 17, 1903.

3 Sullivan, "Chiefly among Women," 334.

4 Tyrrell, "Old Faith and the New Woman."

5 Appleby, *Church and Age Unite*, 5.

6 Cott, *Grounding of Modern Feminism*, 39. See also Bordin, *Alice Freeman Palmer*, 2–3; Woloch, *Women and the American Experience*, 269–307; and Matthews, *Rise of the New Woman*.

7 MacCorrie, "War of the Sexes," 606–7.

8 "Shakespere [*sic*] and the New Woman," 160, 162, 169.

9 Rössler, "Woman," 687–88, 692, 694.

10 Tyrrell, "Old Faith and the New Woman," 632, 634.

11 Rössler, "Woman," 694. For more discussion of Catholics' organic conception of society, see McGreevy, *Catholicism and American Freedom*.

12 Tyrrell, "Old Faith and the New Woman," 641, 643.

13 See biographical sketches of Margaret Buchanan Sullivan in M. [Mother] Seraphine, *Immortelles*, 380, and O'Mahoney, *Famous Irishwomen*, 182–83; see also Conway, "Margaret F. Sullivan"; "Margaret Sullivan Dies," *Chicago Daily Tribune*, December 29, 1903, 4; "The Death of Mrs. Margaret F. Sullivan," *New World* (Chicago), January 2, 1904; and Josephine Byrne Sullivan, "A Brilliant Coterie of Women," *New World* (Chicago), September 11, 1909. Additional biographical information about Sullivan was supplied by Sullivan's great-grand-nephew, Peter Buchanan of Berkley, Michigan, on May 14, 2007, in a conversation with Martha Curry, RSCJ. I am indebted to Curry for sharing this information with me and for introducing me to Peter Buchanan.

14 Margaret Sullivan's burial services were held at Holy Trinity. "Obituary," *Chicago Inter-Ocean*, January 1, 1904, 12.

15 Conway, *Lalor's Maples*, 17.

16 [Margaret Buchanan Sullivan], "The Tabernacle Society," *New World* (Chicago), June 13, 1903.

17 In a letter to James A. McMaster, editor of the *Freeman's Journal*, Sullivan recalls that she submitted a poem as a child; Sullivan to McMaster, May 15, 1876, JAMC.

18 L. R. McCabe, "A Chicago Lady Journalist," *New World* (Chicago), May 27, 1893.

19 P. J. Keeffe, "Margaret Sullivan Dead," *New World* (Chicago), January 2, 1904; Conway, "Margaret F. Sullivan," 220; Byrne Sullivan, "Brilliant Coterie of Women."

20 A. J., "The Woman Who Writes: Margaret F. Buchanan, of the Chicago Post," *Woman's Journal*, January 6, 1872, 2.

21 Quoted in ibid. I am indebted to Martha Curry, RSCJ, who confirmed that Margaret Buchanan was a "parlor boarder" at the Sacred Heart Convent on Taylor Street in Chicago.

22 Quoted in the *Western Catholic* (Chicago), April 13, 1872.

23 Conway, "Margaret F. Sullivan," 221.

24 Newspaper articles reveal two addresses for Alexander and Margaret Sullivan: 378 Oak Street (after 1909, 37 East Oak Street), and 240 N. State Street (850 N. State Street). Both addresses fell within the parish boundaries of Holy Name Cathedral, where Sullivan's funeral Mass was held in 1903. I am indebted to Ellen Skerrett for converting these addresses to present-day ones.

25 Conway, "Margaret F. Sullivan," 220. Conway includes the quotation from Rev. Dorney, who later preached the sermon at Sullivan's funeral. "Funeral of Mrs. Sullivan," *Chicago Daily Tribune*, December 30, 1903, 5.

26 Funchion, "Irish Nationalists and Chicago Politics."

27 "A Moment's Madness," August 8, 1876, *Chicago Daily Tribune*.

28 "Mrs. Sullivan's Plea," *Chicago Inter-Ocean*, June 18, 1889.

29 Sullivan, *Ireland of To-day*; see also Sullivan's articles in the *ACQR* 3 (1878): 104–31, and 6 (1881): 51–91, 508–20, 668–82.

30 Davitt, *Fall of Feudalism in Ireland*, 716. I am indebted to Joe Lee for supplying this reference. Katherine Conway mentions that Sullivan was a friend of Davitt's. Conway, "Margaret F. Sullivan," 220.

31 Sullivan to McMaster, May 15, 1876, JAMC.

32 Middleton, "List of Catholic and Semi-Catholic Periodicals," 216.

33 Sullivan, "Chiefly among Women," 321.

34 "Salutory," 4.

35 M. F. S., "General Banks," 354. In her May 15, 1876, letter to James McMaster, Sullivan identifies herself as the author of this article.

36 *Convention of the Apostolate of the Press*, 8–9.

37 McDannell, "Catholic Women Fiction Writers," 389. Browne and Meline quoted in ibid.

38 Quoted in M. Seraphine, *Immortelles*, 524.

39 Quoted in "Chicago's Great Catholic Writer," *New World* (Chicago), January 9, 1904.

40 "Mrs. Sullivan on the Woman's Congress," *Citizen* (Chicago), May 27, 1893;

[Margaret Buchanan Sullivan], "A Summing Up," *New World* (Chicago), October 25, 1902.

41 M. Seraphine, *Immortelles*, 14.

42 Mozans, *Woman in Science*, 406.

43 M. Seraphine, *Immortelles*, 395.

44 Adams, "Men and Things" (1897); Adams, "Men and Things" (1898), 2.

45 "Suggestions from Our Prize Contestants," 182.

46 Toomy, "Some Noble Work," 234.

47 Sullivan, "Chiefly among Women," 340. The best source on Marie de l'Incarnation is Davis, *Women on the Margins*.

48 Shea, "Catholic Church in American History."

49 See, for example, Sullivan's essay "Distinguished Catholic Prelates as American Diplomats," reprinted in *Our Church and Country*, 81–86. I have been unable to locate the original, which was unsigned. In another article Sullivan rejoiced that Irish Catholic John Barry had been restored to his rightful position as "father of the American navy." [Margaret Buchanan Sullivan], "A Conspiracy Ended," *New World* (Chicago), February 14, 1903.

50 Moreau, "Rise of the (Catholic) American Nation," 68.

51 Ibid.

52 *Sadlier's Excelsior Studies*, 21, quoted in Moreau, "Rise of the (Catholic) American Nation," 75.

53 *Our Church and Country*, 107.

54 Shea, "Columbus Centenary of 1892," 694.

55 Quoted in Moloney, *American Catholic Lay Groups*, 15.

56 For more on Christopher Columbus, see Kauffman, "Christopher Columbus and American Catholic Identity."

57 Starr, *Isabella of Castile*, 103; Donnelly, "Woman in Literature," 83.

58 Lummis, *Daughters of the Faith*, 39.

59 Barton, *Columbus the Catholic*, 13.

60 Onahan, "Isabella the Catholic," 33.

61 Religious of the Ursuline Community, *Life of the Venerable Mother Mary of the Incarnation*, 323. When calls for Isabella's canonization did come in the late twentieth century, they were predictably problematic. See Woodward, "Saint Isabella?," 67.

62 Clark, *Voices from an Early American Convent*.

63 Greer, "Colonial Saints."

64 *Sadlier's Excelsior Studies*, 101.

65 Mahon and Hayes, *Trials and Triumphs*, 230.

66 Sister Mary Celeste, *American History*, 115; Franciscan Sisters of Perpetual Adoration, *History of the United States*, 68.

67 Sadlier, *Women of Catholicity*, 180.

68 M. A. C., "Education in Louisiana in French Colonial Days," 418.

69 Ibid., 397.

70 O'Brien, "Ursulines," 105; Franciscan Sisters of Perpetual Adoration, *History of the United States*, 44.

71 M. A. C., "Education in Louisiana in Spanish Colonial Days," 267, 270.

72 Vogel, "Ursuline Nuns in America," 213–14.

73 See the chapters "Three Saintly Ladies" and "Venerable Margaret Bourgeois" in Mahon and Hayes, *Trials and Triumphs*, 216–42, 420–40, and Crowley, *Daughter of New France*.

74 John Carroll later became the first U.S. bishop, and Margaret Sullivan wrote about Carroll's mission to show how "distinguished American prelates" helped to save the Republic during times of war. Sullivan, "Distinguished Catholic Prelates as American Diplomats," 81–86.

75 Sadlier, *Women of Catholicity*, 239–40.

76 Ibid., 264, 3.

77 Sadlier, *Elizabeth Seton*, 1.

78 Murray, *Lives of Catholic Heroes and Heroines*, 721–22.

79 Reville, *First American Sister of Charity*, 37.

80 Murray, *Lives of Catholic Heroes and Heroines*, 713–14.

81 O'Brien, *Daughters of the Faith*, 39.

82 Reville, *First American Sister of Charity*, 35.

83 Elliott, "St. Vincent de Paul and the Sisters of Charity," 28.

84 Brunowe, *Famous Convent School*, 28, 31.

85 McCann, *Mother Seton*, 66.

86 Seton's nephew, James Roosevelt Bayley, became the first bishop of Newark, New Jersey, and he established Seton Hall College in 1856. Her grandson Robert Seton became archbishop of Heliotrope.

87 Clarke, "Beatification Asked," 809.

88 Greer, "Colonial Saints," 326n9.

89 Provincial Annals, ASJPH, August 3, 1882. Gibbons's specification that the "first movement must naturally begin here" refers to the fact that initial appeals could not come from the hierarchy. Even though the sainting process has changed a great deal in recent years, it remains one of the most democratic processes in the church. For more information, see Higgins, *Stalking the Holy*, 30.

90 See, for example, Henry Moeller, archbishop of Cincinnati, to Rev. J. P. Cribbins, C.M., July 7, 1913, directing the Sisters of Charity of St. Vincent DePaul to write a history of their order, microfilm reel 6, CLSC.

91 Belloc, *Historic Nuns*, 187.

92 Greer, "Natives and Nationalism"; Walworth, *Life and Times*.

93 Mahon and Hayes, *Trials and Triumphs*, 329.

94 Walworth, *Life and Times*, 253.

95 Pope John Paul II beatified Kateri Tekakwitha in 1980. For more information, see Woodward, *Making Saints*, 117–18, 208, 217. Seton was beatified in 1963 and canonized in 1975, becoming the first native-born American saint. Frances Cabrini had been canonized in 1946, the first American so honored.

96 On this particular occasion, Sullivan was named as the author of the essay. McDevitt, "Boards of Education," 4. See original in "Notes on 'Have Women Souls?,' " box 5, folder 33, PRMC/ND.

97 McDevitt, "Boards of Education," 5.

98 Translation of the first sentence: "For there stood up in this synod a certain man among the Bishops who said, that a woman was not able to be called a human." The remainder of the passage reads: "But still he was satisfied with the rationale accepted by the Bishops: that which says, that where the Old Testament of the Holy Bible teaches, that in the beginning, there was man from God the Creator; male and female he created them, and called them Adam because he is a human from the earth; and so from there calling them woman or man: for he said that both are human. But also Our Lord Jesus is called, according to this [the Bible], the son of man, because he is the son of a virgin, which is to say the son of a woman, and with this argument of his refuted by many other testimonies the man was satisfied."

99 McDevitt, "Boards of Education," 7.

100 Ibid., 7.

101 Ibid., 3.

102 Bebel, *Woman and Socialism*, <www.marxists.org/archive/bebel/1879/woman-socialism/ch03.html>.

103 Gage, *Woman, Church and State*, 56.

104 Matthews, *Rise of the New Woman*, 69 (emphasis in original).

105 Holman, " 'New Woman,' " 438.

106 Donnelly, "Have Women Souls?," 302; Gilman, "History of Love," 910; George, "Notes on the Intelligence of Woman," 721. See also "Catholic Apologetics—Historical Myths; Letters to Newspapers re: Misstatements," box 5, folder 24, PRMC/ND. This folder contains a clipping of an article from the October 26, 1922, *New York Evening World* that referred to it as Nicea; folder 33, "Notes to Have Women Souls," contains a copy of a letter from Edward Walsh to the editor of the *Ecclesiastical Review*, June 8, 1916, that reports a reference to the debate at Trent; "Has a Council Denied."

107 "Women's Position in the Catholic Church," *Watson's Magazine*, December 1912, 78, quoted in Nordstrom, *Danger on the Doorstep*, 113.

108 *Sadlier's Excelsior Studies*, 5; "Shakespere [sic] and the New Woman," 378; "New Home of the Summer-School," 82; *World's Columbian Catholic Congresses*, 29; Grimes, "Woman in History," 124.

109 Blakely, "Topics of Interest."

110 Edselas, "Institute for Women's Professions," 378.

111 Sadlier, "Women in the Middle Ages," 60, 88.

112 Gibbons, "Relative Condition of Woman," 656, 657.

113 Coogan, "Occupations for Women," 289.

114 Husslein, "New Woman after God's Heart."

115 McSorley, "Saint Chantal," 572–73.

116 Ibid., 572.

117 Sullivan, "Chiefly among Women," 332 (emphasis added).

118 Repplier, *Mère Marie of the Ursulines*, 286.

119 Gibbons, "Relative Condition of Woman," 656, 657 (emphasis added).

120 Murphy, "Opportunities of Educated Catholic Women," 612.

121 Carrigan, "Higher Education of Catholic Women," 418.

122 Shields, "Teachers College," 324.

123 Appleby, *Church and Age Unite*, 13.

124 Mozans, *Woman in Science*, 80, 75.

125 Ibid., 391; Russett, "Preface to the 1991 Edition," xvii.

126 Carrigan, "Higher Education of Catholic Women," 417.

127 Walsh, *Education*, 286; Murphy, "Opportunities of Educated Catholic Women," 613.

128 Gleason, *Keeping the Faith*, 19–20.

129 Walsh, "Some Women of a Medieval Century," 616; Walsh, *The Thirteenth, Greatest of Centuries*, esp. chap. 20.

130 Walsh, "Some Women of a Medieval Century," 622.

131 Onahan, "Catholic Women in Philanthropy," 106.

132 *New World* (Chicago), October 17, 1903, quoted in Shanabruch, *Chicago's Catholics*, 133.

133 Campbell, "Origins of Charitable Institutions."

134 Spalding, "Should Catholic Associations," 282 (emphasis added).

135 Walsh to McDevitt, June 6, 1911, box 5, PRMC/PA; Flick, *Life of Bishop McDevitt*, 126.

136 Donnelly, "Have Women Souls?," 304.

137 See, for example, "Fear of Committee-ment," *Chronicle of Higher Education*, November 16, 2001, <http://chronicle.com/jobs/2001/11/2001111602c.htm>, and Nolan, "Myth of Soulless Women."

138 George, "Notes on the Intelligence of Woman," 721.

139 Walsh to McDevitt, June 9, 1908, box 1, PRMC/PA; Walsh, *Education*, 292.

140 "Chicago's Great Catholic Writer," *New World* (Chicago), January 9, 1904.

141 Sullivan, "Chiefly among Women," 335.

142 Onahan, "Catholic Women in Philanthropy," 106.

143 [Margaret Buchanan Sullivan], "The New Pope Seen at Harvard," *New World* (Chicago), August 22, 1903.

144 Sullivan, "Chiefly among Women," 341.

145 Sullivan, "Twentieth Century Woman," 649–50.

146 Reprinted in M. Seraphine, *Immortelles*, 224.

147 Reprinted in ibid., 296.

148 O'Dea, *History of the Ancient Order of Hibernians*, 1123.

149 Mrs. Morrogh-Bernard was actually Mother Mary Arsenius (1842–1932) of the Irish Sisters of Charity. In Ireland, the title "Mrs." did not always refer to marital status and could be used to imply maturity or seniority. It was often used in reference to professed nuns. For more information on Agnes Morrogh-Bernard, see Finlan, "Cocking a Snook at Patriarchy to Create an Industrial Marvel," *Irish Times* (Dublin), May 8, 1992, 12; Gallagher, *Courageous Irishwomen*, 73–77. I am indebted to Walter Nugent for supplying this reference.

150 Moore, "New Woman's Work," 458.

151 "Not the New Woman," 196.

152 Doyle, "Striking for Ireland on the New York Docks," 358.

153 Sullivan, "Twentieth Century Woman," 652; Moore, "New Woman's Work," 451, 458.

154 Tynan (after her marriage, Katharine Tynan-Hinkson) was one of the most prolific Irish women writers, publishing 184 volumes over the course of her career. See Colman, "Far from Silent," 203, and Tynan, "Higher Education for Catholic Girls," 620.

155 A Chronicler, "Words for Women."

156 Walsh, "City of Learned Women," 596–97, 598, 608.

157 Onahan, "Catholic Women in Philanthropy," 105–6. Catherine of Alexandria is not a doctor of the church, and it is unclear on what basis Onahan believed that she was. The first woman doctor of the church was Catherine of Siena, who was declared such in 1970. Saint Teresa of Avila also received that honor later that year. In 1997, John Paul II declared Thérèse of Lisieux to be a doctor of the church.

158 Nixon, "Saintly Scholar," 452.

159 Ibid.; Blake, "Blessed Daughter," 309.

160 See, for example, O'Reilly, "One of Philadelphia's Soldiers in the Mexican War," and "One of Philadelphia's Soldiers in the War of 1812," 419.

161 Judith Stone observes that "the valiant tale of Joan of Arc played an important role in *fin-de-siecle* Catholic sensibility—the female savior of France who

defended royal, male power, promoting the king's cause as a Christian crusade. . . . The struggle over who rightly possessed Joan was part of a broader rhetorical, cultural and political competition over whether clericals or anticlericals could better embody and defend France." See Stone, "Gender Identities and the Secular/Clerical Conflict," quoted with permission of author.

162 O'Reilly, "Maid of Orleans."

163 O'Mahoney, *Famous Irishwomen*, 7, 14, 191.

164 Ibid., 59. See also Anna Sadlier's biographical sketch of O'Carroll, in which she argued that "O'Carroll's life revealed Ireland in all of its 'glory and greatness.' " Sadlier, *Women of Catholicity*, 24–25.

165 Brundage, " 'In Time of Peace, Prepare for War,' " 324.

166 Curtis, *American Catholic Who's Who*, 492; *Records of the Proceedings of the Ladies Auxiliary of the Ancient Order of Hibernians in America*, 105, 111, 125.

167 Repplier, "Catholicism and Authorship," 173; Repplier, *Varia*, 1–2.

168 Repplier, *Mère Marie of the Ursulines*, 12, 187.

169 Ibid., 24.

170 "Biographical Sketch," Agnes Repplier Papers, University of Pennsylvania. <http://www.library.upenn.edu/collections/rbm/mss/repplier/repplierbio>.

171 See list in *RACHSP* 6 (1895): 27.

172 Campbell, "Women Scholars of the Middle Ages," 246.

173 Campbell, "Woman and the Ballot," 191.

174 See, for example, Campbell, "Origins of Charitable Institutions," and Baille, "Some Women of Bologna."

175 Lummis, *Daughters of the Faith*, 10–11.

176 For a study of how these tensions shaped American Catholic literature in the first two-thirds of the twentieth century, see Cadegan, *All Good Books Are Catholic Books*.

177 Lummis, *Daughters of the Faith*, ix; constitution quoted on xi–xii.

178 It was, for example, reprinted in the *Catholic Mind* 14 (1916): 319–49.

179 Sullivan, "Chiefly among Women," 327.

CHAPTER TWO

1 Waggaman, "Catholic Life in Washington," 837–38.

2 Conway, *New Footsteps*, 210.

3 Seton, "Higher Education of Women," 147.

4 O'Mahoney, *Famous Irishwomen*, 123–24.

5 SJM to Superiors, January 1896, quoted in Bosler, "Preparation of Sister Teachers," 129.

6 As Philip Gleason has explained, it is difficult to determine the exact number of Catholic colleges that existed at this time because of the uncertainty about what type of institution constituted a college as opposed to an academy. He also pointed out that this problem is not unique to Catholic institutions. See Gleason, *Contending with Modernity*, 3.

7 Bowler, "History of Catholic Colleges for Women," 19.

8 The School Sisters of Notre Dame should not be confused with the Sisters of Notre Dame de Namur. The motherhouse of the former was in Munich, and the American province was based in Milwaukee.

9 Cameron, *College of Notre Dame of Maryland*, 56–58.

10 Gleason, *Contending with Modernity*, 70.

11 Oates, "Development of Catholic Colleges for Women," 414; Hayes, "Founding of Trinity College," 84.

12 SJM to SME, April 1897, transcribed into Sister Mary Euphrasia, "Sketch of the Foundation," 62, TCA.

13 Englemeyer, "Maryland First," 196; Bowler, "History of Catholic Colleges for Women," 49, 31; Gleason, *Contending with Modernity*, 89–90.

14 The University of Notre Dame, for example, had opened in 1842 but did not differentiate between preparatory and graduate work until the 1880s, and the preparatory school remained on the campus until the 1920s. Gleason, *Contending with Modernity*, 4, 6.

15 As Suellen Hoy observed in her history of Irish nuns, "obscurity and invisibility, though not uncommon in the study of women's lives in general, are particularly troublesome when they are sought after and considered measures of success." Hoy, "Journey Out," 65.

16 SJM to the Sisters of Trinity, February 1901, FY.

17 Carol Coburn and Martha Smith note that nuns' achievements and influence are routinely attributed to "Father" or "beloved Bishop." Coburn and Smith, *Spirited Lives*, 223.

18 O'Mahoney, *Famous Irishwomen*, 127.

19 Sister Helen Louise, *Sister Julia*, 5.

20 Sister of Notre Dame de Namur, *American Foundations*, x–xvi; Mullaly, *Trinity College*, 7.

21 Quoted in Sister Helen Louise, *Sister Julia*, 25, 30.

22 Sister of Notre Dame de Namur, *Historical Sketch*, 9; Keenan, *Three against the Wind*, 15–29.

23 Bosler, "Preparation of Sister Teachers," 119.

24 Hoy, "Journey Out," 64–98; Diner, *Erin's Daughters in America*, 130.

25 Hilliard, "Investigation of Selected Events," 62–64; Bosler, "Preparation of Sister Teachers," 138–41.

26 Woloch, *Women and the American Experience*, 276–77. See also Solomon, *In the Company of Educated Women*, and Palmieri, *Adamless Eden*.

27 Sister Mary Euphrasia, "In the Midst of Things," *Notre Dame Quarterly*, September 2, 1910, copy in TCA.

28 SJM to SME, September 2, 1897, copied into Sister Mary Euphrasia, "Sketch of the Foundation," 236.

29 Sister of Notre Dame de Namur, *Historical Sketch*, 10.

30 Gleason, *Contending with Modernity*, 28, 89.

31 Sister Mary Euphrasia, "Sketch of the Foundation," 1–3.

32 Ibid., 3 (emphasis in original).

33 Ibid., 10. For a discussion of the twenty women applicants, see Cohen, "Early Efforts," 4–6, and Gleason, *Contending with Modernity*, 28.

34 Sister Mary Euphrasia, "Sketch of the Foundation," 8. Most Catholic colleges were single-sex until the 1970s.

35 Gleason, *Contending with Modernity*, 25.

36 P. J. Ryan to My Dear Mother Julia, 1897, quoted in Sister Helen Louise, *Sister Julia*, 284.

37 O'Malley, "College Work for Catholic Girls," 162.

38 Ibid.

39 Sister Mary Euphrasia's account of the meeting appears in her "Sketch of the Foundation," 41–45.

40 Ibid., 56. The fact that Sister Mary Euphrasia recorded this statement further testifies to congregational pride as a motivating factor.

41 Ibid., 63.

42 Gibbons to SJM, 21 June 1897, TCA.

43 Mullaly, *Trinity College*, 26.

44 *New York Times*, June 16, 1897, 6; Mullaly, *Trinity College*, 30–32.

45 Archbishop John Ireland to SJM, July 16, 1897, SJMC.

46 Gleason, *Contending with Modernity*, 7–12.

47 Fogarty, *Vatican and the American Hierarchy*, 158–59; Hogan, *Catholic University of America*, 6.

48 Litoff and McDonnell, *European Immigrant Women*, 149.

49 Spalding, "Woman and the Higher Education," 29, 38, 26.

50 Gibbons to SJM, June 21, 1897, SJMC.

51 Quoted in Bugg, "Trinity College," 379.

52 Pace, "College Woman," 287.

53 Quoted in Mullaly, *Trinity College*, 27.

54 J. N. E., "The 'New Woman' at the 'University,'" August 11, 1897, *Das Herold des Glaubens*, translation in FY. Evidence that Schroeder was behind this letter can be found in a letter from Sr. Angela Elizabeth, SND, to Sr. Sheila

Doherty, June 2, 1972, TCA. "J. N. E." is most likely John N. Enzelberger, a German priest from Illinois and the editor of *Das Herold des Glaubens*.

55 Sr. Mary Euphrasia to editors of *Das Herold des Glaubens*, August 28, 1897, copy in TCA.

56 Satolli to Gibbons, August 15, 1897, translation in Hogan, *Catholic University of America*, 97 (original in Italian in Baltimore Archdiocesan Archives).

57 Martinelli to Gibbons, August 23, 1897, quoted in Hogan, *Catholic University of America*, 97.

58 Sister Mary Euphrasia, "Sketch of the Foundation," 192–95.

59 See Clippings file, TCA.

60 Mullaly, *Trinity College*, 36.

61 Sister Mary Euphrasia, "Sketch of the Foundation," 209–16.

62 SJM to SME, September 2, 1897, in ibid., 236.

63 "Trinity College Journal," unpublished manuscript, 17, TCA.

64 Sr. Agnes Loretto to Sr. Superior [Sr. Mary Borgia], September 15, 1897, TCA; Sister Helen Louise, *Sister Julia*, 273.

65 Sister Mary Euphrasia, "Sketch of the Foundation," 241–43.

66 SJM to Ferrata, September 8, 1897, copy in TCA; SJM to Aloisi-Masella, September 1897, copy in TCA.

67 Bosler, "Preparation of Sister Teachers," 128.

68 SJM to Rampolla, September 8, 1897, copy in TCA.

69 SME to Satolli, August 26, 1897, copy in TCA.

70 SJM to Ferrata, September 8, 1897; SJM to Aloisi-Masella, September 1897. Rooker's advice appears in Sister Mary Euphrasia, "Sketch of the Foundation," 241–42.

71 Sr. Agnes Loretto to Sr. Superior [Sr. Mary Borgia], September 25, 1897, TCA.

72 SME to Satolli, August 26, 1897, copy in TCA.

73 SJM to Rampolla, September 8, 1897, copy in TCA.

74 Gibbons to Martinelli, August 25, 1897; Gibbons to Satolli, September 5, 1897, quoted in Hogan, *Catholic University of America*, 98.

75 M. C. M., "Columbian Reading Union," 861–63.

76 Sr. Agnes Loretto to Sr. Superior [Sr. Mary Borgia], September 15, 1897, TCA.

77 Rampolla to Martinelli, November 1897; letter was received at the Apostolic Delegate on November 27; translation quoted in Hogan, *Catholic University of America*, 98.

78 "Trinity College Journal," 16.

79 Ibid., 17.

80 Sr. Agnes Loretto to Sr. Superior [Sr. Mary Borgia], October 26, 1897, TCA.

81 Schroeder officially resigned on December 29, 1897. Gleason, *Contending with Modernity*, 10; Fogarty, *Vatican and the American Hierarchy*, 158–59.

82 Quoted in "Trinity College Journal," 16–17.

83 Keenan, *Three against the Wind*, 112.

84 Bosler, "Preparation of Sister Teachers," 129.

85 The fullest account of this incident is found in Keenan, *Three against the Wind*, 131–36.

86 Ibid., 134.

87 Hayes, "Founding of Trinity College," 81; Sister Mary Euphrasia, "Sketch of the Foundation," 202.

88 Sr. Julia to Dr. Garrigan, April 18, 1898, SJMC.

89 Minutes of the Ladies Auxiliary Board, April 3, 1899, LAB.

90 "A Summary of Questions Most Frequently Asked," November 28, 1899, pamphlet, FY.

91 Sr. Julia to American sisters, December 1897, reprinted in Sister Helen Louise, *Sister Julia*, 330.

92 Sr. Julia to American sisters, December 26, 1889, quoted in Sister Helen Louise, *Sister Julia*, 174.

93 SJM to Ferrata, September 8, 1897, SJMC.

94 Sr. Julia to Dr. Philip Garrigan, April 18, 1898, SJMC.

95 Minutes of the Ladies Auxiliary Board, March 31, 1898, April 3, 1899, LAB; "A Summary of Questions Most Frequently Asked," FY.

96 Minutes of the Ladies Auxiliary Board, April 13, 1898, LAB.

97 "Trinity College Organizations," pamphlet, FY.

98 Mullaly, *Trinity College*, 45–46.

99 Open Letter from Olive Risley Seward, president of the Ladies Auxiliary Board, April 18, 1898, in "First Fund-Raising Appeals," LAB.

100 Bugg, "Trinity College," 383.

101 Minutes of the Ladies Auxiliary Board, November 7, 1898; Mullaly, *Trinity College*, 50.

102 "Trinity College Journal," reprinted in Mullaly, *Trinity College*, 50.

103 Minutes of the Ladies Auxiliary Board, December 16, 1898, LAB.

104 Spalding, "Woman and the Higher Education," 25–47.

105 Slayden, *Washington Wife*, 29.

106 Minutes of the Ladies Auxiliary Board, March 3, 1899, May 10, 1899, LAB; Sister of Notre Dame de Namur, *Historical Sketch*, 18.

107 Sister of Notre Dame de Namur, *Historical Sketch*, 18; Mullaly, *Trinity College*, 56.

108 Keenan, *Three against the Wind*, 129.

109 Sister Helen Louise, *Sister Julia*, 281.

110 Sister of Notre Dame de Namur, *Historical Sketch*, 19; "Laying the Cornerstone of Trinity College, Washington, DC," *Pilot* (Boston), December 16, 1899.

111 Emma Forbes Cary to SME, May 3, 1900, Emma Forbes Cary folder, LAB.

112 Gasson, "Women and the Higher Intellectual Life," 67.

113 Quoted in Mullaly, *Trinity College*, 59.

114 Howe, "Trinity College," 321–22; "Report of the Ladies Auxiliary Board of *Trinity College*," January 1911, LAB.

115 Mullaly, *Trinity College*, 58.

116 Obituary, Ellen Carter folder, LAB; Sen. Thos. Carter to ELD, June 28, 1906, ELD folder, LAB; Nelly Feely, "Auxiliary Board of Regents of Trinity College: Historical Sketch," February 18, 1934, typescript, 4–5, LAB.

117 "Miss Dorsey's Expense Account (recapitulation)," app. 4, Mullaly, *Trinity College*, 551–53; minutes of the Ladies Auxiliary Board, December 3, 1900, LAB.

118 Minutes of the Ladies Auxiliary Board, May 9, 1901, LAB.

119 Ibid., November 6, 1899, LAB, quoted in Mullaly, *Trinity College*, 62.

120 ELD to Sr. Lidwine, November 5, 1901, ELD folder, LAB.

121 For a complete account of the crises with the Ladies Auxiliary Board, see Cummings, "We Owe It to Our Sex."

122 Obituary, *Trinity College Record* 30 (Winter 1936), clipping in ELD folder, LAB.

123 ELD to SJM, January 14, 1901, ELD folder, LAB.

124 ELD to Sr. President [Sr. Julia of the Trinity], February 13, 1932, ELD folder, LAB.

125 ELD to Sr. Georgiana, February 26, 1902, October 25, 1902, August 13, 1902, ELD folder, LAB.

126 Sister Helen Louise, *Sister Julia*, 347.

127 Ibid., 298–99.

128 SJM to SME, April 1897, in Sister Mary Euphrasia, "Sketch of the Foundation," 62.

129 Sister Helen Louise, *Sister Julia*, 299–300.

130 Sister of Notre Dame de Namur, *Historical Sketch*, 35; Mullaly, *Trinity College*, 71.

131 Sister of Notre Dame de Namur, *Historical Sketch*, 35, quoted in Bugg, "Trinity College," 380.

132 Sr. Agnes Loretto to SME, September 2, 1897, in Sister Mary Euphrasia, "Sketch of the Foundation," 239; SME to Satolli, August 26, 1897, copy in TCA.

133 SJM to Ferrata, September 8, 1897, copy in TCA.

134 Quoted in Mullaly, *Trinity College*, 40.

135 M. C. M., "Columbian Reading Union," 862.

136 "Trinity College Prospectus," in FY.

137 SJM to SME, April 1897, copied into Sister Mary Euphrasia, "Sketch of the Foundation," 63; minutes of the Ladies Auxiliary Board, May 10, 1899, LAB; Keenan, *Three against the Wind*, 124.

138 Bugg, "Trinity College," 377.

139 Mullaly, *Trinity College*, 266.

140 McDevitt, "Trinity College and Higher Education," 389.

141 Rev. Thomas Beaven, archbishop of Springfield, Massachusetts, to Sr. Julia, July 14, 1897, FY. Excerpts of this letter were reprinted in a publicity pamphlet.

142 Sr. Agnes Loretto to SME, September 2, 1897, TCA.

143 Garrigan to SME, in Sister Mary Euphrasia, "Sketch of the Foundation," 27.

144 SJM to SME, August 11, 1897, in Sister Mary Euphrasia, "Sketch of the Foundation," 187.

145 Howe, "Trinity College," 323; Bugg, "Trinity College," 382.

146 Trinity would share some faculty members with Catholic University until the 1930s, when the accrediting agencies objected to the sharing of resources. Mullaly, *Trinity College*, 87.

147 *Trinity College Catalogue*, 1898, TCA.

148 Minutes of the Advisory Board, May 9, 1901, TCA; Mullaly, *Trinity College*, 314.

149 Litoff and McDonnell, *European Immigrant Women*, 149, 111, 45; Smith, "American Irish Women in Education."

150 Sister of Notre Dame de Namur, *Historical Sketch*, 61; minutes of the Advisory Board of Trinity College, May 13, 1905, May 31, 1906, TCA.

151 Sister of Notre Dame de Namur, *Historical Sketch*, 21–22. Irish surnames predominated on later class rosters as well. "Degrees Conferred, 1904–1925," *Trinity College Catalogue*, 1925, TCA.

152 Trinity's inaugural class roster lists Helen Loretto O'Mahoney of Lawrence, Massachusetts. Lawrence is also the hometown of Katharine O'Keeffe O'Mahoney. Sister of Notre Dame de Namur, *Historical Sketch*, 21–22.

153 Sr. Agnes Loretto to Sr. Superior [Sr. Mary Borgia], September 15, 1897, TCA.

154 *Trinity College Catalogue*, 1898, TCA.

155 SME to SJM, May 25, 1897, in Sister Mary Euphrasia, "Sketch of the Foundation," 135–36 (emphasis in original).

156 "Rambles in Ireland," illustrated lecture by Rev. M. F. Foley of Baltimore, February 20, 1910, in Ellen Carter folder, LAB.

157 Upton, "House on the Aventine," 633; Mullaly, *Trinity College*, 45; Eliza Allen Starr, pamphlet, FY.

158 Mullaly, *Trinity College*, 313; Bugg, "Trinity College," 388. For Bugg's status as a student, see SJM to Sisters of Trinity, February 1901, SJMC.

159 Quoted in Sister Helen Louise, *Sister Julia*, 350.

160 Quoted in Mullaly, *Trinity College*, 31.

161 Landy, "Colleges in Context," 66.

CHAPTER THREE

1 An account of the competition is provided in Sister M. Stanislaus [Quigley], "The Most Reverend Philip R. McDevitt: Founder of High Schools," box 4, folder 2, SEC.

2 Miss Mary Donohue, "A Home Art," June 1905, "Prize Papers in Christian Doctrine," box 1, folder 1, SAMC (emphasis in original).

3 Catholic sisters' labor was technically not unpaid, as they received room and board, and some pastors remitted a sum for each parish teacher to the community. One early scholar of Catholic education estimated that the amount paid to a teaching sister was, on average, one-third to one-half less of what either male religious or female public school teachers received. See Burns, "Training of the Teacher," 8.

4 For other scholarship on nuns as "workers," see Wall, *Unlikely Entrepreneurs*, and essays by Morrow and Clark in Delfino and Gillespie, *Neither Lady nor Slave*.

5 Dolan, *American Catholic Experience*, 289.

6 Burns, "Development of Parish School Organization," 428–29; Flick, *Life of Bishop McDevitt*, 74–85.

7 Burns, *Catholic Education*, 58.

8 Information on the McEvoy family is gleaned from census records of 1850 (roll M432–812, p. 39, image 79) and from Sister M. Franceline, SSJ, "Sister M. Assisium, S.S.J.," typescript, SAMC. Information on Cedar Ward can be found in Gillette, "Emergence of the Modern Metropolis," 7, 11. On the demographics of St. Patrick's, see Nolan, "Francis Patrick Kenrick," 157–58. In her community history of the Sisters of St. Joseph, Logue described St. Patrick's as a "parish of serving girls" in the mid-nineteenth century. Logue, *Sisters of St. Joseph*, 115. One of the wealthier members of St. Patrick's was Thomas Cahill, a Catholic benefactor. See *Souvenir Sketch of St. Patrick's Church*, 46–47.

9 Fessenden, "Nineteenth-Century Bible Wars."

10 Meenagh, "Archbishop John Hughes."

11 See Jorgenson, *State and the Non-Public School*, esp. chap. 5, and Meenagh, "Archbishop John Hughes," 42.

12 The incident is recorded both in Sister Franceline's biographical essay on McEvoy, "Sister M. Assisium, S.S.J.," and in Mahony, *Historical Sketches*, 65. More details are included in *Souvenir Sketch of St. Patrick's Church*, 16, 17.

13 *Souvenir Sketch of Saint Patrick's Church*, 24. On the Irish background of the SSJs, a list of professed sisters dating from 1857 has fifty-four names. Thirty-five of the sisters listed had been born in Ireland, three in Germany, and the rest had been born in the United States and had Irish surnames. The profession book of 1860 shows similar proportions. I obtained these figures courtesy of Sister Mary Helen Kashuba, SSJ, who is writing an updated history of the congregation.

14 Sister Assisium's memorandum of Neumann's visit is quoted in Logue, *Sisters of St. Joseph*, 117.

15 See Coburn and Smith, *Spirited Lives*, 56–60. See also Byrne, "Sisters of St. Joseph," 257–58.

16 *Catholic Standard* (Philadelphia), September 1, 1883, quoted in Donaghy, *Philadelphia's Finest*, 84. For Catholics' objection to public schools, see Gleason, *Keeping the Faith*, 119–29.

17 State law, church efforts to "Americanize" immigrants, the propaganda campaign of World War I, and a decline in immigration in the 1920s all contributed to the demise of the ethnic school by the 1930s. Walch, *Parish School*, 76–83. See Ryan, "Missing Piece of the 1918 Dewey Report," 58–78.

18 "Decrees of the Third Plenary Council of Baltimore (1884)," reprinted in McCluskey, *Catholic Education in America*, 94.

19 Philadelphia was elevated to a metropolitan see in 1875.

20 Ryan stated that "any rector of a parish whose annual diocesan statement shows that he can establish such a school, and who shall not have one in operation by September 1905, shall be subject to removal to an inferior parish, at that date." Quoted in Martino, "Study of Certain Aspects," 389.

21 "Table Showing Progress of Philadelphia Diocese from 1884 to 1903," in Kirlin, *Life of Most Reverend Patrick John Ryan*, 35.

22 See Walch, *Parish School*, chap. 6. Though Ryan was less vociferous in his criticism of Ireland than was McQuaid or Corrigan, he disagreed vehemently with Ireland's position. See P. J. R., "Editorial Note," 642.

23 Ireland, "On the Occasion of the Fiftieth Anniversary," 154.

24 There were remarkably few dissenting voices after 1893. Ryan, *Are Parochial Schools the Answer?*

25 Appleby, Byrne, and Portier, *Creative Fidelity*, 55.

26 Ireland, "On the Occasion of the Fiftieth Anniversary," 155.

27 Stewart, "Women Religious in America," 1496. See also Stewart's *Marvels of Charity*, esp. tables on 322, 564, 565.

28 Gibbons, "School Supervision," 165, 168. Thomas Shields and Edward Pace wrote to the American hierarchy in March 1908, recommending that all

bishops appoint school superintendents to foster progress. Gorman, *Celebrating the Journey*, 166. See also Jacobs, "U.S. Catholic Schools," 17–18.

29 Mother Clement Lannen, SSJ, to Rev. Fisher, December 7, 1889, quoted in Logue, *Sisters of St. Joseph*, 191. The sister or brother who was appointed to this office had no other responsibilities; just as bureaucratization and specialization shaped corporate and industrial work, they also shaped the work of people who were "removed from the world." Dries, "Americanization of Religious Life," 17–18.

30 O'Hara, "Supervision of Catholic Schools," 216.

31 Burns, "Development of Parish School Organization," 430; Gibbons, "School Supervision," 178–79.

32 In 1908, the superintendent of Cincinnati's parochial schools urged that "permission be granted to organize a Board of Inspectors, such as they have in Philadelphia." *Annual Report of the Superintendent of the Parochial Schools of the Archdiocese of Cincinnati*, 7. In 1912, the superintendent of the Diocese of Hartford, Connecticut, told McDevitt that he had succeeded in getting communities to appoint inspectors. See W. J. Fitzgerald to McDevitt, December 17, 1912, in box 3, PRMC/PA.

33 Thompson, "Validation of Sisterhood," 38–78.

34 Logue, *Sisters of St. Joseph*, 174–75.

35 Augenstein, *Lighting the Way*, 15.

36 The first Catholic layman was appointed in Manchester, New Hampshire, in 1919. Jacobs, "U.S. Catholic Schools," 18.

37 As David Tyack observed in his study of education in urban America, the hierarchical organization of schools replicated the gender patterns of society at large. The separation of male administration and female teaching staff fit the male chauvinism of the larger society "as hand to glove." Tyack, *One Best System*, 60.

38 M. de Chantal to Ryan, August 31, 1890, PJRC, copy in box 22, folder 45, MMDCP.

39 Sr. M. Anastasia, IHM, to McDevitt, 1910, in "Letters from Religious," box 2, folder 37, PRMC/ND.

40 See, for example, S. M. Ubalda to McDevitt, October 14, 1916, in "Letters from Religious," box 2, folder 37, PRMC/ND.

41 McDevitt to Howard, May 20, 1909, quoted in Augenstein, *Lighting the Way*, 15–16.

42 McDevitt to S. Edwin Megargee, Esq., November 27, 1912, box 3, PRMC/PA.

43 McDevitt to Rev. P. J. Scott, n.d. [1915?], box 11, PRMC/PA.

44 Gibbons, "School Supervision," 172.

45 Burns, "Training of a Teacher," 8.

46 McDevitt to S. Edwin Megargee, January 27, 1914, box 5, PRMC/ND.

47 Mother Bonaventure Stimson to Rev. Matthew Hand, January 27, 1912, box 4, folder 4, SAMC.

48 In Philadelphia, school reformers created a centralized system in the "Revolution of 1905." Hoffman, *Woman's True Profession*, 212; Issel, "Modernization in Philadelphia School Reform," 358–83.

49 For Dewey's vision, see Crunden, *Ministers of Reform*, 58–63.

50 Woods, *Church Confronts Modernity*, 98.

51 Hayes, "Need of Religious Vocations," 221.

52 McDevitt's annual report for 1899–1900 lists 713 teachers in the 112 schools in the archdiocese; 686 were religious, and 27 were lay. See *ARSPS*, *Sixth Annual Report*, 14.

53 The IHMs had arrived in the diocese from Monroe, Michigan, at the invitation of Neumann in 1858. The IHMs would eventually be separated into three congregations, one in Monroe, one in Philadelphia, and one in Scranton, Pennsylvania. A history of all three congregations, *Building Sisterhood*, was compiled by the Sisters, Servants of the Immaculate Heart of Mary and published by Syracuse University Press in 1997. The Philadelphia mother-house was established near West Chester, Pennsylvania, in 1872. The best source for the Philadelphia IHMs for the first half century is the congregational history written by Sister Maria Alma, IHM, *Sisters, Servants of the Immaculate Heart of Mary*.

Neumann had also been responsible for the foundation of Franciscans in Philadelphia when he encouraged three local German American women to form a religious community. Like most German American clerics, Neumann was particularly concerned that the children of Philadelphia's German immigrants be educated in their native language. For an account of the founding, see Gorman, *Celebrating the Journey*, chaps. 1 and 2. The motherhouse was moved from Philadelphia to Glen Riddle, Pennsylvania, in 1872.

54 Mother M. Katharine Drexel to Mother M. St. Ursula, September 29, 1939, box 5, folder 2, SAMC.

55 McEvoy's letters to McDevitt are found in both PRMC/ND and PRMC/PA. The dates of their correspondence range from October 24, 1901, until 1935, when McEvoy composed a poem in honor of McDevitt's golden jubilee (poem in box 4, folder 2, SEC). I found far fewer of McDevitt's letters to McEvoy. See, for example, SA to McDevitt, February 7, 1912, box 2, PRMC/PA; SA to McDevitt, September 13, 1913, in box 3, PRMC/PA; SA to McDevitt, May 24, 1917, box 2, folder 28, PRMC/ND. On December 21, 1925, Sister Assisium

writes to McDevitt that "just to claim your friendship is a great honor"; box 2, folder 37, PRMC/ND.

56 SA to McDevitt, September 23, 1921, box 2, folder 45, PRMC/ND.

57 Philip McDevitt, "Sermon, Diamond Jubilee of the Sisters, Servants of the Immaculate Heart of Mary (1921)," box 6, folder 27, PRMC/ND.

58 Ibid.

59 SA, "Meditation on Vocation" and "Mediation on the Vows," Instructions to Tertians, box 1 and 2, SAMC.

60 SA to McDevitt, October 6, 1925, box 2, folder 36, PRMC/ND.

61 As Mary Oates notes, this feminization of the teaching profession paralleled trends in secular education fifty years earlier. Oates, "Organized Voluntarism," 152.

62 Mother Mary Monica Felici, superior general of Felician Sisters of the OSFs, August 22, 1890, box 7, PJRC; contract, Sisters of the Holy Family at Nazareth, approved by Ryan, June 25, 1892, box 7, PJRC.

63 Statistics were obtained from the *Official Catholic Directory* and ARSPS, *Ninth Annual Report* (1903).

64 Mother de Chantal often delayed the entry of new postulants until more space could be added to the building. Sister M. Blanche, *Mother Mary de Chantal*, 58.

65 Most Rev. P. J. Ryan to Mother M. de Chantal, July 18, 1888, box 22, no. 36, MMDCP.

66 Rev. J. S. Noel to Mother Superior, May 6, 1891; Most Rev. Wm. H. Gross, C.S.S.R., to Sr. Mary Ambrose (with request to forward to Mother Superior), May 6, 1891; Archbishop Ryan to Mother M. de Chantal, May 31, 1891, box 22, folders 53, 48, 49, MMDCP.

67 Sister M. Blanche, *Mother Mary de Chantal*, 87.

68 McDevitt's annual reports record the OSFs with twenty schools in 1900 and twenty-three in 1919. Presumably canonical status helped to limit the number of schools the order accepted as well; its rule was approved in 1907. See Gorman, *Celebrating the Journey*, chap. 6, "Toward Papal Approbation." These sisters opened orphanages, hospitals, and schools in Oregon, Idaho, Maryland, and Delaware. For a complete list, see ibid., app. 3, "Apostolic Missions, 1855–1975," 444.

69 See drafts of letters to Shanahan, December 5, 1902, April 16, 1905, in box 4, folder 4, SAMC. Logue clarifies that the schools in these three cities were consolidated into one, Sacred Heart School at Conewago. Logue, *Sisters of St. Joseph*, 217.

70 Shanahan to McDevitt, November 7, 1911, box 2, PRMC/PA.

71 See, for example, *ARSPS, Tenth Annual Report* (1904), where McDevitt observes, "The overcrowding evil, I regret to say, shows little abatement in the parish schools. . . . In several of my reports I have dwelt on this defect of overcrowding" (20); Rev. J. A. Connelly to McDevitt, November 27, 1913, box 2, PRMC/PA.

72 Statistics are provided by McDevitt in *ARSPS, Eleventh Annual Report* (1905), in tables on pp. 114–19. In 1895, there were 86 schools and 33,060 students; ten years later, there were 106 schools and 50,974 students.

73 Matt. 9:37–38, quoted in *ARSPS, Eleventh Annual Report* (1905), 21; *ARSPS, Fourteenth Annual Report* (1908), 18.

74 O'Reilly "Necessity and Means," 264.

75 Schrembs, "Vocations to the Teaching Orders," 106. Schrembs's essay was later reprinted in pamphlet form.

76 Ibid., 107; Rev. Mother M. Anselm, *Catholic Teacher's Role*, 9.

77 M. Mary St. Andrew, SHCJ, to McDevitt, January 24, 1917, box 2, folder 37, PRMC/ND.

78 Hayes, "Need of Religious Vocations," 226.

79 Quoted in O'Reilly, *Out of Many Hearts*, 34.

80 O'Reilly, "Necessity and Means," 255.

81 Schrembs, "Vocations to the Teaching Orders," 107.

82 Hayes, "Need of Religious Vocations," 226.

83 Ibid.

84 A Sister of the Holy Cross, "Vocations for the Religious Life," 486.

85 McDevitt, "Need of Religious Teachers," quoted in O'Reilly, *Out of Many Hearts*, 35; Schrembs, "Vocations to the Teaching Orders," 107.

86 "Resolutions," 33.

87 Burns, "Condition of Catholic Secondary Education," 213–14; Burns, *Catholic Education*, 72, 75.

88 *ARSPS, First Annual Report* (1895), 10–11.

89 Spalding, "Normal Schools for Catholics," 95.

90 Bishop Bernard McQuaid, quoted in O'Reilly, *Out of Many Hearts*, 36.

91 Tyack provides the approximate statistics: the percentages of women teachers increased from 59 percent in 1870, to 70 percent in 1900, to 86 percent in 1920. The percentage of female teachers was higher in elementary schools. By 1905 only 2 percent of teachers in elementary schools were men, whereas 38 percent of elementary school principals were men. Tyack, *One Best System*, 61.

92 Ibid., 59–65; Brown, "Fear of Feminization."

93 Horsa, "Need of Male Teachers," 286–88.

94 McDevitt's response is found in *CEAB* 10 (1913): 295. As for the age, Shanahan specified that sisters would "labor under serious disadvantages" if teaching boys older than twelve. Others placed the age at thirteen or fourteen. See
   Rev. J. F. Lambert, *CEAB* 10 (1913): 292.

95 Rev. Mother M. Anselm, *Catholic Teacher's Role*, 5–6.

96 Quoted in Gorman, *Celebrating the Journey*, 162.

97 Brother Anthony, "Pastor and the School," 256, quoted in O'Reilly, "Necessity
   and Means," 266.

98 In his annual report for 1904–5, McDevitt lists 46 teaching brothers and 812
   teaching sisters in the archdiocese. The 1907–8 report shows 43 teaching
   brothers and 914 teaching sisters. The annual report for 1919 shows 43 teaching brothers and 1,571 teaching sisters. *ARSPS*, *Eleventh Annual Report* (1905),
   130; *Fourteenth Annual Report* (1908), 142; *Twenty-fifth Annual Report* (1919),
   155. Oates discusses the dwindling supply of teaching brothers in "Organized
   Voluntarism," 151–52. On the dearth of vocations to the teaching brotherhoods at the national level for a period that extends beyond that covered by
   this chapter, see the citations in Kreidler, "Fostering of Religious Vocations
   for the Brotherhood."

99 Rt. Reverend Camillus P. Maes, *CEAB* 5 (1908–9): 274.

100 Egan, "Importance of Vocation," quoted in O'Reilly, *Out of Many Hearts*, 2;
    Francais, "Vocations to Brotherhoods," quoted in O'Reilly, *Out of Many Hearts*,
    17; Brother Edward, FSC, *CEAB* 17 (1920): 229.

101 See comments by Rev. Leo Gassler and Brother Philip, FSC, in *CEAB* 10
    (1913): 291, 294.

102 Burns, *Catholic Education*, 118.

103 Barbian, "Plea for the Man Teacher."

104 In Philadelphia, at least, no effort appears to have been made to enlist laywo-
    men as teachers. McDevitt referred all inquiries about teaching vacancies by
    laywomen to the superiors of individual communities. Whether he did this
    because he deferred to their judgment or because he did not see enlisting
    laywomen as a viable option is unclear. See Elizabeth McClay to McDevitt,
    December 15, 1909, and McDevitt's reply to McClay, December 20, 1909, in
    box 1, PRMC/PA; McDevitt to Miss Madeleine Glynn, January 4, 1910; Mc-
    Devitt to Margaret McCarthy, June 23, 1911, box 2, PRMC/PA.

105 "Notes to Tertians," boxes 1 and 2, SAMC.

106 Quoted in O'Reilly, "Necessity and Means," 263–64.

107 Schrembs, "Vocations to the Teaching Orders," 108–9 (emphasis in original).

109 O'Reilly, "Necessity and Means," 256–57.

109 Power, "Thorough Formation of Our Teachers," 356–57.

110 "Very Singular Fact."

111 See, for example, SEJ, quoted in Sister Mary Barnaba, *Diamond Crown for Christ the King*, 147, in box 38, folder 1, ROPM.

112 Bro. Denis, "Vocations to the Teaching Orders," 31.

113 *ARSPS, Fifteenth Annual Report* (1909), 18–19; O'Reilly, too, insisted that "there is no question here of forcing vocations on children who have no calling." O'Reilly, "Necessity and Means," 261.

114 I am most indebted to Joseph Chinnici, Order of Friars Minor, for his assistance on this question. Lahitton, *La vocation sacerdotale*; O'Malley, "Spiritual Formation for Ministry," 90. O'Malley cites a passage from an entry on vocation in *Dictionnaire de théologie catholique*, cols. 3171–74. An account of the Lahitton controversy, as well as a copy of Cardinal Merry De Val's letter settling it, is included in Vermeersch, *Religious and Ecclesiastical Formation*, 74–84.

115 Delaunay, *Religious Teacher*, 14.

116 Rev. Mother M. Anselm, *Catholic Teacher's Role*, 13. The Lahitton resolution is also mentioned in Sauer, "On Vocations to the Teaching Brotherhoods," 304.

117 Hayes, "Need of Religious Vocations," 225.

118 Brother Philip, F.S.C., *CEAB* 10 (1913): 294. Schrembs exhorted sisters to remember that their solicitude and watchful care in fostering vocations should extend to girls as well as boys." Schrembs, "Vocations to the Teaching Orders," 8.

119 O'Reilly, "Necessity and Means," 267; Rev. Mother M. Anselm, "Catholic Teacher's Role," 10.

120 Power, "Thorough Formation of Our Teachers," 355.

121 O'Reilly, "Necessity and Means," 260.

122 Schrembs, "Vocations to the Teaching Orders," 113; O'Reilly, "Necessity and Means," 266; Brother Justin in commentary on O'Reilly, "Necessity and Means," 272.

123 Thomas Magennis to Archbishop William O'Connell, January 10, 1908, quoted in Oates, "Professional Preparation," 61.

124 Delaunay, *Religious Teacher*, 17.

125 M. Bonaventure to Rev. Ar. Prendergast, September 21, 1914, and Sr. M. of St. Bernadina, OLCGS, to Prendergast, June 21, 1915, in box 9, EPC.

126 Though this is widely assumed, it is little documented. Research for a period later than this one shows that a majority of women religious first began to consider religious life because of the influence of another sister. Hoedl, *Types of Secondary Schools*, 91–92. According to one estimate, between 50 and 90 percent of candidates for religious life had been educated by religious teachers, often those from the same order. O'Reilly, "Necessity and Means," 256.

That an area contained "good prospects for vocations" was often a carrot to open schools. See, for example, Rev. F. Borman, Diocese of Sioux Falls, South Dakota, to Mother Superior, IHM, March 10, 1920, box 23, folder 43a, MMJP.

127 [Sister Assisium], pamphlet commemorating anniversary of St. Mary's, Bayonne, New Jersey, typescript August 1915, box 5, folder 1, SAMC.

128 Rev. Mother M. Anselm, *Catholic Teacher's Role*, 8.

129 Ibid., 12.

130 Renamed John Hallahan High School in 1926.

131 *ARSPS, Seventh Annual Report* (1901), 5–7. For the SSJs, see Rev. M. Clement to Superiors at Missions, July 31, 1900, and September 3, 1900, box 4, folder 1, SEC. For the OSFs, see S. M. Cleta to McDevitt, July 9, 1900, box 1, PRMC/PA.

132 The Sisters of Notre Dame de Namur also opened a center in 1903.

133 Philip McDevitt to Mother Clement, June 20, 1900, quoted in Logue, *Sisters of St. Joseph*, 240. Writing to Rev. Robert Brown of Grand Rapids, McDevitt recalled that "each [congregation] followed their own way" in the high school centers; January 13, 1912, box 2, PRMC/PA.

134 McDevitt to Rev. William Cunningham, March 27, 1911, box 2, PRMC/PA.

135 See letters from Mother Aloysia, OSF, to McDevitt, May 19, 1911, and May 26, 1911, in box 1, PRMC/PA.

136 M. Mary Paul, Provincial, SHCJ, to McDevitt, November 21, 1911, and M. St. Michael to McDevitt, February 13, 1912, both in box 4, PRMC/PA. I found no correspondence between McDevitt and the SNDs, but they were not part of the original faculty.

137 McDevitt to Fr. Joseph McClancy, December 14, 1925, box 3, folder 1, PRMC/ND.

138 Delaunay, *Religious Teacher*, 28.

139 Sr. M. Stephanie to SEJ, May 8, 1924, box 6, folder 5, SEJC.

140 Sister M. Blanche, *Mother Mary de Chantal*, 83.

141 The "Report of the Mistress of Novices, 7th General Chapter, July 1916," lists 4 graduates from commercial high schools, 16 graduates from schools outside the city, 8 from the public high schools, 6 from Mount St. Joseph Academy, 75 from the high school, 5 from McSherrystown. ASSJ.

142 Sister St. Anne, SSJ, "Points Regarding His Excellency, the Late Philip R. McDevitt," and Sister Stanislaus, SSJ, "Most Reverend Philip McDevitt," box 4, folder 2, SEC.

143 See, for example, an invitation to the graduates of the centers, 1907, and program for a "Weekend Retreat given to the Alumnae of the Sisters of the Immaculate Heart of Mary, June 18–21, 1915," in box 3, folder 1, PRMC/ND; Sister Assisium's "Notebook of Catholic Girls' High School Retreats, 1915–

1927," box 1, folder 8, SAMC. Mother Aloysia of the OSFs believed that the congregations' constitution made no provision for outsiders to remain in the convent overnight and would not allow retreats. See Gorman, *Celebrating the Journey*, 176.

144 SSJ, "Suggestions as to the Government of the Catholic Girls' High School," box 2, folder 50, PRMC/ND.

145 Rev. John Flood, D.D., *CEAB* 17 (1920): 230.

146 Rev. Mother M. Anselm, *Catholic Teacher's Role*, 12.

147 "Instructions to Tertians," SAMC.

148 The *Official Catholic Directory* for 1903 shows 500 Sisters of St. Joseph, 312 Sisters, Servants of the Immaculate Heart of Mary, and 319 Franciscans in the Archdiocese of Philadelphia. In 1925, those numbers are 1,081, 922, and 360, respectively. Another way to measure growth is by looking at the proportion of women religious among the Catholic population. In 1884, there was one sister for every 294 Catholics in Philadelphia. By 1921, there was one sister for every 195 Catholics.

149 Stewart, *Marvels of Charity*, 565.

150 Hayes, "Need of Religious Vocations," 218, 224.

151 A Sister of the Holy Cross, "Vocations," 489.

152 Rev. Mother M. Anselm, *Catholic Teacher's Role*, 3.

153 *ARSPS, Twenty-Fifth Annual Report* (1919), 15.

154 Pastoral Letter of the American Hierarchy 1919, quoted in Rev. Mother M. Anselm, *Catholic Teacher's Role*, 16.

155 Quoted in Sister M. Blanche, *Mother Mary de Chantal*, 88.

156 *ARSPS, Eighth Annual Report* (1902), 4–6; *ARSPS, Seventeenth Annual Report* (1911), 21–22. In a letter to James Burns, McDevitt defined "more teachers" and "better teachers" as the two most urgent needs of Catholic education. "Better equipment" was identified as a third need. Burns quotes the letter in *Catholic Education*, 68.

157 *ARSPS, Thirteenth Annual Report* (1907), 11.

158 *ARSPS, Sixteenth Annual Report* (1910), 10.

159 McDevitt to Scott [1915], box 11, PRMC/PA.

160 SA to McDevitt, December 22, 1920, box 2, folder 45, PRMC/ND.

161 "Conferences, April 16, 1913," SAMC (emphasis in original).

162 SA to McDevitt, December 22, 1920, box 2, folder 45, PRMC/ND.

163 Summary of sermon preached to SSJs by Rev. Father Matheo in Chapel of Chamber, December 8, 1921, box 1, folder 5, SAMC.

164 Luke 10:41–42.

165 See, for example, Maus, "Address at Reception of Sisters of Mercy," 896.

166 Leo XIII's *Conditae a Christo* (1900) recognized active sisters as real religious

despite their lack of cloister and solemn vows. McNamara, *Sisters in Arms*, 613; Dries, "Americanization of Religious Life," 20.

167 Sister of St. Joseph, *Gleanings in Historic Fields*, 6.

168 Meyers, *Education of Sisters*, 9.

169 Sister M. Blanche, *Mother Mary de Chantal*, 55; SA, untitled typescript, December 1923 (transcribed from manuscript), box 5, folder 4, SAMC.

170 See Sister Eberharda's Mission Card, ASSFP, and U.S. Census of 1870.

171 Sister Eberharda Jones, "Handwritten Notes to Young Teachers," box 16, folder 8, SCSE.

172 Sister M. Eberharda, "Supervising Principal and the Teacher," 286.

173 McDevitt to Reverend Mother Aloysia, September 7, 1915, box 20, folder 5, SCSE.

174 Biographical material on Mother Camilla is found in box 23, folder 21a, MMCP, and Sister Maria Alma, *Sisters, Servants*, 240–41. The quotation from McDevitt is found in *ARSPS, Fourteenth Annual Report* (1913), 22.

175 Gorman reports that Archbishop Ryan notified all communities in 1893 that "the training of teachers was imperative because dioceses were increasingly conscious of the need for credentialed instruction." Gorman, *Celebrating the Journey*, 157; see also Burns, "Training of the Teacher," 23.

176 *ARSPS, Ninth Annual Report* (1903), 9–10.

177 Dr. Shaeffer, *Report of Commissioner of Education for 1903*, I, 1099, quoted in Meyers, *Education of Sisters*, 15.

178 Burns, "Development of Parish School Organization," 430–31.

179 Chinnici, "Religious Life," 33.

180 Ryan, sermon at Villa Maria, quoted in Sister M. Blanche, *Mother Mary de Chantal*, 75.

181 Summary of sermon preached to SSJs by Rev. Father Matheo in Chapel of Chamber, December 8, 1921, box 1, folder 5, SAMC.

182 Donaghy, *Philadelphia's Finest*, 119; *ARSPS, Third Annual Report* (1897), v–vii; *ARSPS, Eighth Annual Report* (1902), 6.

183 "Biographical Material, Mother Camilla," box 23, folder 21a, MMCP; Sister Maria Alma, *Sisters, Servants*, 241.

184 Draft, letter to Shanahan, April 1905, box 4, folder 4, SAMC.

185 Stimson to Ryan, September 21, 1914, EPC.

186 Gorman, *Celebrating the Journey*, 160.

187 Power, "Thorough Formation of Our Teachers," 341, 359.

188 Ei, "Difficulties Encountered by Superiors," 371.

189 *ARSPS, Fifteenth Annual Report* (1909), 17–18.

190 On Hofer's concern, see Gorman, *Celebrating the Journey*, 160. This period covered Hofer's first term as superior. The lone exception was St. Peter's

School in New Castle, Delaware, to honor a commitment made by Mother Agnes Bucher, Hofer's predecessor as superior. See ibid., 167. Note that the request for teachers to staff Catholic Girls' High School came in 1911, which may explain why Hofer was initially so reluctant to promise faculty.

191 Sr. Marilla Stoddard to Rev. Heuser, November 3, 1909, quoted in Gorman, *Celebrating the Journey*, 168.

192 "Instructions to Tertians," SAMC.

193 "Rules for Sister Teachers," in "Instructions to Tertians," SAMC.

194 Sister M. Blanche, *Mother Mary de Chantal*, 29; Mother Mary de Chantal, "Letters and Talks on the Spiritual Life, 1890," reprinted in Sister M. Blanche, *Mother Mary de Chantal*, 111.

195 Sister Eberharda Jones, "Notes on Retreat, July 23–31, 1911," box 6, folder 4, SEJC.

196 This poem was found among Sister Assisium's papers, and though she did not sign it, it is reasonable to assume that she was the author; box 1, folder 5, SAMC.

197 "Community Items," box 1, folder 5, SAMC.

198 Sister Mary Adele, "Mother Camilla," and Sister M. Cyrilla, "Mother Mary Camilla," in box 23, folder 21a, MMCP.

199 Sister Eberharda Jones, "Remote and Immediate Preparation of the Teacher," typescript, box 16, folder 9, SCSE.

200 Hofer, Mother Aloysia, letter to sisters in hospital ministry, February 11, 1914, quoted in Gorman, *Celebrating the Journey*, 173 (emphasis in original).

201 Sr. M. Carmela, CSJ, to SA, January 2, 1917, box 5, folder 1, SAMC.

202 SEJ to Sr. Valerie, October 16, 1919, box 6, folder 5, SEJC.

203 M. Camilla to M. Kostka, September 30, 1909, box 23, folder 6, MMCP.

204 Sister Mary Eberharda, A.B., "The Training of the Religious Teacher" (M.A. thesis, Mount Saint Mary's College, 1921), 1, box 16, folder 8, SCSE.

205 "Meditation on Vocation," SAMC.

206 "Holy Rule" and "Meditation on the Vows," SAMC.

207 "Holy Rule, Part 1," box 1, folder 12, SAMC.

208 "Mediation on the Vows," SAMC.

209 SA to McDevitt, December 22, 1920, box 2, folder 45, PRMC/ND.

210 Sister M. Blanche, *Mother Mary de Chantal*, 98, 83.

211 Sister Eberharda Jones, "Training of the Religious Teacher," 30.

212 Logue, *Sisters of St. Joseph*, 243; Gibbons also noted that while teaching communities labored in a common cause, they were "practically segregated" from one another. See Gibbons, "School Supervision," 168.

213 Mother Clement to Superiors, July 31, 1900, box 4, folder 1, SEC.

214 Sister M. Blanche, *Mother Mary de Chantal*, 84.

215 Flick, *Life of Bishop McDevitt*, 137.

216 McDevitt to McClancy, December 14, 1925, box 3, folder 1, PRMC/ND. See also Gibbons on this point, who identified one of the benefits that would accrue from closer collaboration among teaching communities as a "healthy emulation." Gibbons, "School Supervision," 168.

217 Quoted in Flick, *Life of Bishop McDevitt*, 138.

218 Spalding, "Normal Schools for Catholics," 88–97; Burns, "Training of the Teacher," 34–35; *ARSPS, Tenth Annual Report* (1904), 16–18.

219 *ARSPS, Sixteenth Annual Report* (1910); McDevitt to Rev. J. F. Sheehan, December 12, 1913, box 3, PRMC/PA.

220 "Convent News," *Messenger of Our Lady of Angels* (1900), mentions McDevitt's visit to the novitiate school, where he "spoke to the novices about their duties in the schoolroom as teachers" and "urged them to study well now and read much"; box 13, folder 3, SCSE.

221 Copies of school reports can be found in PRMC/PA. In one representative letter to the superintendent, Sister Irene, IHM, acknowledges her mistakes and promises improvement. Feast of Pentecost [May] 1907, box 1, PRMC/PA.

222 B. Ellen Burke to McDevitt, September 20, 1913, box 3, PRMC/PA. In 1913, for example, McDevitt sponsored one lecture on Tennyson and another on German literature; McDevitt to M. Bonaventure, SSJ, January 5, 1913; McDevitt to Dr. Remy, March 28, 1913, box 3, PRMC/PA. Other references to such lectures can be found in a letter to McDevitt from J. C. Monahan, April 29, 1909, and McDevitt to Reverend Mothers, January 4, 1910, box 1, PRMC/PA.

223 Stimson to Hand, January 27, 1912, box 4, folder 4, SAMC.

224 A. Duncan Yocum to McDevitt, May 11, 1911; McDevitt to Yocum, May 18, 1911, box 2, PRMC/PA.

225 Oates, "Professional Preparation," 65.

226 Sister Eberharda Jones, "Training of the Teacher," 10; T. E. Shields to SA, November 21, 1916, SAMC; SA to McDevitt, May 24, 1917, PRMC/ND; Donaghy, *Philadelphia's Finest*, 169.

227 Report of the Mistress of Novices, 7th General Chapter, July 1916, ASSJ.

228 Burns, *Catholic Education*, 72.

229 Quoted in A Sister of St. Dominic, "Our First Year," 435.

230 "Acct of Sisters Studies up to 1928," 24, ASSJ.

231 Ibid., 42.

232 Sister Maria Alma, *Sisters, Servants*, 256.

233 A Sister of St. Joseph [SA], "Attendance of Sisters," 475; typescript in SAMC.

234 Sister Eberharda Jones, "Educational Reorganization," 538–39; original in ASSFP.

235 Blakely, "Do we Want 'Prussianized' Schools?," 106; McGinnis, "State and Education," 105.

236 McDevitt, "State and Education," 82.

237 Sister Eberharda Jones, "Educational Reorganization," 537.

238 SEJ to Bishop McDevitt, n.d. [1919], and McDevitt's reply to SEJ, n.d. [1919], box 6, folder 5, SEJC.

239 Donaghy, *Philadelphia's Finest*, 182.

240 Sister Mary Adele, "Mother Camilla," and Sister Mary Albina, "Mother Mary Camilla," in box 23, folder 21a, MMCP.

241 Molloy, "Catholic Colleges for Women," 236.

242 McDevitt to Rev. H. C. Boyle, January 3, 1910, box 1, PRMC/PA. A similar controversy erupted when the Philadelphia Normal School announced it would only be accepting graduates of Philadelphia's public schools. McDevitt responded with letters to the *Public Ledger*, many of which are available in box 7, PRMC/PA.

243 For the most succinct summary of McDevitt's arguments, see his "State and Education," 74–99; see also McDevitt to Megargee, November 27, 1912, box 3, PRMC/PA.

244 *ARSPS, Ninth Annual Report* (1903), 9.

245 McDevitt, "State and Education," 82.

246 Sister St. Anne, SSJ, "Points Regarding His Excellency," box 4, folder 2, SEC; McDevitt, "State and Education," 85.

247 A Sister of St. Joseph [SA], "Attendance of Sisters," 475.

248 "Educating in the things of time as well as eternity" was identified as "the root idea of Catholic schools." See *Homiletic Monthly and Catechist* 4 (August 1904): xi.

249 Shields, "Catholic Education," 17; Shields, "Some Relations," 53.

250 A Sister of St. Dominic, "Our First Year," 439.

251 Tracy, "Church as an Educational Factor," 213.

252 *ARSPS, Sixteenth Annual Report* (1910), 20; McDevitt, "State and Education," 99.

253 Burns, *Catholic Education*, 16, 21 (emphasis in original); Carrigan, "Higher Education for Catholic Women," 417; see also Pace, "Papacy and Education," 2.

254 *ARSPS, Tenth Annual Report* (1904), 6. The essay contest continued at least until McDevitt's consecration as bishop. See sample essays in box 2, folder 46, PRMC/ND. For more information on the essay contest as well as the catechetical exhibit, see Sister St. Anne, "Points Regarding His Excellency."

255 In 1890, John Lancaster Spalding had suggested that Catholic teachers use "new methods" to make it more attractive and more central. Spalding, "Nor-

mal School for Catholics," 91. See also Bellord, *Religious Education and Its Failures*, 6–7, 17.

256 *ARSPS, Ninth Annual Report* (1903), 13–14.

257 Mother Clement to missions, December 13, 1901, quoted in Logue, *Sisters of St. Joseph*, 225.

258 S.S.J. [Sister Assisium McEvoy], preface to *Course of Christian Doctrine*; A Sister of St. Joseph of Philadelphia, "Objective Method."

259 *ARSPS, Ninth Annual Report* (1903), 14; *ARSPS, Tenth Annual Report* (1904), 21; Logue, *Sisters of St. Joseph*, 225–27.

260 See letters from, among others, Whelan, Shanahan, Workman, Etchemandy, Sr. Cordula, and Burke to SA in "Commendations of Religious and Lay Catechists," box 4, folder 4, SEC.

261 For Sister Assisium's travels and presentations, see Rev. Wm. J. McConnell to Superiors of Parish Schools, October 8, 1912, box 3, PRMC/PA; McConnell to McDevitt, October 8, 1912, box 3, PRMC/PA; Wm. J. McConnell to SA, October 12, 1918, in "Correspondence regarding Catechism and Mass Charts," and SA to McDevitt, May 29, 1911, both in box 5, folder 2, SAMC. Logue also discusses the popularity of the book in *Sisters of St. Joseph*, 227.

262 Sr. Eugenia to SA, November 22, 1923, box 4, folder 4, SEC.

263 Rev. Charles Carmody to Sr. Benigna Consolota, January 13, 1979, box 4, folder 4, SEC. Carmody had read the paper in the *CEAB* and was writing to inquire about the name of the author, who was listed only as "A Sister of Saint Joseph of Philadelphia." The text he pointed to reads: "Again, in teaching about the Passion, too much emphasis is often given to the point that Our Lord was crucified by Jews. Verbally, this is true; but in reality, it is sinners, including ourselves, who, knowing them better than they did, have crucified, and still crucify him by our transgressions." A Sister of St. Joseph of Philadelphia, "Objective Method," 284.

264 Sr. Cordula, Ursuline Academy, Great Falls, Montana, to SA, September 15, 1918, box 4, folder 4, SEC.

265 A Sister of Charity, "Misleading Graphs," 69–70.

266 McDevitt to SA, November 13, 1917, and Rev. J. A. Dillon, superintendent of schools in Newark, New Jersey, October 31, 1917, box 4, folder 5, SEC.

267 SA to McDevitt, May 25, 1932, PRMC/ND.

268 *ARSPS, Tenth Annual Report* (1904), 6; Sister Eberharda Jones, "Methods in Teaching," typescript, n.d., box 16, folder 10, SCSE.

269 Sister Eberharda Jones, "Educational Reorganization," 528.

270 Kathryn L. Abraham to Sr. M. Adele Francis Gorman, April 26, 1984, box 6, folder 5, SEJC.

271 Reher, "Review of Thomas Woods' *The Church Confronts Modernity*," 394.

272 Schuler, "Reaction of American Catholics," 4.

273 Hubbert, "'For the Upbuilding of the Church,'" 828–29.

274 Rev. Herman J. Heuser to Mother Clement and to SA [1904], box 4, folder 4, SEC.

275 H. J. Heuser to SEJ, July 29, 1915, box 20, folder 2, SCSE; F. A. Diehl, OSA, to SEJ, June 4, 1923, box 20, folder 3, SCSE.

276 Rev. Joseph A. Hickey, OSA, to SEJ, June 29, 1926, box 20, folder 9, SCSE.

277 Burns, "Training of a Teacher," 22–23; Meyers, *Education of Sisters*, 15.

278 ARSPS, *Fifteenth Annual Report* (1909), 19; ARSPS, *Twelfth Annual Report* (1906), 21–22.

279 ARSPS, *Thirteenth Annual Report* (1907), 21.

280 Burns, "Training of the Teacher," 18, 20.

281 Horsa, "Need of Male Teachers," 285–86.

282 Mullany, "Catholic Nun in the Classroom," 97.

283 Shields, "Catholic Education," 17.

284 Sister Eberharda Jones, "Handwritten Notes to Young Teachers," 24; Sister Eberharda Jones, "Training of the Teacher," 24.

285 Power, "Thorough Formation of Our Teachers," 339; Gibbons, "School Supervision," 172–73.

286 McDevitt, "Diamond Jubilee," box 6, folder 27, PRMC/ND.

287 ARSPS, *Tenth Annual Report* (1904), 21.

288 Burns, "Training of the Teacher," 19.

289 Power, "Thorough Formation of Our Teachers," 349.

290 Shields, "Some Relations," 61–62; Shields, "Catholic Education," 15.

291 Guthrie, "Catholic School," 548; Mullany, "Catholic Nun in the Classroom," 97.

292 Burns, "Training of a Teacher," 19–21.

293 Shields, "Teachers Salaries," 419.

294 Stimson to Hand, January 27, 1912, box 4, folder 4, SAMC.

295 Copy of Dougherty's letter to pastors, December 27, 1919, in box 23, folder 35, MMJP.

296 In particular, sisters bristled at Dougherty's strict enforcement of the six-year maximum assignment on any particular mission. In a letter to McDevitt, Sister Assisium referred to the "cyclonic nature" of the revised code: "Sixteen of our superiors have to hear the mighty 'Go.'" SA to McDevitt, September 3, 1925, PRMC/ND. Correspondence of the IHMs contains similar complaints.

In response to a questionnaire sent by the education committee of the National Catholic Welfare Conference, created in 1919, Mother Mary James Rogers of the SSJs stated that certification of teachers by ecclesiastical authorities would be far preferable to certification by the state. Mother Mary James's reply to questionnaire sent by Edward Pace, September 2, 1921, SEC.

297 SA to McDevitt, May 4, 1931, box 2, folder 45, PRMC/ND; D. J. M. Callahan, SJ, to SA, May 17, 1929, box 4, folder 1, SAMC.

298 SA to McDevitt, August 3, 1930, and October 12, 1930, in PRMC/ND.

299 Morris, *American Catholic*, 165–95.

300 SA to McDevitt, February 25, 1927, October 17, 1921, October 6, 1925, September 3, 1925, PRMC/ND.

301 SA to McDevitt, October 8, 1922, PRMC/ND.

302 SA to McDevitt, May 23, 1922, PRMC/ND.

303 SA to McDevitt, February 25, 1927, PRMC/ND.

304 SA to McDevitt, November 6, 1923, and May 29, 1924, PRMC/ND.

305 Molloy, "Catholic Colleges for Women," 245.

306 Sr. Stanislaus Quigley to SA, June 16, 1930, box 4, folder 1, SEC (emphasis in original).

307 SA to McDevitt, January 12, 1928, PRMC/ND.

308 Dries, "Americanization of Religious Life," 18–19.

CHAPTER FOUR

1 Conway, *Way of the World*, 148.

2 [Conway], "Catholics and Woman's Day," *Pilot* (Boston), June 3, 1893, 5.

3 See, for example, Blair, *Clubwoman as Feminist*; Muncy, *Creating a Female Dominion in American Reform*; Higginbotham, *Righteous Discontent*; and Palmieri, *In Adamless Eden*.

4 Kenneally, "Eve, Mary and Historians," 204–5.

5 Kenneally, "Question of Equality"; Diner, *Erin's Daughters in America*, 149–53.

6 Kenneally, "Catholic and Feminist," 253.

7 Lerner, "Editor's Introduction," xvi; Jablonsky, *Home, Heaven, and Mother Party*; Marshall, *Splintered Sisterhood*.

8 Kenneally, *History of American Catholic Women*, 133, 135; Kane, *Separatism and Subculture*, 231; Diner, *Erin's Daughters in America*, 154–55.

9 Conway, "The Cultured Catholic Woman and Her Political Duty," 7, n.d. [1924?], typescript, box 6, folder 14, KECC/BC; Conway, "Catholic Literary Societies," 204.

10 Conway, "Blessed among Women," box 6, folder 3, KECC/BC, later published in *Rosary Magazine*.

11 Brekus, "Introduction," 26; Rymph, *Republican Women*.

12 Biographical information on Conway is drawn from the following sources:

Curtis, *American Catholic Who's Who*, 115; Sr. M. Eleanore, "Passing of a Valiant Woman"; Driscoll, "In Memoriam."

For a comparison between Rochester and New England in terms of treatment of Irish Catholics, see Conway, "Right Reverend Bernard J. McQuaid, First Bishop of Rochester, New York: A Memoir," 24, typescript, BJMC. For her views on racial and religious prejudice in New England, see Conway, "John Boyle O'Reilly," 198.

13 For Conway's views of Catholic schools, see her letters to McQuaid, especially December 14, 1896, and June 29, 1892, BJMC.

14 Conway, "Right Reverend Bernard J. McQuaid," 4–5.

15 Lord, *History of the New England Women's Press Association*, 98; George E. Ryan, "Pilot's Only Woman Editor Fought for Dignity," *Pilot* (Boston), August 5, 1961. Although Eliza Allen Starr taught at Saint Mary's in the late nineteenth century, Conway became the first layperson to hold the rank of professor at the college. Sr. Bernadette Marie to Dr. William Hickey, 1986, KECC/SMCA.

16 KEC, Diary, November 25, 1908, February 14, 1912, KECC/BC; "56th Annual Commencement," *Saint Mary's Chimes*, June 1911, 192, SMCA. Conway, *New Footsteps*, 210. Conway was a member of Trinity's Associate Board in Boston. Reference to her attendance at meetings and her monetary contributions are found in the Emma Forbes Cary folder, LAB. Conway promoted the college in *Pilot* articles as well as in the *London Ontario Record*. Keenan, *Three Against the Wind*, 205n4. Conway also worshiped with the Sisters of Notre Dame de Namur in Boston and admired the congregation's founder, Mother Julie Billiart. See KEC, Diary, January 3, 1907, KECC/BC.

17 Sr. M. Eleanore, "Passing of a Valiant Woman," 411; Cullen, *Story of the Irish in Boston*, 277–78. Conway identifies Louise Imogen Guiney as the author of her profile in Cullen's book in a letter to McQuaid, September 1, 1889, BJMC. She also reports that she wrote several other essays and biographical sketches in this collection. Neither Conway nor Guiney received attribution, as all the contributors listed are men.

18 Annette S. Driscoll, a friend of Conway's, wrote that McQuaid noticed her paying rapt attention during his sermons at the cathedral. Other sources describe him as a family friend. Driscoll, "In Memoriam," 484; McNamara, *Diocese of Rochester*, 228–29. Conway, "Right Reverend Bernard J. McQuaid." There are approximately thirty letters from Conway to McQuaid in the Archives of the Diocese of Rochester. Unfortunately, none of McQuaid's letters to Conway are extant.

19 Nolan, *Servants of the Poor*; Cullen, *Story of the Irish in Boston*, 278.

20 Diner, *Erin's Daughters in America*, 70–73.

21 Obituary, Mary Conway, *New York Times*, September 10, 1903; "Memorial to Miss Mary Conway in Buenos Aires," *Pilot* (Boston), February 27, 1904, 7.

22 KEC to McQuaid, December 14, 1886, and June 15, 1892, BJMC; Thomas Hogan to Daniel Hudson, August 30, 1898, box 10, folder 4, DEHC; KEC to McQuaid, December 2, 1905, BJMC; Helene Conway to Edward Henry, June 30, 1974, KECC/SMCA. Conway records frequent visits to her brother in her diaries. Another sister had died at a young age. See "In Memory of Lena," in Conway, *On the Sunrise Slope*, 67.

23 KEC to McQuaid, June 15, 1892, BJMC.

24 Diner, *Erin's Daughters in America*, 15.

25 Conway, "The Difficulties and Triumphs of the Church in America," lecture, reprinted in Conway, *Some Illustrative Literature*, 435.

26 McManamin, *American Years of John Boyle O'Reilly*, 1, 19, 31, iii; Walsh, "Boston *Pilot*," 186–87, 192.

27 See, for example, John Boyle O'Reilly, "Women and Men" and "Woman Suffrage," in O'Reilly, *Watchwords*, 13, 20; KEC to McQuaid, September 18, 1886, and December 14, 1886, BJMC; "Conferring of the Laetare Medal," *Notre Dame Scholastic*, May 25, 1907, UNDA.

28 Fanning, *Exiles of Erin*, 241.

29 John J. Fitzgerald to Sisters of the Holy Cross, June 13, 1912, reprinted in *Saint Mary's Chimes*, June 1912, 213, SMCA.

30 Fanning, *Exiles of Erin*, 93.

31 Ibid., 241.

32 Conway, *Lalor's Maples*.

33 Fanning, "Woman of the House," 85–89.

34 Conway, *New Footsteps*, 217, 219 (emphasis in original).

35 Shelley, "Twentieth Century American Catholicism and Irish Americans," 575; Meagher, "Irish, American, Catholic"; Skerrett, "Development of Catholic Identity."

36 Sister Helen Louise, *Sister Julia*, 74; SA to Philip McDevitt, December 27, 1921, in box 2, folder 45, PRMC/ND.

37 Conway, "Catholic Church in Boston," 121.

38 Conway, "Why Always Catholic," 31; KEC to Sister M. Madeleva, May 14, 1925, KECC/SMCA.

39 Conway, "Priest and Author," 10, 11.

40 Conway, "Mending Old Roads," 77, 81, 83.

41 Skerrett, "Development of Catholic Identity," 137.

42 Dogherty, *'Scusa Me Teacher*, 103–4; Hoffman, *Woman's "True" Profession*, 257.

43 KEC, Diary, February 1, 1907, April 23, 1907, March 13, 1902, June 14, 1911, KECC/BC.

44 Carr, "Catholic Woman and Suffrage," 293.

45 Toomy, Donnelly, and Conway, "Woman Question among Catholics," 669–81; Farinholt et al., "Public Rights of Women"; Saunders et al., "Present Aspect of Woman Suffrage."

46 Evans, *Born for Liberty*, 122–23.

47 "Archbishop on Women's Suffrage."

48 "Gibbons against Suffrage," *New York Times*, August 9, 1913; Gibbons, "Restless Woman." For more on bishops and suffrage, see Iadorola, "American Catholic Bishops and Woman," 460–61.

49 Haines, "Catholic Womanhood and the Suffrage," 55.

50 Ibid., 57, 66. For more on Campbell and McPike, see Kenneally, *History of American Catholic Women*, 134–35, and Naccarelli, "Guided by their Conscience."

51 "Woman Suffragists Are Undaunted," *New York Times*, October 5, 1894, 8.

52 See also Bucy, "Catherine Kenny," 198–213.

53 Diner, *Erin's Daughters in America*, 139.

54 Rorke, *Letters and Addresses on Woman Suffrage*, 9.

55 Dunne, "Woman Suffrage," 225.

56 Anthony and Harper, *History of Women's Suffrage*, 4.

57 Conway, "Catholic Writers and Literary Success," *The Tidings*, n.d., clipping, KECC/BC.

58 Conway, "Cultured Catholic Woman and Her Political Duty," 3, KECC/BC; KEC to McQuaid, June 15, 1892, BJMC; Driscoll, "In Memoriam," 482.

59 Toomy, Donnelly, and Conway, "Woman Question among Catholics," 682. This article was later reprinted as "The Normal Christian Woman" in Donnelly, *Girlhood's Handbook*, 149–55.

60 Toomy, Donnelly, and Conway, "Woman Question among Catholics," 681.

61 Dowd, "Public Rights of Women," 319.

62 Conway, *Christian Gentlewoman*, 21.

63 M. B. O'S., "Why Are Women Paid Less Than Men?," 211; Conway, "Our Girls as Bread Winners," 228.

64 Seawell, *Ladies' Battle*, 72.

65 Saunders et al., "Present Aspect of Woman Suffrage," 394; Conway, "Cultured Catholic Woman and Her Political Duty," 1.

66 For more on antisuffragist arguments, see Woloch, *Women and the American Experience*, 341.

67 Marshall, *Splintered Sisterhood*, 4–5.

68 KEC to William Onahan, February 19, 1893, box 9, folder 1, WJOC; Hopkins, "People in Print."

69 Jablonsky, *Home, Heaven and Mother Party*, 53.

70 KEC to Onahan, February 12, 1893, and July 7, 1893, box 9, folder 1, WJOC.

71 [Conway], "Catholics and Woman's Day," *Pilot* (Boston), June 3, 1893, 5.

72 Conway, *Bettering Ourselves*, 78.

73 Conway, *Christian Gentlewoman*, 13.

74 Ibid., 20.

75 Toomy, Donnelly, and Conway, "Woman Question among Catholics," 683.

76 Quoted in Sr. M. Eleanore, "Passing of a Valiant Woman," 410.

77 Conway, "Margaret F. Sullivan," 220–21.

78 Conway, *Christian Gentlewoman*, 14.

79 Deland, "Change in the Feminine Ideal," 298.

80 Conway criticized Deland and her novels in "Vital Problems in Modern Literature," typescript, box 6, folder 15, 7–11, KECC/BC.

81 Deland, "Change in the Feminine Ideal," 299.

82 "Woman Suffragists Are Undaunted," *New York Times*, October 5, 1894.

83 McGreevy, *Catholicism and American Freedom*, 95–96.

84 Evans, *Born for Liberty*, 155–56; Newman, *White Woman's Rights*.

85 M. C. O'Neil to Philip McDevitt, February 15, 1915, PRMC/ND.

86 "The Suffragettes Again," *New World* (Chicago), March 16, 1912.

87 Shields, "Teachers' Salaries," 419; Shields, *Education of Our Girls*, 18.

88 Conway, "Catholic Summer School and the Reading Circles," 106.

89 Saunders et al., "Present Aspect of Woman Suffrage," 394.

90 Conway, *Christian Gentlewoman*, 43.

91 KEC to Onahan, February 12, 1893, WJOC.

92 Conway, "Catholic Summer School and Reading Circles," 106.

93 "College Women on Dr. Abbott's Trail," *New York Times*, December 12, 1908, 6.

94 Seawell, *Ladies' Battle*, 71; McKee, "Shall Women Vote?," 53.

95 Avery, "Woman Suffrage." For more background on Avery, see Allitt, *Catholic Converts*, 144–47.

96 D'Arnoux, "Woman Suffrage and Religion," 48.

97 Seawell, *Ladies' Battle*, 73; McKee, "Shall Women Vote?," 53–54; "That Women's Bible," *Catholic Standard*, December 14, 1895, 14.

98 Avery, "Genesis of Woman Suffrage," 5.

99 Avery, "Women and Religion," 112.

100 Stanton, *Woman's Bible*, 195, 200; Kern, *Mrs. Stanton's Bible*, 67.

101 Avery, "Woman Suffrage," 652.

102 Conway, "The Blessed among Women," 5; Toomy, Donnelly, and Conway, "Woman Question among Catholics," 683.

103 Murphy, "How the Church Understands and Upholds," 79, 91; Evenson, "Blanche E. Murphy."

104 Blake, "True Solution," 420–21; Kenneally, "Catholic and Feminist," 229–37.

105 "Catholic Woman," *Donahoe's Magazine*.

106 Conway, *Christian Gentlewoman*, 27.

107 Conway, "Some Christian Ideas. Read for the Women's Educational and Industrial Union, Boston, February 3, 1889," 52, box 6, folder 2, KECC/BC.

108 Conway, *Christian Gentlewoman*, 9; Conway, "Difficulties and Triumphs," 435; Conway, "Cultured Catholic Woman and Her Political Duty," 5.

109 Conway, *New Footsteps*, 210.

110 Quoted in Kenneally, *American Catholic Women*, 61.

111 Toomy, Donnelly, and Conway, "Woman Question among Catholics," 678, 680, 681.

112 Chung, "Who Is Mary for Today's Asian Woman?," 75.

113 Dowd, "Public Rights of Women," 314, 318.

114 Farinholt et al., "Public Rights of Women," 305. For a short biography of Spellissy, see M. Seraphine, *Immortelles*, 245.

115 Conway, "Blessed among Women," 1.

116 Cunneen, *In Search of Mary*, 261–63.

117 Cary, "Elevation of Womanhood," 296.

118 Conway to Hudson, September 10, 1889, box 10, folder 3, DEHC.

119 Kane, *Separatism and Subculture*, 230.

120 Evans, *Born for Liberty*, 170–72.

121 Conway, "Cultured Catholic Woman and Her Political Duty," 1–2.

122 Ibid., 7.

123 "Prominent Clergymen Tell Catholic Club Women to Vote," *New World* (Chicago), October 25, 1913.

124 "Catholic Women at the Polls," 215.

125 Ryan, "Suffrage and Women's Responsibility," 260–61; "Prominent Clergymen Tell Catholic Club Women to Vote," *New World* (Chicago), October 25, 1913.

126 Cott, *Grounding of Modern Feminism*, 15.

127 Murphy, "What Women Wanted," 128.

128 Avery, "Genesis of Woman Suffrage," 5, 6; "Fallacies on Feminism," 725; F. E. T., " Work of the Sisters," 26.

129 Kenneally notes that of sixty subjects classified as feminists in *Notable American Women* (Cambridge: Harvard University Press, 1971), only three were Catholic, and of those, two had left the church. James J. Kenneally, "Eve, Mary and Historians," 204–5.

130 Cott, *Grounding of Modern Feminism*, 5, 9.

131 Helene Conway to Edward Henry, June 30, 1974, KECC/SMCA. Helene was

Conway's favorite niece and heir. In a letter to Saint Mary's president she recalled how happy her aunt had been during her years at Saint Mary's.

132 "Laetare Medalist for 1907," *Notre Dame Scholastic*, March 16, 1907, UNDA; "Conferring of the Laetare Medal," *Notre Dame Scholastic*, May 25, 1907, UNDA; KEC, Diary, May 31, 1911, KECC/BC.

133 Sister M. Madeleva, *My First Seventy Years*, 41; Sister M. Eleanore, "Passing of a Valiant Woman," 411; Mandell, *Madeleva*, 65; "School of Journalism Opened," *Saint Mary's Chimes*, October 1912, SMCA; Bowler, "History of Catholic Colleges for Women," 49.

134 For information about Conway's later years, see KEC to Sr. M. Madeleva, May 14, 1925, and October 8, 1926, KECC/SMCA; see also Kane, *Separatism as Subculture*, 224–25.

135 KEC to McQuaid, January 22, 1890, BJMC.

136 KEC to McQuaid, July 9, 1892, BJMC.

137 KEC to McQuaid, December 29, 1904, BJMC.

138 KEC to McQuaid, December 29, 1904; "Congrats to *Pilot*'s New Management," *Pilot* (Boston), April 8, 1905.

139 Kane, *Separatism and Subculture*, 123; KEC to McQuaid, December 2, 1905, BJMC.

140 Tobias, *Faces of Feminism*, 139.

141 Kane, *Separatism and Subculture*, 227.

142 Mary Ann Glendon, "The Pope's New Feminism," <http://www.tcrnews2.com/glendon.html>.

143 Cummings, "Change of Habit," 38.

144 Prejean, *Dead Man Walking*, 6.

Bibliography

MANUSCRIPT COLLECTIONS

Aston, Pennsylvania
    Archives of the Sisters of St. Francis of Philadelphia
        Sister Eberharda Jones Collection
        Special Collections—Sister Eberharda Jones
Boston, Massachusetts
    John J. Burns Library, Boston College Archives
        Katherine E. Conway Collection
Chestnut Hill, Pennsylvania
    Archives of the Sisters of St. Joseph of Philadelphia
        Account of Sisters Studies, 1928
        Sister Assisium McEvoy Collection
        Reports of the Mistress of Novices
        Sisters' Education
Emmitsburg, Maryland
    Archives of the Daughters of Charity
        Archives of the St. Joseph Provincial House
Immaculata, Pennsylvania
    Archives of the Sisters, Servants of the Immaculate Heart of Mary
        Mother Mary Camilla Papers
        Mother Mary de Chantal Papers
        Mother Mary James Papers
Notre Dame, Indiana
    Saint Mary's College Archives
        Katherine E. Conway Collection
        Saint Mary's Chimes
        University of Notre Dame Archives
        Daniel E. Hudson Collection

Philip R. McDevitt Collection

James A. McMaster Collection

Notre Dame Scholastic

William James Onahan Collection

Religious Orders Printed Material

Charles Leon Souvay Collection

Philadelphia, Pennsylvania

Philadelphia Archdiocesan Historical Records Center

Philip R. McDevitt Collection

Archbishop Edmond Prendergast Collection

Archbishop Patrick J. Ryan Collection

Rochester, New York

Archives of the Diocese of Rochester

Bishop Bernard McQuaid Collection

Washington, D.C.

Trinity College Archives

Sister Mary Euphrasia, SND. "A Sketch of the Foundation of Trinity College for the Higher Education of Catholic Women, Washington, D.C.," unpublished manuscript, 1897

Founding Years

Ladies Auxiliary Board Collection

Sister Julia McGroarty Correspondence

"Trinity College Journal," unpublished manuscript

Trinity College Record

NEWSPAPERS

Catholic Standard (Philadelphia)

Chicago Daily Tribune

Chicago Inter-Ocean

Citizen (Chicago)

Irish Times (Dublin)

New York Times

New World (Chicago)

Pilot (Boston)

Western Catholic (Chicago)

Woman's Journal (Boston)

PUBLISHED PRIMARY SOURCES

Adams, Henry Austin. "Men and Things." *Donahoe's Magazine* 38 (1897): 409–10.

——. "Men and Things." *Donahoe's Magazine* 39 (1898): 1–3.

Annual Report of the Superintendent of the Parochial Schools of the Archdiocese of Cincinnati. Cincinnati: Archdiocese of Cincinnati, 1908.

Annual Reports of the Superintendent of Parochial Schools of the Archdiocese of
Philadelphia. Vols. 1–25. Philadelphia: M. P. Lewis, Jr. and Co., 1895–1919.

Anthony, Bro., F.S.C. "The Pastor and the School: The Teacher's Point of View."
Catholic Educational Association Bulletin 4 (1907): 255–71.

Anthony, Susan B., and Ida Husted Harper. The History of Women's Suffrage. Vol. 4.
Indianapolis: Hollenbeck Press, 1902.

"An Archbishop on Women's Suffrage." Ave Maria 76 (1913): 468.

Avery, Martha Moore. "Genesis of Woman Suffrage." America, October 16, 1915, 5–6.

———. "Woman Suffrage: Six Papers." Catholic Mind 18 (1915): 625–56.

———. "Women and Religion." America, November 14, 1914, 111–13.

Baille, Gertrude Stewart. "Some Women of Bologna." Women's Progress in
Literature, Science, Education and Art (Philadelphia) 4 (1895): 67–70.

Barbian, J. "A Plea for the Man Teacher." Catholic Educational Review 6 (1913): 35–40.

Barton, George. Columbus the Catholic. Baltimore: John Murphy and Co., 1893.

Belloc, Bessie R. Historic Nuns. London: Duckworth and Co., 1899.

Bellord, James. Religious Education and Its Failures. Notre Dame, Ind.: Ave Maria
Press, 1901.

Blake, Mary Elizabeth. "A Blessed Daughter of the People." Catholic World 49
(1889): 293–309.

———. "True Solution of the Woman Question." Donahoe's Magazine 29 (1893):
417–21.

Blakely, Paul, S.J. "Do We Want 'Prussianized' Schools?" America, November 9,
1918, 106–7.

———. "Topics of Interest: Has Woman a Soul?" America, July 24, 1915, 365.

Brunowe, Marion J. [Mary Browne]. A Famous Convent School. New York: Meany
Co., 1897.

Bugg, Lelia Hardin. "Trinity College." Rosary Magazine 18 (April 1901): 377–88.

Burns, Rev. James A., C.S.C. Catholic Education: A Study of Conditions. New York:
Longmans, Green and Co., 1917.

———. "Condition of Catholic Secondary Education in the U.S." Catholic
Educational Review 10 (1915): 204–23.

———. "The Development of Parish School Organization." Catholic Educational
Review 3 (1912): 428–29.

———. "The Training of the Teacher." Educational Briefs 5 (1904): 3–38. Reprinted
from American Catholic Quarterly Review 28 (1903): 664–83.

C., M. A. [Mother Mary Austin Carroll]. "Education in Louisiana in French
Colonial Days." American Catholic Quarterly Review 11 (1886): 395–418.

———. "Education in Louisiana in Spanish Colonial Days." American Catholic
Quarterly Review 12 (1887): 253–77.

Campbell, Jane. "Origins of Charitable Institutions." *Women's Progress in Literature, Science, Education and Art* (Philadelphia) 1 (June 1893): 149–56.

———. "Woman and the Ballot." In *Girlhood's Handbook of Woman*, edited by Eleanor C. Donnelly, 189–203. St. Louis: B. Herder, 1914.

———. "Woman Scholars of the Middle Ages." *American Catholic Quarterly Review* 43 (1918): 237–46.

Carr, Eva Dorsey. "The Catholic Woman and Suffrage." *America*, December 29, 1917, 293.

Carrigan, Thomas C. "Higher Education of Catholic Women." *Catholic Educational Review* 4 (1912): 416–29.

Cary, Emma Forbes. "Elevation of Womanhood through the Veneration of the Blessed Virgin." In *Immortelles of Catholic Columbian Literature*, edited by M. [Mother] Seraphine [Leonard], 295–303. Chicago: D. H. McBride and Co., 1896.

"The Catholic Woman." *Donahoe's Magazine* 26 (1891): 363–64.

"Catholic Women at the Polls." *America*, December 8, 1917, 214–15.

A Chronicler. "Words for Women." *Donahoe's Magazine* 34 (1895): 1050.

Clarke, R. H. "Beatification Asked for American Servants of God." *Catholic World* 40 (1885): 808–20.

The Convention of the Apostolate of the Press: Report of Papers and Letters. New York: Columbus Press, 1892.

Conway, Katherine E. *Bettering Ourselves.* Thomas J. Flynn and Co., 1904.

———. "Blessed among Women." *Rosary Magazine* 2 (1892): 720–25; 3 (1892): 2–6, 106–10.

———. "The Catholic Church in Boston." In *The Story of the Irish in Boston*, edited by James Bernard Cullen, 121–64. Boston: James B. Cullen and Co., 1889.

———. "Catholic Literary Societies." In *Summer School Essays.* 1:203–15. Chicago: D. H. McBride and Co., 1896.

———. "The Catholic Summer School and the Reading Circles." In *The World's Columbian Catholic Congresses*, 106–11. Chicago: J. S. Hyland and Co., 1893.

———. *The Christian Gentlewoman and the Social Apostolate.* Boston: Thomas J. Flynn and Co., 1904.

———. "John Boyle O'Reilly." *Catholic World* 53 (1891): 198–218.

———. *Lalor's Maples.* Boston: Pilot Publishing Co., 1901.

———. "Margaret F. Sullivan, Journalist and Author." *Donahoe's Magazine* 51 (1904): 220–23.

———. "Mending Old Roads and Making New Ones." In *The Convention of the Apostolate of the Press: Report of Papers and Letters*, 76–85. New York: Columbus Press, 1892.

———. *New Footsteps in Well-Trodden Ways.* Boston: Pilot Publishing Co., 1899.

——. *On the Sunrise Slope*. New York: Catholic Publication Society, 1881.

——. "Our Girls as Bread Winners." *Donahoe's Magazine* 29 (1893): 226–29.

——. "Priest and Author." In *An Appreciation of Dr. John Talbot Smith*, edited by Rev. John Cavanaugh, 10–13. New York: Catholic Summer School, 1924.

——. *Some Illustrative Literature of Church History*. South Bend, Ind.: Tribune Publishing Co., 1912.

——. *The Way of the World and Other Ways: A Story of Our Set*. Boston: Pilot Publishing Co., 1900.

——. "Why Always Catholic." *Columbia Magazine*, May 1925, 31.

Coogan, M. T. "Occupations for Women." *Donahoe's Magazine* 39 (1898): 289–91.

Crowley, Mary Catherine. *A Daughter of New France*. Boston: Little, Brown, and Co., 1901.

Cullen, James Bernard, ed. *The Story of the Irish in Boston*. Boston: James B. Cullen and Co., 1889.

Curtis, Georgina Pell, ed. *American Catholic Who's Who*. St. Louis: B. Herder, 1911.

D'Arnoux, C. E. "Woman Suffrage and Religion." *Fortnightly Review* 20 (1913): 48–50.

Davitt, Michael. *The Fall of Feudalism in Ireland*. New York: Harper and Brothers, 1904.

Deland, Margaret. "The Change in the Feminine Ideal." *Atlantic Monthly*, March 1910, 289–302.

Delaunay, Rev. John B., CSC. *The Religious Teacher and the Work of Vocations*. Hartford, Conn.: St. Augustine Novitiate, 1918.

Denis, Bro. "Vocations to the Teaching Orders." *Catholic Educational Review* 7 (1914): 24–32.

Dogherty, Marian A. *'Scusa Me Teacher*. Francestown, N.H.: Marshall Jones Co., 1943.

Donnelly, Eleanor C., ed. *Girlhood's Handbook of Woman*. St. Louis: B. Herder, 1914.

——. "Woman in Literature." In *The World's Columbian Catholic Congresses*, 83–87. Chicago: J. S. Hyland and Co., 1893.

Donnelly, Rev. F. P., S.J. "Have Women Souls?" *The Messenger*, March 1906, 302–5.

Driscoll, Annette S. "In Memoriam—Katherine E. Conway." *Catholic World* 126 (1927–28): 481–87.

Dunne, Finley Peter. *Mr. Dooley and the Chicago Irish: The Autobiography of a Nineteenth-Century Ethnic Group*. Edited by Charles Fanning. Washington, D.C.: Catholic University of America Press, 1987.

Dunne, Rt. Rev. E. M. "Woman Suffrage." *Fortnightly Review* 20 (1913): 225–26.

Edselas, F. M. "Institute for Woman's Professions." *Catholic World* 57 (1893): 373–80.

Ei, Very Rev. J. C. "Difficulties Encountered by Superiors in the Professional Training of Their Teachers." *Catholic Educational Association Bulletin* 10 (1913): 362–79.

Elliott, Rev. Walter, C.S.P. "St. Vincent dePaul and the Sisters of Charity." *Catholic World* 70 (1899): 13–28.

"Fallacies on Feminism." *Ave Maria* 75 (1912): 723–25.

Farinholt, F. C., Mary A. Spellissy, Katherine F. Mullaney, and Mary A. Dowd. "Public Rights of Women: A Second Round Table Conference." *Catholic World* 59 (1894): 299–320.

Franciscan Sisters of Perpetual Adoration. *A History of the United States for Catholic Schools.* Chicago: Scott, Foresman and Co., 1914.

Gage, Matilda Joslyn. *Woman, Church and State: A Historical Account of the Status of Woman through the Christian Ages with Reminiscences of the Matriarchate.* Rev. ed. Watertown, Mass.: Persephone Press, 1980. Originally published by C. H. Kerr, 1893.

Gasson, Rev. Thomas, S.J. "Women and the Higher Intellectual Life." In *Higher Education for Catholic Women: A Historical Anthology,* edited by Mary Oates, C.S.J., 49–67. New York: Garland, 1987.

George, W. L. "Notes on the Intelligence of Woman." *Atlantic Monthly,* December 1915, 721–30.

Gibbons, J. Cardinal. "Restless Woman." *Ladies' Home Journal,* January 1902, 6.

Gibbons, James. "Relative Condition of Woman under Pagan and Christian Civilization." *American Catholic Quarterly Review* 11 (1886): 656–57.

Gibbons, Rev. E. F. "School Supervision—Its Necessity, Aims and Methods." *Catholic Educational Association Bulletin* 2 (1905): 164–81.

Gilman, Lawrence. "A History of Love." *North American Review* 201 (1915): 910.

Grimes, Rev. John J., S.M. "Woman in History." *Catholic Mind* 11 (1913): 119–35.

Guthrie, William D. "The Catholic School." *Catholic Mind* 13 (1915): 537–48.

Haines, Helen. "Catholic Womanhood and the Suffrage." *Catholic World* 102 (1915): 55–57.

"Has a Council Denied That Women Have Souls?" *Fortnightly Review* 22 (1915): 742–43.

Hayes, Rev. Ralph L. "The Need of Religious Vocations for the Teaching Orders." *Catholic Educational Association Bulletin* 17 (1920): 217–31.

Holman, Mrs. T. P. "The 'New Woman.'" *Gospel Advocate,* July 9, 1896, 438.

Hopkins, William. "People in Print." *Donahoe's Magazine* 37 (1897): 73–79.

Horsa, Rev. Bede, O.S.B. "The Need of Male Teachers in Our Parish Schools." *Catholic Educational Association Bulletin* 10 (1913): 281–89.

Howe, Sarah Willard. "Trinity College." *Donahoe's Magazine* 44 (1900): 315–23.

Husslein, Joseph, S.J. "The New Woman after God's Heart." *America* 13 (May 8, 1915): 91–92.

Ireland, John. "On the Occasion of the Fiftieth Anniversary of Sisters of St. Joseph in St. Paul, Minn." *Homiletic Monthly and Catechist* 3 (1902): 154–61.

Kirlin, Rev. Joseph Louis J. *The Life of Most Reverend Patrick John Ryan, D.D., L.L.D.* Philadelphia: Gibbons Publishing Co., 1903.

Lahitton, Joseph. *La vocation sacerdotale: Traité théorique et practique.* Paris: Gabriel Beauchesne, 1914.

Ludden, Rt. Rev. P. A., D.D. Introduction to *The Pioneer Church of the State of New York,* by Rev. John F. Mullany, LL.D. Syracuse, N.Y.: St. John's Rectory, 1897.

Lummis, Eliza O'Brien. *Daughters of the Faith: Serious Thoughts for Catholic Women.* New York: Robert Greir Cook, 1907.

M., M. C. "The Columbian Reading Union." *Catholic World* 65 (1897): 860–64.

MacCorrie, John Paul. "The War of the Sexes." *Catholic World* 63 (1896): 605–18.

Mahon, P. J., and Rev. J. M. Hayes, S.J. *Trials and Triumphs of the Catholic Church in America.* Chicago: J. S. Hyland and Co., 1907.

M. Anselm, Rev. Mother, O.S.D. *The Catholic Teacher's Role in the Fostering of Vocations.* Notre Dame, Ind.: Brothers of the Congregation of Holy Cross, n.d.

Mary Celeste [Leger], Sister. *American History.* New York: Macmillan, 1926.

Mary Eberharda [Jones], Sister. "Educational Reorganization from the Catholic Viewpoint." *Catholic Educational Association Bulletin* 20 (1923): 525–39.

———. "The Supervising Principal and the Teacher." *Catholic Educational Association Bulletin* 19 (1922): 286–89.

Maus, Rev. H. P. "Address at Reception of Sisters of Mercy." *Homiletic Monthly and Catechist* 5 (1905): 896–900.

McCann, Sister Mary Agnes. *Mother Seton: Foundress of the Sisters of Charity.* Mount St. Joseph-on-the-Ohio: Sisters of Charity, 1909.

McDevitt, M. "Trinity College and Higher Education." *Catholic World* 79 (1904): 387–91.

McDevitt, Rev. Philip. "Boards of Education and Historical Truth: 'Chiefly among Women' by Mrs. Margaret Sullivan." *Educational Briefs* 13 (1906): 3–10.

McDevitt, Rt. Rev. Msgr. P. R. "The State and Education." *Catholic Educational Association Bulletin* 12 (1915): 74–99.

McGinnis, Rev. C. F. "The State and Education." *Catholic Educational Association Bulletin* 12 (1915): 102–10.

McKee, Joseph. "Shall Women Vote?" *Catholic World* 102 (1915): 45–54.

McSorley, Rev. Joseph. "Saint Chantal: A Type of Christian Womanhood." *Catholic World* 76 (1903): 571–78.

M. Eleanore [Brosnahan], Sister, C.S.C. "The Passing of a Valiant Woman." *America,* February 5, 1927, 410–12.

Meyers, Sister Bertrande, Ph.D. *The Education of Sisters: A Plan for Integrating the Religious, Social, Cultural, and Professional Training of Sisters*. New York: Sheed and Ward, 1941.

Middleton, Fr. Thomas. "List of Catholic and Semi-Catholic Periodicals Published in the U.S. from Earliest Dates." *Records of the American Catholic Historical Society of Philadelphia* 4 (1893): 213–42.

M. Madeleva [Wolff], Sister, C.S.C. *My First Seventy Years*. New York: Macmillan, 1959.

Molloy, Mary. "Catholic Colleges for Women." *Catholic Educational Association Bulletin* 15 (1918–19): 233–36.

Moore, Marguerite. "A New Woman's Work in the West of Ireland." *Catholic World* 64 (1897): 451–58.

Mozans, H. J. [John A. Zahm]. *Woman in Science*. Rev. ed. Notre Dame, Ind.: University of Notre Dame Press, 1991. Originally published in 1913 by D. Appleton.

Mullany, Rev. John F., LL.D. "The Catholic Nun in the Classroom." In *The Pioneer Church of the State of New York*, 85–128. Syracuse, N.Y.: St. John's Rectory, 1897.

Murphy, Blanche E. "How the Church Understands and Upholds the Rights of Women." *Catholic World* 15 (1872): 78–91.

Murphy, Edward F. "What Women Wanted." *America*, November 20, 1915, 128–30.

Murphy, John T. "The Opportunities of Educated Catholic Women." *American Catholic Quarterly Review* 23 (1898): 611–17.

Murray, John O'Kane. *Lives of Catholic Heroes and Heroines of America*. New York: J. Sheehy, 1879.

"The New Home of the Summer-School at Plattsburgh." *Catholic World* 57 (1893): 67–84.

Nixon, Mary F. "A Saintly Scholar: St. Catherine of Alexandria." *Catholic World* 67 (1898): 447–62.

"Not the New Woman." *Donahoe's Magazine* 38 (1897): 195–96.

Oates, Mary, C.S.J., ed. *Higher Education for Catholic Women: A Historical Anthology*. New York: Garland, 1987.

O'Brien, James, S.J. "The Ursulines." *Queen's Work* 3 (1915): 103–9.

O'Dea, John. *History of the Ancient Order of Hibernians and Ladies' Auxiliary*. Vol. 3. New York: National Board of the AOH, 1923.

Official Catholic Directory of the Philadelphia Archdiocese. Philadelphia: Catholic Standard and Times, 1925.

O'Hara, Joseph M. "The Supervision of Catholic Schools by Community Superiors." *Catholic Educational Association Bulletin* 18 (1921): 209–16.

O'Mahoney, Katharine O'Keeffe. *Famous Irishwomen*. Lawrence, Mass.: Lawrence Publishing Co., 1907.

O'Malley, Austin, M.D., L.L.D. "College Work for Catholic Girls." *Catholic World* 68 (1898): 161–67.

Onahan, Mary Josephine. "Catholic Women in Philanthropy." In *Girlhood's Handbook of Woman*, edited by Eleanor C. Donnelly, 90–108. St. Louis: B. Herder, 1914.

———. "Isabella the Catholic." In *The World's Columbian Catholic Congresses*, 28–33. Chicago: J. S. Hyland and Co., 1893.

O'Reilly, Bernard. *The Mirror of True Womanhood*. New York: P. F. Collier, 1877.

———. "Necessity and Means of Promoting Vocations to the Teaching Orders." *Catholic Educational Association Bulletin* 5 (1908–9): 253–71.

O'Reilly, Brother Aidan, C.S.C. *Out of Many Hearts: Thoughts on the Religious Vocation*. Notre Dame, Ind.: Brothers of the Congregation of Holy Cross, 1908.

O'Reilly, Isabel M. "The Maid of Orleans and the New Womanhood." *American Catholic Quarterly Review* 19 (1894): 582–606.

———. "One of Philadelphia's Soldiers in the Mexican War." *Records of the American Catholic Historical Society of Philadelphia* 13 (1902): 137–64, 257–84, 411–53.

———. "One of Philadelphia's Soldiers in the War of 1812." *Records of the American Catholic Historical Society of Philadelphia* 12 (1901): 294–321, 419–51.

O'Reilly, John Boyle. *Watchwords from John Boyle O'Reilly*. Edited by Katherine E. Conway. Boston: Joseph George Cupples, 1891.

O'S., M. B. [Mary Blanche O'Sullivan]. "Why Are Women Paid Less Than Men?" *Donahoe's Magazine* 30 (1893): 210–11.

Our Church and Country: The Catholic Pages of American History. New Haven, Conn.: Catholic Historical League of America, 1908.

Pace, Rev. Edward. "The College Woman." *Donahoe's Magazine* 52 (1904): 285–88.

———. "The Papacy and Education." *Catholic Educational Review* 1 (1911): 2–9.

Power, Rev. William, S.J. "The Thorough Formation of Our Teachers in the Spirit and Observances of Their Respective Orders, an Indispensable Condition to Sound and Successful Pedagogics." *Catholic Educational Association Bulletin* 10 (1913–14): 339–62.

R., P. J. [Patrick James Ryan]. "Editorial Note: The Pope's Letter to the American Bishops on the School Question." *American Catholic Quarterly Review* 18 (1893): 642–43.

Records of the Proceedings of the Ladies Auxiliary of the Ancient Order of Hibernians in America. Cleveland: Martin Printing Co., 1916.

A Religious of the Ursuline Community. *Life of the Venerable Mother Mary of the Incarnation*. Dublin: James Duffy and Sons, 1880.

Repplier, Agnes. "Catholicism and Authorship." *Catholic World* 90 (1909): 167–74.

———. *Mère Marie of the Ursulines: A Study in Adventure.* Garden City, N.Y.: Doubleday, Doran and Co., 1931.

———. *Varia.* Boston: Houghton, Mifflin and Co., 1897.

"Resolutions." *Catholic Educational Association Bulletin* 2 (1905): 33–35.

Reville, Rev. John C., S.J. *The First American Sister of Charity.* New York: America Press, 1921.

Rorke, Margaret Hayden, ed. *Letters and Addresses on Woman Suffrage by Catholic Ecclesiastics.* New York: Devin-Adair, 1914.

Rössler, Augustine. "Woman." *Catholic Encyclopedia* (1914), 687–88, 692, 694. Reprinted in *Gender Identities in American Catholicism*, edited by Paula Kane, James Kenneally, and Karen Kennelly, 56–57. Maryknoll, N.Y.: Orbis Books, 2001.

Ryan, John A. "Suffrage and Women's Responsibility." *America*, December 22, 1917, 260–61.

S., M. F. [Margaret Frances Buchanan Sullivan]. "General Banks as a Historian." *American Catholic Quarterly Review* 1 (1876): 353–76.

Sadlier, Agnes. *Elizabeth Seton, Foundress of the American Sisters of Charity: Her Life and Work.* Philadelphia: H. L. Kilner and Co., 1904.

Sadlier, Anna T. "Women in the Middle Ages." In *Girlhood's Handbook of Woman*, edited by Eleanor C. Donnelly, 60–89. St. Louis: B. Herder, 1914.

———. *Women of Catholicity.* New York: Benziger Brothers, 1885.

Sadlier's Excelsior Studies in the History of the United States, for Schools. New York: W. H. Sadlier, 1879.

"Salutory." *American Catholic Quarterly Review* 1 (1876): 1–4.

Sauer, Bro. George. "On Vocations to the Teaching Brotherhoods." *Catholic Educational Association Bulletin* 18 (1921): 301–12.

Saunders, Charles R., Julia Howe, Evelyn Greenleaf Sutherland, and Katherine E. Conway. "Present Aspect of Woman Suffrage: A Symposium." *Donahoe's Magazine* 35 (1896): 388–94.

Schrembs, Rt. Rev. Joseph, D.D. "Vocations to the Teaching Orders." *Catholic Educational Review* 1 (1911): 105–15.

Seawell, Molly Elliot. *The Ladies' Battle.* New York: Macmillan, 1911.

Seraphine [Leonard], M. [Mother], OSU, ed. *Immortelles of Catholic Columbian Literature.* Chicago: D. H. McBride and Co., 1897.

Seton, William. "The Higher Education of Women and Posterity." *Catholic World* 73 (1901): 147–49.

"Shakespere [sic] and the New Woman." *Catholic World* 64 (1896): 158–69.

Shea, John Gilmary. "The Catholic Church in American History." *American Catholic Quarterly Review* 1 (1876): 148–73.

——. "Columbus Centenary of 1892." *American Catholic Quarterly Review* 14 (1889): 691–700.

Shields, Thomas. "Catholic Education: The Basis of True Americanization." *Catholic Educational Review* 19 (1921): 3–19.

——. *The Education of Our Girls*. New York: Benziger Brothers, 1907.

——. "Some Relations between the Catholic School System and the Public School System." *Catholic Educational Association Bulletin* 53 (1916): 51–62.

——. "Teachers College of the Catholic University of America." *Catholic Educational Review* 6 (1913): 314–37.

——. "Teachers' Salaries." *Catholic Educational Review* 8 (1914): 413–24.

A Sister of Charity. "The Misleading Graphs." *America*, October 27, 1917, 69–70.

A Sister of St. Dominic. "Our First Year at the Sisters College." *Catholic Educational Review* 3 (1912): 435–44.

A Sister of St. Joseph [Sister Assisium McEvoy]. "The Attendance of Sisters at State Normal Schools." *Catholic Educational Association Bulletin* 17 (1920): 474–77.

——. *Gleanings in Historic Fields, 1650–1798*. Philadelphia: Sisters of St. Joseph of Philadelphia, 1925.

A Sister of St. Joseph of Philadelphia. "The Objective Method of Teaching Religion." *Catholic Educational Association Bulletin* 11 (1914): 277–85.

A Sister of the Holy Cross. "Vocations for the Religious Life." *Catholic Educational Association Bulletin* 17 (1920): 485–90.

Sisters of the Third Order of St. Francis of the Perpetual Adoration. *A History of the United States for Catholic Schools*. New York: Scott, Foresman and Co., 1914.

Slayden, Ellen Maury. *Washington Wife: Journal of Ellen Maury Slayden from 1897–1919*. New York: Harper and Row, 1963.

The Souvenir Sketch of St. Patrick's Church, Philadelphia, 1842–1892. Philadelphia: Hardy and Mahony, 1892.

Spalding, Henry, S.J. "Should Catholic Associations of Charity Associate with Other Similar Institutions?" *Queen's Work* 1 (1914): 280–82.

Spalding, Rev. John Lancaster. "Normal Schools for Catholics." *Catholic World* 51 (1890): 88–97.

——. "Woman and the Higher Education." In *Higher Education for Catholic Women: A Historical Anthology*, edited by Mary J. Oates, C.S.J., 25–47. New York: Garland, 1987.

S.S.J. [Sister Assisium McEvoy]. *Course of Christian Doctrine: A Handbook for Teachers*. Philadelphia: Dolphin Press, 1904.

Stanton, Elizabeth Cady. *The Woman's Bible*. 1895. Amherst, N.Y.: Prometheus Books, 1999.

Starr, Eliza Allen. *Isabella of Castile, 1492–1892*. Chicago: C. V. Waite and Co., 1889.

"Suggestions from Our Prize Contestants." *Donahoe's Magazine* 38 (1897): 181–82.

Sullivan, Margaret Buchanan [An American Woman, pseud.]. "Chiefly among Women." *Catholic World* 21 (1875): 324–40.

Sullivan, Margaret F. [Buchanan]. *Ireland of To-day: The Causes and Aims of Irish Agitation*. Philadelphia: J. C. McCurdy and Co., 1881.

———. "The Twentieth Century Woman." *Donahoe's Magazine* 30 (1893): 649–52.

T., F. E. "Work of the Sisters during the Epidemic of Influenza, October 1918." *Records of the American Catholic Historical Society of Philadelphia* 30 (1919): 25–63.

Toomy, Alice Timmons, Eleanor C. Donnelly, and Katherine E. Conway. "The Woman Question among Catholics: A Round Table Conference." *Catholic World* 57 (1839): 669–84.

Toomy, L. A. [Lily Alice]. "Some Noble Work of Catholic Women." *Catholic World* 57 (1893): 234–43.

Tracy, John. "The Church as an Educational Factor." *Catholic Educational Review* 6 (1913): 207–14.

Tynan, Katharine. "The Higher Education for Catholic Girls." *Catholic World* 51 (1890): 616–21.

Tyrrell, George, S.J. "The Old Faith and the New Woman." *American Catholic Quarterly Review* 22 (1897): 630–45.

Upton, Sara Carr. "The House on the Aventine." *Catholic World* 67 (1898): 633–43.

Vermeersch, Rev. Dr. Arthur, S.J. *Religious and Ecclesiastical Formation*. Translated from Latin by Joseph G. Kempf. St. Louis: B. Herder, 1925.

"A Very Singular Fact." *American Catholic Historical Researches* 22 (1905): 149–50.

Vogel, Ettie Madeline. "Ursuline Nuns in America." *Records of the American Catholic Historical Society of Philadelphia* 2 (1886–88): 214–43.

Waggaman, Mary T. "Catholic Life in Washington." *Catholic World* 66 (1898): 821–38.

Walsh, James Joseph. *Education: How Old the New*. New York: Fordham University Press, 1910.

———. "Some Women of a Medieval Century." *Donahoe's Magazine* 57 (1907): 616–28.

———. *The Thirteenth, Greatest of Centuries*. 2nd ed. New York: Catholic Summer School Press, 1909.

Walsh, Marie Donegan. "A City of Learned Women." *Catholic World* 75 (1902): 596–608.

Walworth, Ellen Hardin. *The Life and Times of Kateri Tekakwitha: The Lily of the Mohawks, 1656–1680*. Buffalo, N.Y.: Peter Paul and Brother, 1890.

The World's Columbian Catholic Congresses. Chicago: J. S. Hyland and Co., 1893.

Allitt, Patrick. "American Women Converts and Catholic Intellectual Life." *U.S. Catholic Historian* 13, no. 1 (1995): 57–79.

———. *Catholic Converts: British and American Intellectuals Turn to Rome.* Ithaca, N.Y.: Cornell University Press, 1997.

Anderson, M. Christine. "Negotiating Patriarchy and Power: Women in Christian Churches." *Journal of Women's History* 16, no. 3 (2004): 187–96.

Appleby, R. Scott. *Church and Age Unite: The Modernist Impulse in American Catholicism.* Notre Dame, Ind.: University of Notre Dame Press, 1992.

Appleby, R. Scott, Patricia Byrne, and William Portier, eds. *Creative Fidelity: American Catholic Intellectual Traditions.* Maryknoll, N.Y.: Orbis Books, 2004.

Augenstein, John J. *Lighting the Way, 1908–1935: The Early Years of Catholic School Superintendency.* Washington, D.C.: National Catholic Educational Association, 1996.

Baylor, Ronald, and Timothy J. Meagher, eds. *The New York Irish.* Baltimore: Johns Hopkins University Press, 1996.

Becker, Penny Edgell. " 'Rational Amusement and Sound Instruction': Constructing the True Woman in the *Ave Maria*, 1865–89." *Religion and American Culture* 8. no. 1 (1998): 55–90.

Blair, Karen J. *The Clubwoman as Feminist: True Womanhood Redefined, 1868–1914.* New York: Holmes and Meier, 1980.

Bordin, Ruth. *Alice Freeman Palmer: The Evolution of a New Woman.* Ann Arbor: University of Michigan Press, 1993.

Boylan, Anne M. *The Origins of Women's Activism: New York and Boston, 1794–1840.* Chapel Hill: University of North Carolina Press, 2002.

Braude, Ann. *Radical Spirits: Spiritualism and Women's Rights in Nineteenth-Century America.* Bloomington: Indiana University Press, 2001.

———. "Review of Anne M. Boylan's *The Origins of Women's Activism: New York and Boston, 1794–1840*." *Catholic Historical Review* 91, no. 1 (2005): 183–84.

———. "Women's History *Is* American Religious History." In *Retelling U.S. Religious History*, edited by Thomas A. Tweed, 87–107. Berkeley: University of California Press, 1997.

Brekus, Catherine A. "Introduction: Searching for Women in Narratives of American Religious History." In *The Religious History of American Women: Reimagining the Past*, edited by Catherine A. Brekus, 1–50. Chapel Hill: University of North Carolina Press, 2007.

Brown, Dorothy M., and Elizabeth McKeown. *The Poor Belong to Us: Catholic Charities and American Welfare.* Cambridge, Mass.: Harvard University Press, 1997.

Brown, Victoria Bissell. "The Fear of Feminization: Los Angeles High Schools in the Progressive Era." *Feminist Studies* 16, no. 3 (1990): 493–518.

Brundage, David. " 'In Time of Peace, Prepare for War': Key Themes in the Social Thought of New York's Irish Nationalists." In *The New York Irish*, edited by Ronald Baylor and Timothy J. Meagher, 321–34. Baltimore: Johns Hopkins University Press, 1996.

Bucy, Carole Stanford. "Catherine Kenny: Fighting for the Perfect Thirty-sixth." In *Ordinary Women, Extraordinary Lives: Women in American History*, edited by Kriste Lindenmeyer, 197–213. Wilmington, Del.: Scholarly Resources, 2000.

Byrne, Patricia. "The Sisters of St. Joseph: The Americanization of a French Tradition." *U.S. Catholic Historian* 5, nos. 3–4 (1986): 241–72.

Cadegan, Una M. *All Good Books Are Catholic Books: Censorship and the Cultural Work of Catholic Literature*. Forthcoming.

Cameron, Sister Mary David. *The College of Notre Dame of Maryland, 1895–1945*. New York: Declan X. McMullen Co., 1947.

Camhi, Jane Jerome. *Women against Women: American Anti-Suffragism, 1880–1920*. Brooklyn, N.Y.: Carlson Publishing Co., 1994.

Chinnici, Joseph P., O.F.M. "Religious Life in the Twentieth Century: Interpreting the Languages." *U.S. Catholic Historian* 22, no. 1 (2004): 27–47.

Chung, Hu Kyung. "Who Is Mary for Today's Asian Woman?" In *Struggle to Be the Sun Again: Introducing Asian Women's Theology*, 74–84. Maryknoll, N.Y.: Orbis Books, 1990.

Clark, Emily, ed. *Voices from an Early American Convent: Marie Madeleine Hachard and the New Orleans Ursulines*. Baton Rouge: Louisiana State University Press, 2007.

Coburn, Carol, and Martha Smith. *Spirited Lives: How Nuns Shaped Catholic Culture and American Life, 1836–1920*. Chapel Hill: University of North Carolina Press, 1999.

Cohen, Lucy M. "Early Efforts to Admit Sisters and Lay Women to the Catholic University of America." In *An Introduction to Pioneering Women at the Catholic University of America*, edited by E. Catherine Dunn and Dorothy A. Mohler, 1–18. Washington, D.C.: Catholic University Press, 1990.

Colman, Anne. "Far from Silent: Nineteenth Century Irish Women Writers." In *Gender Perspectives in Nineteenth Century Ireland: Public and Private Spheres*, edited by Margaret Kelleher and James H. Murphy, 203–11. Dublin: Irish Academic Press, 1997.

Connelly, James F. *The History of the Archdiocese of Philadelphia*. Philadelphia: Archdiocese of Philadelphia, 1976.

Cott, Nancy F. *The Grounding of Modern Feminism*. New Haven, Conn.: Yale University Press, 1987.

Crunden, Robert M. *Ministers of Reform: The Progressives' Achievement in American Civilization*. Urbana: University of Illinois Press, 1984.

Cummings, Kathleen Sprows. "Change of Habit." *Notre Dame Magazine*, Autumn 2003, 34–39.

———. "'We Owe It to Our Sex as Well as Our Religion': The Sisters of Notre Dame de Namur, the Ladies Auxiliary, and the Founding of Trinity College, 1898–1904." *American Catholic Studies* 115, no. 2 (2004): 21–36.

Cunneen, Sally. *In Search of Mary: The Woman and the Symbol*. New York: Ballantine Books, 1996.

Curtis, Sarah. *Educating the Faithful: Religion, Schooling and Society in Nineteenth-Century France*. University Park: Pennsylvania State University Press, 2000.

Davis, Natalie Zemon. *Women on the Margins: Three Seventeenth Century Lives*. Cambridge, Mass.: Harvard University Press, 1995.

De Hart, Jane Sherron, and Linda K. Kerber. "Introduction: Gender and the New Women's History." In *Women's America: Refocusing the Past*, edited by Linda K. Kerber and Jane Sherron De Hart, 1–23. New York: Oxford University Press, 2004.

Delfino, Susanna, and Michele Gillespie, eds. *Neither Lady nor Slave: Working Women in the Old South*. Chapel Hill: University of North Carolina Press, 2002.

Diner, Hasia R. *Erin's Daughters in America: Irish Immigrant Women in the Nineteenth Century*. Baltimore: Johns Hopkins University Press, 1983.

Dolan, Jay P. *The American Catholic Experience: A History from Colonial Times to the Present*. Notre Dame, Ind.: University of Notre Dame Press, 1992.

Donaghy, Thomas J., F.S.C. *Philadelphia's Finest: A History of Education in the Catholic Archdiocese, 1692–1970*. Philadelphia: American Catholic Historical Society, 1972.

Doyle, Joe. "Striking for Ireland on the New York Docks." In *The New York Irish*, edited by Ronald Baylor and Timothy J. Meagher, 357–73. Baltimore: Johns Hopkins University Press, 1996.

Dries, Angelyn, O.S.F. "The Americanization of Religious Life: Women Religious, 1872–1922." *U.S. Catholic Historian* 10, nos. 1–2 (1992): 13–24.

Englemeyer, Sister Brigid. "A Maryland First." *Maryland Historical Magazine* 78 (Fall 1983): 196.

Evans, Sara M. *Born for Liberty: A History of Women in America*. New York: Free Press, 1997.

Evenson, Ardy. "Blanche E. Murphy and the Rights of Women." *Records of the American Catholic Historical Society of Philadelphia* 103, no. 1 (1992): 17–26.

Fanning, Charles, ed. *Exiles of Erin: Nineteenth-Century Irish-American Fiction*. Notre Dame, Ind.: University of Notre Dame Press, 1987.

———. "The Woman of the House: Aspects of Irish-American Fiction." *The Recorder* 1 (1985): 82–115.

Fessenden, Tracy. "The Nineteenth-Century Bible Wars and the Separation of
    Church and State." *Church History* 74, no. 3 (2005): 784–811.

Fitzgerald, Maureen. *Habits of Compassion: Irish Catholic Nuns and the Origins of
    New York's Welfare System.* Urbana: University of Illinois Press, 2006.

Flanagan, Maureen A. *America Reformed: Progressives and Progressivisms, 1890s–
    1920s.* New York: Oxford University Press, 2007.

Flick, Ella Marie. *The Life of Bishop McDevitt.* Philadelphia: Dorrance and Co., 1940.

Fogarty, Gerald P. *The Vatican and the American Hierarchy from 1870–1965.*
    Wilmington, Del.: Michael Glazier, 1985.

Funchion, Michael. "Irish Nationalists and Chicago Politics in the 1880s." *Eire-
    Ireland* 10, no. 2 (1975): 3–18.

Gallagher, John. *Courageous Irishwomen.* Mayo, Ireland: Fiona Books, 1995.

Gillette, Howard, Jr. "The Emergence of the Modern Metropolis: Philadelphia in
    the Age of Its Consolidation." In *The Divided Metropolis: Social and Spatial
    Dimensions of Philadelphia, 1800–1975,* edited by William W. Cutler III and
    Howard Gillette Jr., 3–25. Westport, Conn.: Greenwood Press, 1980.

Gleason, Philip. *Contending with Modernity: Catholic Higher Education in the
    Twentieth Century.* New York: Oxford University Press, 1995.

———, ed. *Keeping the Faith: American Catholicism Past and Present.* Notre Dame,
    Ind.: University of Notre Dame Press, 1989.

———. "The New Americanism in Catholic Historiography." *U.S. Catholic Historian*
    11, no. 3 (Summer 1993): 1–18.

Gorman, Sister Adele Francis, OSF (with Sister Emily Ann Herbes, OSF).
    Celebrating the Journey. Vol. 2, *History of the Sisters of St. Francis of Philadelphia,
    1855–1970.* Glen Riddle, Pa.: Sisters of St. Francis of Philadelphia, 2005.

Greer, Allan. "Colonial Saints: Gender, Race, and Hagiography in New France."
    William and Mary Quarterly 57 (April 2000): 323–48.

———. "Natives and Nationalism: The Americanization of Kateri Tekakwitha."
    Catholic Historical Review 90, no. 2 (2004): 260–72.

Hayes, Mary, S.N.D. de N. "The Founding of Trinity College, Washington, D.C."
    U.S. Catholic Historian 10, nos. 1–2 (1992): 79–86.

Helen Louise [Nugent], Sister, SND. *Sister Julia [Susan McGroarty], Sister of Notre
    Dame de Namur.* New York: Benziger Brothers, 1928.

Higginbotham, Evelyn Brooks. *Righteous Discontent: The Women's Movement in the
    Black Baptist Church, 1880–1920.* Cambridge, Mass.: Harvard University Press,
    1993.

Higgins, Michael W. *Stalking the Holy: The Pursuit of Saint-Making.* Toronto:
    Anansi, 2006.

Hoedl, Sr. M. Celestine. *Types of Secondary Schools and the Development of Religious
    Vocations.* Mendham, N.J.: Assumption College for Sisters, 1962.

Hoffman, Nancy. *Woman's True Profession: Voices from the History of Teaching*. Old Westbury, N.Y.: Feminist Press, 1981.

Hogan, Peter E., S.S.J. *The Catholic University of America, 1896–1903: The Rectorship of Thomas J. Conaty*. Washington, D.C.: Catholic University of America Press, 1949.

Hoy, Suellen. *Good Hearts: Catholic Sisters in Chicago's Past*. Urbana: University of Illinois Press, 2006.

———. "The Journey Out: The Recruitment and Emigration of Irish Religious Women to the United States, 1812–1914." *Journal of Women's History* 6/7, no. 4/1 (1995): 64–98.

Iadorola, Annette. "The American Catholic Bishops and Woman: From the Nineteenth Amendment to ERA." In *Women, Religion, and Social Change*, edited by Yvonne Yazbeck Haddad and Ellison Banks Findly, 457–76. Albany: State University of New York Press, 1985.

Issel, William. "Modernization in Philadelphia School Reform." *Pennsylvania Magazine of History and Biography* 94 (1970): 358–83.

Jablonsky, Thomas. *The Home, Heaven, and Mother Party: Female Anti-Suffragists in the United States, 1868–1920*. Brooklyn, N.Y.: Carlson Publishing Co., 1994.

Jacobs, Richard M., O.S.A. "U.S. Catholic Schools and the Religious Who Served in Them: Contributions in the First Six Decades of the 20th Century." *Catholic Education* 2 (1998): 15–34.

Jorgenson, Lloyd. *The State and the Non-Public School, 1825–1925*. Columbia: University of Missouri Press, 1987.

Kane, Paula. "Review of John T. McGreevy, *Catholicism and American Freedom: A History*." *American Historical Review* 109, no. 3 (2004): 905.

———. *Separatism and Subculture: Boston Catholicism, 1900–1920*. Chapel Hill: University of North Carolina Press, 1994.

Kane, Paula, James Kenneally, and Karen Kennelly. *Gender Identities in American Catholicism*. Maryknoll, N.Y.: Orbis, 2001.

Kauffman, Christopher. "Christopher Columbus and American Catholic Identity, 1880–1900." *U.S. Catholic Historian* 11 (1993): 93–110.

Keenan, Sister Angela Elizabeth. *Three against the Wind: The Founding of Trinity College, Washington, D.C.* Westminster, Md.: Christian Classics, 1973.

Kenneally, James. "Catholic and Feminist: A Biographical Approach." *U.S. Catholic Historian* 3, no. 4 (1984): 229–53.

———. "Eve, Mary and Historians: American Catholicism and Women." In *Women and American Religion*, edited by Janet Wilson James, 191–206. Philadelphia: University of Pennsylvania Press, 1980.

———. *The History of American Catholic Women*. New York: Crossroad Publishing Co., 1990.

———. "A Question of Equality." In *American Catholic Women: A Historical Exploration*, edited by Karen Kennelly, 125–37. New York: Macmillan, 1989.

Kennelly, Karen, C.S.J., ed. *American Catholic Women: A Historical Exploration*. New York: Macmillan, 1989.

Kern, Kathi. *Mrs. Stanton's Bible*. Ithaca, N.Y.: Cornell University Press, 1999.

Landy, Thomas M. "The Colleges in Context." In *Catholic Women's Colleges in America*, edited by Tracy Schier and Cynthia Russett, 55–97. Baltimore: Johns Hopkins University Press, 2002.

Lerner, Gerda. "Editor's Introduction to the Series." In *Women against Women: American Anti-Suffragism, 1880–1920*, by Jane Jerome Camhi, xi–xix. Brooklyn, N.Y.: Carlson Publishing Co., 1994.

Litoff, Judy Barrett, and Judith McDonnell, eds. *European Immigrant Women in the United States: A Biographical Dictionary*. New York: Garland, 1994.

Logue, Sister Maria Kostka, S.S.J. *Sisters of St. Joseph of Philadelphia: A Century of Growth and Development, 1847–1947*. Westminster, Md.: Newman Press, 1950.

Lord, Myra. *History of the New England Women's Press Association*. Newton, Mass.: Graphic Press, 1932.

Mahony, Daniel H. *Historical Sketches of the Catholic Churches and Institutions in Philadelphia*. Philadelphia: Daniel H. Mahony, 1895.

Mandell, Gail Porter. *Madeleva: A Biography*. Albany: State University of New York Press, 1997.

Maria Alma, Sister, IHM. *Sisters, Servants of the Immaculate Heart of Mary*. Philadelphia: Dolphin Press, 1934.

Marshall, Susan E. *Splintered Sisterhood: Gender and Class in the Campaign against Woman Suffrage*. Madison: University of Wisconsin Press, 1997.

Matthews, Jean V. *The Rise of the New Woman: The Women's Movement in America, 1875–1930*. Chicago: Ivan R. Dee, 2003.

M. Blanche, Sister, IHM. *Mother Mary de Chantal of the Sisters, Servants of the Immaculate Heart of Mary*. Philadelphia: Dolphin Press, 1938.

McAvoy, Thomas Timothy. *The Great Crisis in American Catholic History, 1895–1900*. Chicago: H. Regnery Co., 1957.

McCluskey, Neil G., S.J. *Catholic Education in America: A Documentary History*. New York: Teachers College of Columbia University, 1964.

McDannell, Colleen. "Catholic Women Fiction Writers, 1840–1920." *Women's Studies* 19, no. 3/4 (1991): 385–405.

McGreevy, John T. *Catholicism and American Freedom: A History*. New York: Norton, 2003.

McManamin, Francis G., S.J. *The American Years of John Boyle O'Reilly, 1870–1890*. New York: Arno Press, 1976.

McNamara, Jo Ann Kay. *Sisters in Arms: Catholic Nuns through Two Millennia.* Cambridge, Mass.: Harvard University Press, 1996.

McNamara, Robert F. *The Diocese of Rochester, 1869–1968.* Rochester, N.Y.: Christopher Press, 1968.

McShane, Joseph Michael. *Sufficiently Radical: Catholicism, Progressivism, and the Bishops' Program of 1919.* Washington, D.C.: Catholic University of America Press, 1986.

Meagher, Timothy J. "Irish, American, Catholic: Irish-American Identity in Worcester, Massachusetts." In *From Paddy to Studs: Irish-American Communities in the Turn of the Century Era, 1880–1920,* edited by Timothy J. Meagher, 53–74. Westport, Conn.: Greenwood Press, 1986.

Meenagh, Martin L. "Archbishop John Hughes and the New York Schools Controversy of 1840–43." *American Nineteenth Century History* 5, no. 1 (Spring 2004): 34–65.

Moloney, Deirdre M. *American Catholic Lay Groups and Transatlantic Social Reform in the Progressive Era.* Chapel Hill: University of North Carolina Press, 2002.

Moreau, Joseph. "Rise of the (Catholic) American Nation: United States History and Parochial Schools, 1878–1925." *American Studies* 38, no. 3 (1997): 67–91.

Morris, Charles R. *American Catholic: The Saints and Sinners Who Built America's Most Powerful Church.* New York: Times Books, 1997.

Morrow, Diane Batts. *Persons of Color and Religious at the Same Time: The Oblate Sisters of Providence, 1828–1860.* Chapel Hill: University of North Carolina Press, 2002.

Mullaly, Sister Columba, S.N.D. *Trinity College, Washington, D.C.: The First Eighty Years, 1897–1977.* Westminster, Md.: Christian Classics, 1987.

Muncy, Robyn. *Creating a Female Dominion in American Reform, 1890–1935.* New York: Oxford University Press, 1991.

Newman, Louise Michele. *White Woman's Rights: The Racial Origins of Feminism in the United States.* New York: Oxford University Press, 1999.

Nolan, Hugh J. "Francis Patrick Kenrick, First Coadjutor-Bishop." In *The History of the Archdiocese of Philadelphia,* edited by James F. Connelly, 113–208. Philadelphia: Archdiocese of Philadelphia, 1976.

Nolan, Janet. *Servants of the Poor: Teachers and Mobility in Ireland and Irish America.* Notre Dame, Ind.: University of Notre Dame Press, 2004.

Nolan, Michael. "The Myth of Soulless Women." *First Things* 72 (April 1997): 13–14.

Nordstrom, Justin. *Danger on the Doorstep: Anti-Catholicism and American Print Culture in the Progressive Era.* Notre Dame, Ind.: University of Notre Dame Press, 2006.

Nugent, Walter. "A Catholic Progressive? The Case of Judge E. O. Brown." *Journal of the Gilded Age and Progressive Era* 2, no. 1 (2003): 5.

Oates, Mary J., C.S.J. "The Development of Catholic Colleges for Women, 1895–1960." *U.S. Catholic Historian* 7, no. 4 (1988): 413–28.

——. "Organized Voluntarism: Catholic Sisters in Massachusetts, 1870–1940." In *Women and American Religion*, edited by Janet Wilson James, 141–69. Philadelphia: University of Pennsylvania Press, 1980.

——. "The Professional Preparation of Parochial School Teachers, 1870–1940." *Historical Journal of Massachusetts* 12 (January 1984): 60–72.

O'Malley, John W., S.J. "Spiritual Formation for Ministry: Some Roman Catholic Traditions—Their Past and Present." In *Theological Education and Moral Formation*, edited by Richard John Neuhaus, 79–111. Grand Rapids, Mich.: W. B. Eerdmans Publishing, 1992.

Palmieri, Patricia Ann. *In Adamless Eden: The Community of Women Faculty at Wellesley.* New Haven, Conn.: Yale University Press, 1995.

Prejean, Sister Helen. *Dead Man Walking.* New York: Vintage Books, 1994.

Reher, Margaret Mary. "Review of Thomas Woods' *The Church Confronts Modernity: Catholic Intellectuals and the Progressive Era.*" *Catholic Historical Review* 91, no. 2 (2005): 393–94.

Rogers, Rebecca. *From the Salon to the Schoolroom: Educating Bourgeois Girls in Nineteenth Century France.* DeKalb: Northern Illinois University Press, 2005.

Russett, Cynthia. "Preface to the 1991 Edition." In *Woman in Science*, by H. J. Mozans [John A. Zahm]. Notre Dame, Ind.: University of Notre Dame Press, 1991.

Ryan, Francis J. "A Missing Piece of the 1918 Dewey Report on the Philadelphia Polish Community." *Records of the American Catholic Historical Society of Philadelphia* 104, nos. 1–4 (1993): 58–78.

Ryan, Mary Perkins. *Are Parochial Schools the Answer? Catholic Education in the Light of the Council.* New York: Holt, Rinehart and Winston, 1964.

Rymph, Catherine E. *Republican Women: Feminism and Conservatism from Suffrage through the Rise of the New Right.* Chapel Hill: University of North Carolina Press, 2006.

Shanabruch, Charles. *Chicago's Catholics: The Evolution of an American Identity.* Notre Dame, Ind.: University of Notre Dame Press, 1981.

Shelley, Thomas J. "Twentieth-Century American Catholicism and Irish Americans." In *Making the Irish America: History and Heritage of the Irish in the United States*, edited by J. J. Lee and Marion Casey, 574–608. New York: New York University Press, 2006.

Sister of Notre Dame de Namur [Sister Mary Patricia Butler]. *The American Foundations of the Sisters of Notre Dame de Namur.* Philadelphia: Dolphin Press, 1928.

———. *An Historical Sketch of Trinity College, Washington, D.C.: 1897–1925.* Washington, D.C.: Read-Taylor, 1925.

Sisters, Servants of the Immaculate Heart of Mary (Monroe, Mich.). *Building Sisterhood: A Feminist History of the Sisters, Servants of the Immaculate Heart of Mary.* Syracuse, N.Y.: Syracuse University Press, 1997.

Skerrett, Ellen. "The Development of Catholic Identity among Irish Americans in Chicago, 1880 to 1920." In *From Paddy to Studs: Irish-American Communities in the Turn of the Century Era, 1880–1920*, edited by Timothy J. Meagher, 117–38. Westport, Conn.: Greenwood Press, 1986.

Skok, Deborah. *More than Neighbors: Catholic Settlements and Day Nurseries in Chicago, 1893–1930.* DeKalb: Northern Illinois University Press, 2007.

Smith, Sister Doris. "American Irish Women in Education." *Recorder* 34 (1973): 35.

Solomon, Barbara M. *In the Company of Educated Women: A History of Women and Higher Education in America.* New Haven, Conn.: Yale University Press, 1985.

Stewart, George C., Jr. *Marvels of Charity: History of American Sisters and Nuns.* Huntington, Ind.: Our Sunday Visitor, 1994.

———. "Women Religious in America, Demographic Overview." In *Encyclopedia of American Catholic History*, edited by Michael Glazier and Thomas J. Shelley, 1496–98. Collegeville, Minn.: Liturgical Press, 1997.

Tentler, Leslie Woodcock. "On the Margins: The State of American Catholic History." *American Quarterly* 45, no. 1 (March 1993): 104–27.

Thompson, Margaret Susan. "The Validation of Sisterhood: Canonical Status and Liberation in the History of American Nuns." In *A Leaf from the Great Tree of God: Essays in Honor of Ritamary Bradley*, edited by Margot King, 38–78. Toronto: Peregrina Press, 1993.

Tobias, Sheila. *Faces of Feminism: An Activist's Reflections on the Women's Movement.* Boulder, Colo.: Westview Press, 1997.

Tyack, David B. *The One Best System: A History of American Urban Education.* Cambridge, Mass.: Harvard University Press, 1974.

"Vocation." In *Dictionnaire de théologie catholique*, vol. 15, pt. 2, cols. 3148–81. Paris: Letouzey et Ané, 1950.

Walch, Timothy. *Parish School: American Catholic Parochial Education from Colonial Times to the Present.* New York: Crossroad Publishing Co., 1996.

Wall, Barbra Mann. *Unlikely Entrepreneurs: Catholic Sisters and the Hospital Marketplace, 1865–1925.* Columbus: Ohio State University Press, 2005.

White, Deborah Gray. *Too Heavy a Load: Black Women in Defense of Themselves, 1894–1994.* New York: Norton, 1999.

Woloch, Nancy. *Women and the American Experience.* Vol. 2, *From 1860.* New York: McGraw-Hill, 1994.

Woods, Thomas. *The Church Confronts Modernity: Catholic Intellectuals and the Progressive Era.* New York: Columbia University Press, 2004.

Woodward, Kenneth. *Making Saints: How the Catholic Church Determines Who Becomes a Saint, Who Doesn't and Why.* New York: Simon and Schuster, 1996.
———. "Saint Isabella? Not so Fast." *Newsweek,* April 15, 1991, 67.

UNPUBLISHED SOURCES

Bosler, Rosemarie. "The Preparation of Sister Teachers for Selected Schools Sponsored by the Sisters of Notre Dame de Namur." Ed.D. thesis, Catholic University of America, 1991.

Bowler, Sister Mary Mariella, O.S.F. "A History of Catholic Colleges for Women in the United States of America." Ph.D. diss., Catholic University of America, 1933.

Hilliard, Annie P. Toler. "An Investigation of Selected Events and Forces That Contributed to the Growth and Development of Trinity College, Washington, D.C. from 1897 to 1982." Ed.D. thesis, George Washington University, 1984.

Hubbert, Joseph Gerard. " 'For the Upbuilding of the Church': The Reverend Herman Joseph Heuser, D.D., 1851–1933." Ph.D. diss., Catholic University of America, 1992.

Kreidler, Rev. Ildephonse A., O.S.B. "The Fostering of Religious Vocations for the Brotherhood." M.A. thesis, University of Notre Dame, 1933.

Martino, Joseph F. "A Study of Certain Aspects of the Episcopate of Patrick J. Ryan, Archbishop of Philadelphia, 1884–1911." Ph.D. diss., Pontifical Gregorian University, 1982.

Naccarelli, Jennifer. "Guided by Their Conscience: The Evolution of the Catholic Suffrage Movement, 1890–1920." Ph.D. diss., Claremont Graduate University, forthcoming.

Schuler, Paul Julian. "The Reaction of American Catholics to the Foundations and Early Practices of Progressive Education in the United States." Ph.D. diss., University of Notre Dame, 1970.

Stone, Judith. "Gender Identities and the Secular/Clerical Conflict in Fin-de-Siecle France." Paper delivered at the 2006 Annual Meeting of the American Catholic Historical Association, Philadelphia, 2006.

Walsh, Francis Robert. "The Boston *Pilot*: A Newspaper for the Irish Immigrant, 1829–1908." Ph.D. diss., Boston University, 1968.

WEB SITES

Bebel, August. *Woman and Socialism.* New York: Socialist Literature Co., 1879. Translated by Meta L. Stern. <www.marxists.org/archive/bebel/1879/woman-socialism/ch03.html> (accessed December 10, 2006).

"Biographical Sketch." Agnes Repplier Papers, University of Pennsylvania. <http://www.library.upenn.edu/collections/rbm/mss/repplier/repplierbio> (accessed February 2, 2007).

"Fear of Committee-ment," *Chronicle of Higher Education*, November 16, 2001, <http://chronicle.com/jobs/2001/11/2001111602c.htm> (accessed January 15, 2007).

Glendon, Mary Ann. "The Pope's New Feminism." *Traditional Catholic Reflections and Reports*, <http://www.tcrnews2.com/glendon.html> (accessed July 10, 2007).

Index

Democratic Party, 174, 188, 192

Dewey, John, 113

Diner, Hasia R., 66, 161

Diocesan high schools, 47, 109, 114, 127, 153

Dogherty, Marian, 170

Dolan, Jay, 102

Dolphin Press, 147, 149

Domesticity, 5, 6, 18, 101, 185

Donahoe's Magazine, 26, 27, 42, 51–52, 53, 171

Donnelly, Eleanor Cecilia, 30, 185, 186

Donohue, Mary, 101, 127, 151

Dorney, Reverend Maurice, 23

Dorsey, Anna Hanson, 84

Dorsey, Ella Lorraine, 84, 88, 90

Dougherty, Dennis Cardinal, 153

Dowd, Mary Hickey, 175, 186

Drexel, Katharine, 114

Dullaert, Mother Aimee de Jesus, 71, 78, 81–85, 87, 90, 98–99

Dunne, Finley Peter, 5

Ecclesiastical Review, 136

Eckington College, 68, 70

Edmunds, Henry, 38, 40, 47

Education, 5, 44–46, 53, 59–99; coeducation and, 8, 66, 69, 70, 72, 75, 78, 163–64; citizenship and, 10, 144, 146; curriculum standardization and, 109; feminization of teaching and, 121–23; normal schools and, 132, 140, 142–43, 164. *See also* Higher education; Parochial schools; Public schools; Teacher training and credentials; Women's education

"Educational Briefs" (quarterly), 141

Egan, Mr. and Mrs. Maurice Francis, 84

Elizabeth of Hungary, Saint, 8, 46–47, 48

Elliott, Walter, 24–25, 35

England, 17, 47, 64, 66, 83

Enzleberger, John, 75

Equal Rights Amendment, 2, 193, 194

ERA. *See* Equal Rights Amendment

Ethnicity, 5, 6, 14, 15–16; at Trinity College, 96–98; as parochial school growth factor, 107, 108, 116. *See also* Immigrants; Irish American Catholics

Eucharistic Army, 128

Evolution, 44

False vocations, 124

"Famine generation" writers, 166

Famous Irishwomen (O'Mahoney), 55, 63

Fanning, Charles, 166

Farrell, James, 166

Farrell, Reverend John, 69

Felician Sisters, 116

Feminism: women's history and, 2; Catholic women and, 16, 58, 159–62, 189–95; Conway and, 171, 190–95; Mary, mother of Jesus, and, 185–86. *See also* Antifeminism; Woman suffrage movement

Ferrata, Dominic Cardinal, 77, 83, 92

Filiae Fidei, 30, 56, 57

Fitzgerald, John (Honey Fitz), 166, 174

Fitzgerald, Maureen, 2, 15

Flanagan, Maureen, 9

Flanders, Countess of, 82

Flood, Reverend John, 129, 130

Foley, Reverend M. F., 97

Fournier, Mother St. John, 107

France, 49, 54, 74

Franciscans, 122, 139; parochial schools and, 114, 116, 117; senior centers and, 127; union faculty and, 128; teacher training and, 132, 141–42, 143; congregation expansion and, 135, 136–37; nursing and, 138

Sisters of Mercy, 33, 71

Sisters of Notre Dame de Namur, 4, 63, 64–66; Trinity College and, 12, 59–60, 62, 68, 70, 71, 74–84, 87, 93–94; and tensions between American congregation and motherhouse, 81–84, 87, 90, 92

Sisters of Our Lady of Charity of the Good Shepherd, 126

Sisters of St. Joseph of Carondolet, Missouri, 96, 106, 107

Sisters of St. Joseph of Philadelphia, 10, 101, 105–7, 115, 135; parochial schools and, 105, 106–7, 114, 116, 117–18, 127, 128, 153; founding of, 106; diocesan control of, 107; canonical status and, 111; vocations and, 126, 127, 128, 129, 139; senior centers and, 127; teacher training and, 131, 132, 141–42, 143; Christian doctrine curriculum and, 147–48; teacher compensation and, 152; women's college charter for, 154

Sisters of the Blessed Sacrament, 114, 148

Sisters of the Holy Child Jesus, 127, 128, 154

Sisters of the Holy Cross, 62, 69, 190

Sisters of the Holy Family of Nazareth, 116

Skerrett, Ellen, 168, 170

Sketches on the Old Road through France to Florence (Murray), 38–39

Skok, Deborah, 1

Slavery, 15

Smith, Al, 188

Smith, Martha, 1

Smith College, 66, 93

SND. *See* Sisters of Notre Dame de Namur

Social activism, 1, 15, 155

Social class. *See* Class

Socialism, 181–82

Social reform, 10, 157, 159, 194

Social work, 15, 47

Society of the Sacred Heart, 21, 22, 163, 184

Soreno, Jennie, 170

Souls: women's, 38–41, 48, 179, 182

Spalding, Bishop John Lancaster, 72, 73, 74, 86–87, 121–22, 140

Spanish-American War, 85

Spellissy, Mary, 186

SSJ. *See* Sisters of St. Joseph of Philadelphia

Stanton, Elizabeth Cady, 179, 182, 183

Starr, Eliza Allen, 30, 98

"Star-Spangled Banner, The" (Key), 34

Stimson, Mother Bonaventure, 126, 135, 141, 152

Stoddard, Sister Marilla, 136–37

Stowe, Harriet Beecher, 186

Studs Lonigan (Farrell), 166

Suffrage, 2, 3, 10, 56; African American men and, 171, 179; Catholic women and, 188–89, 194. *See also* Woman suffrage movement

Sullivan, Alexander, 22, 23

Sullivan, Margaret Buchanan, 4–5, 8, 11–18, 21–29, 42, 45, 162, 184, 194, 196; pseudonym of, 17; background and youth of, 17, 21; Catholic identity and, 17, 168; "Chiefly among Women," 17–18, 20, 24, 26, 27, 28, 35, 38, 39, 40, 43, 49, 50, 57, 79, 141; journalism career of, 17–18, 21–25, 49, 157–58, 164; marriage of, 22–23; Conway and, 23, 162–63, 178, 190; on Marie de l'Incarnation, 28–29, 31, 32; on Mother Seton, 35; past and precedent and, 49–52; death of, 57